One Small Candle

One Small Candle

*The Plymouth Puritans and the
Beginning of English New England*

FRANCIS J. BREMER

OXFORD

UNIVERSITY PRESS

OXFORD
UNIVERSITY PRESS

Oxford University Press is a department of the University of Oxford. It furthers the University's objective of excellence in research, scholarship, and education by publishing worldwide. Oxford is a registered trade mark of Oxford University Press in the UK and certain other countries.

Published in the United States of America by Oxford University Press
198 Madison Avenue, New York, NY 10016, United States of America.

© Oxford University Press 2020

Library of Congress Cataloging-in-Publication Data
Names: Bremer, Francis J., author.
Title: One small candle : the Plymouth Puritans and
the beginning of English New England / Francis J. Bremer.
Description: New York : Oxford University Press, 2020. |
Includes bibliographical references and index.
Identifiers: LCCN 2019044703 (print) | LCCN 2019044704 (ebook) |
ISBN 9780197510049 (hardback) | ISBN 9780197510063 (epub) |
ISBN 9780197510070
Subjects: LCSH: Pilgrims (New Plymouth Colony). |
Massachusetts—History—New Plymouth, 1620–1691. |
Brewster, William, 1566 or 1567–1644. |
Pilgrims (New Plymouth Colony)—Biography. |
Massachusetts—History—New Plymouth, 1620–1691—Biography.
Classification: LCC F68 .B83 2020 (print) | LCC F68 (ebook) | DDC 974.4/02—dc23
LC record available at https://lccn.loc.gov/2019044703
LC ebook record available at https://lccn.loc.gov/2019044704

1 3 5 7 9 8 6 4 2

Printed by LSC Communications, United States of America

It is now no time to pamper the flesh, live at ease, snatch, catch, scrape and pull, and hoard up but rather to open the doors, the chests and vessels, and say, brother, neighbors, friends, what want thee? Anything I have? Make bold with it, it is yours to command, to do you good, to comfort and cherish you, and glad I am that I have it for you.
—Robert Cushman, sermon in Plymouth, 1621

Contents

One Small Candle

Prologue: Disease and Death in Early Plymouth

Fifty-four-year-old William Brewster stood on the top of the smaller hill overlooking Plymouth harbor on a February day in 1621, mere months after he and his fellow Englishmen had established their settlement. He was one of the leaders of a group of religious reformers who had chosen to leave England because of their views, had spent a decade as refugees in the Netherlands, and now survived the difficult journey to America. In this new land they hoped that they could preserve both their faith and their English identity. He believed that the journey was God's will, but that belief was being sorely tested.

Strong winds blew sleet into his face as he looked down at the *Mayflower* below. He had spent another long day in the common house of the infant Plymouth colony, a shelter that had been turned into an infirmary. Many of his fellow colonists had fallen ill, weakened by the long and difficult journey across the Atlantic in close quarters below deck, food shortages, exposure to harsh weather and wading through freezing water to undertake exploratory missions, the exertion involved in felling trees, building shelters, and unloading their goods from the ship. Most were wracked by "vehement coughs" as a result of their exposure, but many were experiencing the classic symptoms of scurvy—exhaustion, debility, painful legs, swelling of parts of the body, and ulcerated gums.[1]

As William Bradford later recalled in his account *Of Plimoth Plantation*, "in two or three months half of their company died."[2] Eight of the 102 passengers had already died by the end of December 1620. Bradford himself was one of those in jeopardy. On January 11, 1621, he "had been vehemently taken with a grief and pain" shooting from his hip to his ankle, pain so severe that some thought he would have "instantly died."[3] To make matters worse, early in the morning of January

14, smoke had been seen rising from the common house. A fire built to ward off the piercing cold had thrown up a spark, destroying the thatched roof. "The house was as full of beds as they could lie one by another," and the patients scrambled to get to safety. While the roof was lost, the walls of the structure remained intact and the gunpowder stored there was not affected.[4] Still, it was another setback for those already suffering. Eight colonists passed away in January. February would see seventeen more deaths, and thirteen in March.[5] Bradford recorded "there died sometimes two or three of a day," so that by the Spring, "of 100 and odd persons, scarce fifty remained."[6]

"In the time of most distress," wrote Bradford, there were only six or seven individuals able to take care of those on shore who were ill. Among these were "Mr. William Brewster, their reverend Elder, and Myles Standish, their Captain and military commander." In the absence of adequate housing on shore, some settlers and crew were still on the *Mayflower*, where the ill were presumably tended by some of the few surviving women, whose role Bradford, as well as other contemporary writers, consistently overlooks.[7] On shore, Brewster and Standish labored day and night to fetch wood for the fires they burned to keep the patients warm. They made the beds of the sick, dressed them, and changed and washed their soiled clothes. They performed, Bradford reported, "all the homely and necessary offices for them which dainty and queasy stomachs cannot endure to hear named."[8] Miles Standish's wife died. Many families were destroyed, including the entire Martin, Tinker, Ringdale, and Turner households. Thirteen of the twenty-four families that emigrated lost their heads of household; fourteen of eighteen women died; and half of the twenty children. Nine of fourteen male servants died and all of the few female servants. Those who survived endured the heartbreak of losing family and friends.[9]

While the ravages of disease posed the greatest threat to the colonists, there was much more to concern Brewster. In the weeks since the site of settlement had been chosen, the weather had frustrated the effort to build homes and storehouses.[10] On December 23, 1620, men had disembarked from the *Mayflower* in order to begin the task of cutting down trees and carrying the timber to the chosen site. "Frost and foul weather hindered" them and they were "often much troubled with rain and wet." They were finding that the winter was "sharper and longer than in [the] Old [World]."[11] They were unprepared for the fact that in New England the onset of winter frosts, ice, and snow made everyday tasks extremely difficult. Many suffered frozen hands while working in the bitter weather.[12]

Scarcity of provisions was another concern. Delays in setting out from England and the length of the voyage had depleted their supplies. There was no place to replenish them and no expectation of a relief ship. As a later traveler to New England would put it, "once parted with England, you shall meet neither with taverns, nor alehouse, nor butchers, nor grocers, nor apothecaries' shops to help what things you need. . . . Here are neither markets nor fairs to buy what you want."[13] They would have to find and eat quahogs, mussels, and shellfish as well as ground nuts. Brewster and others would have known of the stories of starvation that had almost destroyed the Jamestown settlement, including those told by George Percy, who would recount how when "famine beginning to look ghastly and pale in every face" some were driven to "dig up dead corpses out of graves and to eat them."[14] One of their own number, Stephen Hopkins, had been on the *Sea Venture*, which shipwrecked on Bermuda in 1609 while on a voyage to Virginia. When he and the other survivors eventually reached Jamestown, he witnessed the devastating effects of the "Starving Time" in that colony. Hopkins's tales would have added to the fears of the Plymouth settlers.[15]

Since their first arrival and explorations of the Cape in November 1620 they had been aware of the presence of the Natives and, in fact, had been attacked on the morning of December 7 at what they subsequently named "First Encounter Beach."[16] In the absence of any other contact the colonists were frequently unsettled by the cries of Indians and smoke from distant campfires.[17] They knew of clashes between Englishmen and Natives during the history of the Roanoke settlement and attacks on English traders in the New England region, some of whom had earned the enmity of the local tribes by kidnapping a number of their young men. The fact that in their explorations of the Cape they had uncovered Native burial sites and stolen buried corn may have made them fearful of some sort of retaliation. In addition, they were troubled by the howls of wolves and other wild animals that they might encounter if they strayed too far from their settlement.

There were more failed efforts at colonization than successes. Brewster had read of Humfry Gilbert's failed colony in Newfoundland; the failure of Walter Ralegh's colony in Roanoke and the questions that remained about its Lost Colonists; and negotiations with the Virginia Company would have made it clear that Jamestown's future was still in doubt. Just recently Brewster had learned the fate of Francis Blackwell, once an elder of the main separatist congregation in Amsterdam, who in 1618 had organized an expedition to Virginia for some 180 separatists.[18] Robert Cushman, a deacon in the Leiden congregation and one of the organizers of the *Mayflower* sailing, had reported to Brewster and others that "Mr. Blackwell is dead, and Mr. Maggner the captain, yea, there are dead 130 persons . . . they were packed together like herrings. They had among them the flux so as it is here rather wondered at that so many are alive than that so many are dead."[19]

A life that began in the green countryside of northern England and led William Brewster to the spires of Cambridge's colleges, the court of Queen Elizabeth, and the bustle of Dutch cities had brought him to the bleak winter landscape of Cape Cod. For much of this journey the driving force was his desire to serve his God. But in February 1621 that faith was tested as never before as his own fate and that of his colony were in question.

Introduction

Every November many Americans pause to remember what they have come to call the "First Thanksgiving." In the process they draw on positive and negative stereotypes about the "Pilgrim Fathers" that have developed over the centuries. While the story of those who settled in Plymouth has been told many times in history books, poems, novels, and films, each version carries a different emphasis and perspective, and represents varying degrees of accuracy.[1] In recent years there have been attempts to explore the commercial elements of the establishment of the colony, purported social-economic clashes among the settlers, the deterioration of relations with the Native population, and the transatlantic diplomacy of Edward Winslow, who emerged as one of the colony's leaders, just to name a few. Remarkably few of these examine the religious motivation of those who journeyed on the *Mayflower* and the ways in which their religion shaped their lives and society.[2]

In contrast, this book focuses on the religious lives and ideas of the men and women who gathered to pursue a deeper understanding of God's will in a manor house in Scrooby, England, and how that quest led them to the Netherlands and then to the New England town and colony that we know as Plymouth. These settlers of early Plymouth are commonly referred to as Pilgrims. The application of the term to this group of believers was first employed in the nineteenth century by those who sought to claim a unique identify for these particular colonists, in part to distinguish themselves from the allegedly more rigid puritans of Massachusetts. When the settlers themselves used the term it was only to identify themselves with all searchers for religious truth.[3] This book avoids the term "Pilgrim" in order to emphasize the fact that the colonists are best understood as puritans—part of a broad movement to reform the Protestant Church of England in the sixteenth and seventeenth centuries.[4] Within this movement there were many variations, and the Plymouth congregation differed from others in that movement on various matters. But what united them with fellow puritans was far more important than what divided them, as will become evident from their influence on the religious culture of Massachusetts and other New England colonies.

Focusing on the religious dimension of this story challenges both popular misconceptions and recent scholarly disdain. For much of our history Americans saw puritanism as central to the story of early New England. But mischaracterizations of puritanism began in the later nineteenth century in the search to find the roots of a rigid Victorian cultural code.[5] It was encapsulated in the assessment of the twentieth-century commentator H. L. Mencken, who quipped that puritanism is "the haunting fear that someone, somewhere may be happy." Popular culture came to (mis)understand puritans as theocratic, misogynistic, repressive prudes with bad fashion sense who executed those who disagreed with them and burned witches.[6] They were depicted as hypocrites for claiming religious freedom while denying it to others and as settler colonists who destroyed Native cultures by introducing virulent disease and stealing the land from those who survived those epidemics. Almost every item on that list is at the least an oversimplification, but the best efforts of scholars have done little to dislodge those beliefs.[7]

Since the 1930s scholars have used the voluminous records of seventeenth-century New England to paint a rich picture of that society. Many of the early studies recognized the centrality of religion. But with some notable exceptions, recent students of early America have focused on social, economic, and political themes to the exclusion of religion or, when it is examined, it is mischaracterized.[8] Some who have touched on puritanism have presented it as a superficial justification for actions driven by base secular motives.[9] This in part reflects a recent academic impulse to cast religion in a negative light. Those unable to distinguish the fanaticism of some from the faith of others have tended to deny the religious impulses in society's past and have marginalized the study of religion in America.

Understanding the nature of puritanism does not mean ignoring the negative consequences of some puritan beliefs. In focusing on the subject I bear in mind the instructions that the English puritan Oliver Cromwell is said to have given the artist Sir Peter Lely as Lely prepared to paint the portrait of England's then ruler. Cromwell purportedly told the artist that his portrait should be accurate, including "all these roughnesses, pimples, warts and everything as you see me." Certainly, the finished product, when compared to a surviving death mask of Cromwell, shows that Lely's portrait, warts and all, was accurate. Whether this famous puritan uttered those words or not, it is apt guidance for historians.[10] Too often the dark sides of history, the warts, have been omitted or glossed over in accounts of early New England. But in reaction, many writers retold the history of the puritans by focusing on the warts alone. I hope that this book steers a path between older works that fulsomely celebrated the Pilgrims and writers who have told the history of the puritans by focusing on the warts alone.

The story of *One Small Candle* focuses on a world in which the boundary between the spiritual and the material did not exist. It was a world in which people might feel the direct inspiration of God's spirit, but also sense the presence of the devil. Rather than dismiss the puritans' awareness of the supernatural, we need to understand what that experience meant in the lives of men and women in early modern England and New England.[11] The Plymouth story starts with ordinary men and women such as William and Mary Brewster, who struggled in late sixteenth- and early seventeenth-century England to decide how they should understand and relate to God. Their answers led them to organize themselves into a distinct religious body and separate from the national church, a decision that resulted in persecution by the English church and government. Faced with this hostility, the congregation became refugees, settling in the Netherlands, where they experienced many social, economic, and cultural challenges. During this period they came to refine their beliefs and moved from a rigid separatism to a position that allowed some interaction with puritans who had not separated from the Church of England, as well as other religious groups. When they came to believe that their ability to preserve their values and pass them on to a new generation was threatened, a majority of the congregation determined to move yet again, leading eventually to the settlement of Plymouth.

For most of the 1620s Plymouth was the only substantial settlement in New England. The members of the Scrooby-Leiden congregation (a majority of the settlers) worked to define their faith and religious practice, trying to remain open to further light as they sought the inspiration of the Spirit in their reading of the scriptures. Central to their efforts was a belief in the control of the church by ordinary members, and this Congregationalism shaped political as well as religious institutions.

The first colonists of Massachusetts, arriving in Salem in 1628, turned to Plymouth for advice on how to organize their own churches. What became known as the New England Way—puritan Congregationalism—evolved from this interaction. Plymouth leaders were frequently consulted by their counterparts in Massachusetts and were invited to participate in the clerical assemblies that sought to define New England orthodoxy. Over the years that system was challenged by more radical believers such as Roger Williams on one side, and those seeking a more authoritarian, clergy-dominated Presbyterian system on the other. Plymouth leaders continued to insist on the empowerment of laypeople in their churches and were more moderate than some of their neighbors in the treatment of dissenters such as Roger Williams and Samuel Gorton.

The autonomy of Plymouth came to an end when it was merged with the other colonies in the region into the Dominion of New England, created by King James II in 1684. New Englanders responded to England's Glorious Revolution with their own revolt in 1689, but when William and Mary restored much of the old order, Plymouth was incorporated into Massachusetts under that colony's charter of 1691. This book ends decades earlier, when the distinctive character of Plymouth was lost as the economic and cultural dominance of Massachusetts came to overwhelm the older colony.

Four key themes are woven into this narrative of Plymouth. One is the identification of the Scrooby-Leiden-Plymouth congregation as being solidly within the puritan movement. Another is the importance of lay leadership in the shaping of their religious values and institutions.[12] The central character in this is William Brewster, the layman who led the congregation in its first years in Scrooby and was responsible for religious services during most of the settlers' first decade in the colony. Little of Brewster's own writing has survived, but much of his story can be told from the records and impressions others left behind, and his intellectual development can be illustrated by analyzing the contents of his library.

A third theme is the commitment of these believers to a search for what they referred to as "further light," a better understanding of God and the ways he wanted his saints to live. There were beliefs they considered foundational, but on many issues they were more open to discussion and the toleration of diversity than was the case with many puritans. The evolution of the way they defined their relationship with conforming puritans in the Church of England is a prime example of this.

Finally, this book argues for a greater influence of Plymouth on the religious institutions of Massachusetts than has generally been acknowledged. In his history *Of Plimoth Plantation*, the governor William Bradford claimed of his colony that "as one small candle may light a thousand, so the light here kindled hath shone onto many, yea in some sort to our whole nation."[13] As history has borne out, this was more than an idle boast.

1

The Religious Scene in Early Modern England

The starting point for understanding the events that set William Brewster and other puritans on the journey that took them to Plymouth is the religious turmoil leading to and culminating in the Reformation and in particular the role played by lay Christians. A critical feature of the strain of reform that Brewster came to embrace was a positive valuation of the laity dating back to at least the fourteenth century, when the Oxford priest and theologian John Wycliffe encouraged lay believers, women as well as men, to gather in secret meetings where they "read and discussed the scriptures, heard sermons, and distributed books."[1] The Lollards, as Wycliffe's followers became known, asserted that "every man, holy and predestined to eternal life, even if he is a layman, is a true minister and priest ordained by God to administer the sacraments necessary for the salvation of man, although no bishop shall ever lay hands on him."[2] Lollardy was never completely suppressed, continuing as an underground tradition among friends, families, and neighbors gathering in secret to discuss their understanding of God's will. But for lay believers to act in this fashion it was necessary for such individuals to draw guidance from the scriptures, and thus central to Lollardy was the demand that the scriptures be made available in the vernacular, rather than Latin.

Critical to understanding this belief in lay empowerment is the recognition that in this premodern world there were no hard and fast dividers between the individual self and the spiritual cosmos. Ordinary men and women believed they could be touched by the divine—and potentially by the devil.[3] As John Robinson, Brewster's friend and mentor, explained, due to man's "natural blindness" there were "things left more dark in the Scriptures."[4] This belief that one could be led to truth by the power of the Holy Spirit was the more positive side of a continuum that included belief in demonic possession. As valuable as university training was, natural reason and human learning alone were deemed insufficient to understand scripture. It was possible for ordinary believers, with the guidance of the Holy Spirit, to discern God's will to a degree that could be greater than formally educated clergy.

The Lollard underground would presumably have been encouraged by Martin Luther's call for vernacular Bibles and the "priesthood of all believers." Influenced by Luther, and perhaps the Lollard heritage, the English reformer William Tyndale set out to translate the Bible into English, stating as his goal that he would enable "the boy who drove the plow to know more of the scriptures" than many clergymen, arguing that "there are many found among the laymen which are as wise as their officers."[5] He opposed the monopoly on authority claimed by ordained clergy, and once went so far as to argue that women could preach and administer the sacraments "if necessity required."

Efforts to advance what many perceived as further church reforms continued following Henry VIII's break with Rome, Edward VI's reforms, and the Catholic Counter-Reformation under Mary Tudor, and even into the reign of Elizabeth. Those who were most enthusiastic for further reform demanded changes they believed would purify the church of its Catholic remnants. Their "puritan" agenda included calls for the abandonment of clerical vestments, doing away with signing with the cross in baptism, the provision of an educated preaching ministry in all parishes, and a more rigorous denial of the Lord's Supper to those who were deemed spiritually ineligible.[6]

Such reforms were resisted by England's civil and ecclesiastical leaders, resulting in a tension between the believers' conviction that the spirit of God allowed them to directly understand the demands of scripture and the determination of church authorities to maintain control over doctrine and practice. When Elizabeth I came to the throne in 1558 the Protestant character of the Church of England was restored, but this was reform from the top down, which did not satisfy all reformers. Unable to gain the support of the church hierarchy, those who were seen as the hotter sort of Protestants—"puritans" as they were increasingly referred to—drew on lay support and emphasized the role of the laity. Reforms initiated early in

England's Reformation transferred to lay individuals or groups the right to choose clergy (who had been ordained by a bishop) for parish positions. Some used this right to appoint puritans. In these and other parishes fervent lay believers often pressured their ministers to resist episcopal demands to conform to matters such as wearing traditionally prescribed vestments and requiring that recipients of the Lord's Supper kneel to receive it.

Elsewhere believers, finding themselves in parishes where reform was successfully resisted, separated themselves from the church and began to worship on their own. As the Pilgrim layman Robert Cushman put it, "if the country and kingdom where we live take no public course for preaching, yet the Gospel may still be found in families, and from neighbor to neighbor."[7] Such gatherings, branded conventicles by the authorities, who deemed them illegal, were a way for men and women to engage in proper worship on their own, a position set out by Robert Browne in his *Treatise of Reformation without Tarrying for Any* (1582). Dubbed "Brownists" or separatists, members of some such groups of friends and neighbors could all be lay; in other cases, someone who had held a ministerial living could be part of the group. In the case of Scrooby, Lincolnshire, the layman William Brewster hosted fellow believers for prayer, psalm singing, and the sharing of spiritual insight.[8] After a time, they were joined by ministers who had been deprived of their church livings.

William Brewster was the son of the elder William Brewster of Scrooby, Nottinghamshire, and his wife, Mary Smyth. The exact date of young Brewster's birth is unknown, but would have been in the mid-1560s.[9] At that time, William's father served as master of the royal post in Scrooby, a village on the Great North Road between London and Scotland and the site of one of twenty-five post offices along the route. As postmaster, Brewster Sr. provided government messengers with fresh horses to speed the delivery of dispatches they were carrying and offered refreshments and accommodations to travelers.[10] The post brought men and tales from the centers of the nation's government to the small rural hamlet. In 1575 the elder Brewster was also appointed bailiff and receiver (rent collector) of the manor of Scrooby, a property of the archbishop of York, Edmund Grindal, a sympathizer with the reform movement. From the time of the elder Brewster's appointment the family would have lived in the manor house, the most substantial property in the vicinity.[11]

Young William would likely have been taught by a tutor, perhaps his uncle Henry, who was vicar of Sutton-cum-Lound, and then attended a local grammar school, perhaps the one in Doncaster, a little over ten

Fig. 1.1 Scrooby Church. Drawing by Jeremy D. Bangs.

miles away.[12] Typically, students attended such schools between the ages of seven and fourteen to learn Latin in preparation for university and, according to William Bradford, Brewster "had attained some learning, viz. the knowledge of the Latin tongue and some insight into the Greek."[13] The school year lasted about forty weeks, with five days of instruction from around six in the morning to five in the evening, a half day on Thursdays (perhaps to hear a church lecture), and the Sabbath off for religious services.[14]

On December 3, 1580, William enrolled in Peterhouse College, Cambridge. The daily routine there began as early as 5:00 AM, when members of Peterhouse gathered for morning prayer and a homily. After breakfast he and other students would meet in the room of one of the college tutors to discuss readings from an assigned text. In the afternoon he would have attended college or university disputations. After supper he may have reviewed his day's studies with his tutor until evening prayers around 8:00 PM.[15]

The Cambridge routine brought students and their teachers together in a variety of formal and informal settings, and such contacts were as important as formal lessons in shaping young men. These included conferences in which those attending prayed and discussed matters of religion. Cambridge had come to eclipse Oxford as a center of education for those promoting further reform, and many of those whom Brewster encountered were the "hotter sort of Protestants."[16] John Penry, who became known as the "morning star of the reformation" and founder of nonconformity in Wales, matriculated at Peterhouse on the same day as Brewster. Robert Browne, who was sharply critical of the established church, though not yet advocating separatism, was a preacher at one of the Cambridge churches. Other critics of the national church at Cambridge were John Greenwood and Henry Barrow. Brewster may have also encountered William Perkins, who later established himself as one of the leading lights of Calvinist theology.[17] Francis Johnson, who would be associated with Brewster in later years, was a contemporary of his at the university.[18]

The inventory taken of Brewster's library at the time of his death offers some insight into the shaping of his views during his time at the university and the years immediately following.[19] He acquired some basic works that would have been useful for any student—a

Latin-English dictionary, a Latin-Greek-German dictionary, William Camden's *Britannia*, and Thomas Lupton's *A thousand notable things, on various subjects; disclosed from the secrets of nature and art* (1579). While at Cambridge or later he acquired a 1580 Latin edition of Niccolò Machiavelli's *The Prince*, important not only for its political analysis but also for its material on ancient history.[20]

But most of the works he acquired were related to religion, which was central to the Cambridge curriculum. These included a series of homilies by the Church Father John Chrysostom and two works by Erasmus, including the *Paraphrases*. John Calvin was well represented with seven works, as were works by lesser known figures of the Reformation, such as Theodore Beza, Andrew Musculus, Peter Martyr Vermigli, and John Bale. There were polemics against Catholicism such as an attack on the Spanish Inquisition, a "Dialogue between a gentleman and a papist priest," and a critique of the "Monstrous Popish Mass." The divisions in the English church were represented, with the books he acquired suggesting both an interest in religion and a sympathy for puritan views. He owned the 1572 anti-episcopal *Admonition to Parliament* by John Field and Thomas Wilcox, which advocated presbyterian-style reforms, as well as John Whitgift's *Answer to the Admonition*, Thomas Cartwright's *Reply to Whitgift* and *Second Reply to Whitgift*, and Robert Browne's *Answer to Cartwright*.[21]

Those intending to enter the ministry stayed at university to acquire a bachelor's degree, but most students attended for only a year or two before pursuing a career or returning home to manage their family estates. The last mention of Brewster in the Peterhouse records was in 1581, though he may have attended for a time beyond that date.[22] It was while he was at Cambridge or shortly thereafter that he was "first seasoned with the seeds of grace and virtue," which means that he came to believe that he was blessed with God's saving grace.[23] Sometime in 1583 he entered the employ of William Davison, an envoy in the service of Queen Elizabeth, who had been sent to the Netherlands on a number of occasions between 1576 and 1579. The envoy might have encountered and employed Brewster as he traveled the Great North Road on a mission to Scotland that Elizabeth sent him on in 1583.[24]

Davison was a member of the puritan faction at the center of England's government that included Sir Francis Walsingham, the queen's principal secretary. During his time in Antwerp he had served as an elder to the puritan-inclined church of the English Merchant Adventurers. He helped to secure the employment of the reformer Thomas Cartwright at the Merchant Adventurers' church in Middelburg. When Cartwright relocated in Antwerp, he was supported in part by Davison.[25] On an occasion when the Antwerp congregation needed a new preacher, Davison solicited advice from John Field and the London presbyterian conference as well as from Walsingham's secretary, which led to the appointment of Walter Travers.[26] Davison subsequently corresponded with Travers about church matters. He was also connected to the controversial John Stubbs, who publicly attacked a proposed marriage between Queen Elizabeth and the Catholic brother of the French king. A committed religious reformer, Stubbs wrote to Davison in 1578, claiming that the two of them were united by "this band of Christian love which is between the faithful."[27] Whether Davison employed Brewster because of the young man's existing religious inclinations or other reasons cannot be known, but that Brewster's views were further shaped while he was in service to the envoy is clear. As he accompanied Davison, Brewster was exposed to new lands and new faiths.

This was a time when politics and religion were inseparable, and England was navigating its way in a divided world. In England itself there were Catholics who plotted against Elizabeth. To the north, the Catholic Mary, Queen of Scotland, had been deposed in 1567 by a strong presbyterian faction supported by most of the nobility, which installed James VI as king. Adding to the complexity of the situation was that Elizabeth was childless and her Scottish cousin Mary was heir to the English throne. It was a situation in which Catholics unwilling to wait and hope for a natural succession encouraged plots against Queen Elizabeth. Abroad, England unofficially lent support to the Protestant Dutch, who had rebelled against Catholic Spain in 1568. The Netherlands became not just an ally but also a refuge for many of England's more advanced Protestants.

In 1584 Brewster accompanied Davison on an embassy to the Netherlands to work on a treaty that formalized English military commitments. There Brewster met two of England's military leaders, Sir Philip Sydney and the Earl of Leicester, both of whom were members of the court party that supported further religious reforms, as well as a number of Dutch leaders, including the town secretary of Leiden, Jan van Hout.[28]

No extant record defines Brewster's actual position in Davison's household, but William Bradford would later say that the envoy trusted the young man "above all others that were about him, and only employed him in all matters of greatest trust, and secrecy. He esteemed him rather as a son than a servant, and for his wisdom and godliness (in private) he would converse with him more like a friend and familiar than as a master."[29] Davison entrusted Brewster with the ceremonial keys to the city of Vlissingen (Flushing), which he accepted on Elizabeth's behalf and also with a ceremonial gold chain presented to the envoy at the conclusion of his mission.[30] While in the Netherlands, Davison introduced Brewster to Thomas Cartwright.[31]

Shortly after his return from the continent, Davison was elevated to the post of one of the queen's principal secretaries of state, thus exposing Brewster to the machinations of the court and to many of its principal figures. At this time George Cranmer, the grandnephew of Archbishop Thomas Cranmer, entered Davison's service. One of George Cranmer's close friends was Edwin Sandys, the son of the archbishop of York, Edwin Sandys, whom Brewster's father had served as bailiff.[32] The younger Sandys, who may have already been known to Brewster, would later be a key figure in the Virginia Company. A connection with William Cecil, the queen's chief advisor, is suggested by the fact that Brewster came to own Cecil's personal copy of the 1592 edition of William Lambard's *Eirenarcha*, the popular guide to the work of justices of the peace.[33]

The future looked bright for Davison and his protégé William Brewster in 1586, but their hopes were soon shattered. Davison was deeply engaged in the Privy Council debates over how to deal with Mary, the Catholic queen of Scotland, who had been granted refuge in England but repaid her cousin's hospitality by conspiring against Elizabeth. Mary's very existence as heir to the English throne incited Catholic plots. Late in 1586 Elizabeth appeared to be persuaded that her cousin posed an intolerable threat to her throne. She entrusted Davison with a warrant for Mary's execution, which the secretary dispatched. But when the Scottish queen was executed on February 8,

1587, Elizabeth found it expedient to deny that she had granted the authorization and she made Davison the scapegoat. For a time, it was feared he would be hanged, but in the end the queen imposed a large fine on Davison and imprisoned him, eventually allowing his release in October 1588.

According to Bradford, Brewster continued to serve Davison for "some good time after" his fall from power, "doing him many faithful offices of service in the time of his troubles."[34] Davison was jailed at the Tower of London, and Bradford's statement probably means that Brewster was the member of Davison's household who arranged for the prisoner's amenities and saw to the dispatch of his letters. This means Brewster would have been in London in July 1588, when word arrived that the Spanish Armada had been sighted in the English Channel and when the city cheered the defeat of the enemy's fleet.

Davison's release from the Tower freed Brewster to return to Scrooby to see his ill father. After the elder Brewster's death in the summer of 1590, William assumed his father's duties as postmaster and as the archbishop's bailiff and receiver.[35] When the postmaster-general was found to have offered the post to another candidate, Davison still had sufficient influence at court to have the post confirmed for his protégé.[36] Recent events had denied Brewster the opportunity of a career at court but taught him some useful lessons and left him with some friends in powerful places.

Shortly after his return to Scrooby, William married, and his wife, Mary, gave birth to a son, Jonathan, in August 1593. Three more children were born while the couple lived at the manor. The Brewsters had a comfortable home, if not as grand as some of the residences William had visited and worked in. The manor house had at one time been a palatial residence with more than forty rooms, suitable for entertaining an archbishop and his guests. By Brewster's time many of the buildings had fallen into disrepair and been torn down, but what remained may have been comparable to nearby Gainsborough Old Hall, with its impressive Great Hall, large medieval kitchen, and myriad rooms for the family and servants.[37] The facilities for the post service—stables and an inn—would have been separate. Brewster's position as master of the post carried an income that has been estimated as ten times that of a typical agricultural laborer. While being bailiff and receiver for the archbishop's manor did not pay much, it offered various opportunities to make money. Part of his wealth likely was inherited. His mother came from a well-to-do family. His uncle, John Smythe of Hull, who was also prosperous, named Brewster as one of four individuals to receive Smythe's uncollected debts. His status and his character made him a respected local leader.[38]

At this time Brewster was already identifiable as a puritan, maintaining his membership in the Church of England while pondering the controversies of the age and supporting the cause of further reform. In his household the day would have begun, as set forth in devotional literature, with pious meditation and private devotions followed by gathering the household for communal prayer. After a breakfast of beer, bread, cheese, and leftover meats, William and Mary would have set off on their daily tasks, in his case as Scrooby's postmaster and his supervision of the archbishop's estate. Mary would have marshaled the household's servants for their domestic chores. The midday dinner was the principal meal of the day and would likely have been preceded by a prayer of grace said by Brewster. Likely the type of religious dinner conversation promoted by Martin Luther would have provided a model for discussion at the Brewsters' table. William Teellinck, a Dutch pastor who spent time with English friends in Banbury described life in a pious household that resembled Brewster's. Each member of the family offered a prayer and read a chapter of the Bible before going to work each day. The entire family gathered together around the table for dinner. After a prayer, someone, likely the head of the household, read a scriptural passage, which was discussed during the meal. A similar process was followed at supper, and before retiring individuals meditated on the day's events and offered up prayers. Teellinck also praised the practice of individuals exchanging religious ideas with a companion while traveling. Perhaps what most impressed him was how this piety led to efforts to follow the guidance of the beatitudes in giving to the poor, comforting the sick, and similar acts of charity. The fact that this is well documented in other families makes it likely that this or something similar happened in the Brewster household and those of other pious families in the Scrooby area.[39]

A short distance from the manor house was St. Wilfrid's church, a late medieval building with a choir, a nave, a south aisle, and a tower with a spire. The church graveyard also served as the site for a pound for stray animals and included stocks for the punishment of drunks and other offenders.[40] St. Wilfrid's was under the ecclesiastical supervision of Sutton-cum-Lound, a parish a little over five miles away, where William's brother James Brewster served as the vicar from 1594 to 1614, after succeeding their uncle. James bore the responsibility for choosing a curate to officiate at St. Wilfrid's and seems to have followed William's advice in making appointments, accepting his brother's greater concern for having a curate with a reformist outlook. The living was a poor one, but William seems to have been able to find puritans who sought further church reforms to accept those positions, perhaps by supplementing their income. William Bradford would remember that in terms of "procuring of good preachers to the places thereabout, and drawing on others to assist and help forward in such a work, he himself [was] most commonly deepest in the charge, and sometimes above his ability.[41] This led to the appointment of Thomas Hancock in 1590. Hancock's commitment to reform resulted in him being presented at the archdeacon's court the following year for refusing to wear the surplice, a garment many saw as a remnant of Catholic practice.[42] John Deacon was another such curate, serving both St. Wilfrid's and the parish in nearby Bawtry.

As a result of such efforts Brewster was remembered as one who "did much good in the country where he lived in promoting and furthering religion," not only by attracting and supporting godly preachers, but by "his practice and example."[43] But as he continued to explore what the scriptures required in doctrine and worship he would begin to move down a path that would take him from nonconformity to separatism in his faith, and from Scrooby to New England.

2

To Tarry or Not to Tarry

The path taken by Brewster and others can only be understood by examining the complex nature of the Church of England in the last decades of Elizabeth's reign, and the changes that came during the reign of James I. When Brewster returned to Scrooby most Englishmen, perhaps the vast majority, were content to accept the forms and practices prescribed by the king and his bishops for their worship. But a growing number of clerics and laypeople on opposite ends of the spectrum believed that further changes in the national church were necessary. At one extreme were individuals who challenged the church's broad commitment to a Calvinist theology. At Cambridge in 1595 William Barrett, a chaplain at Caius College, had criticized the teaching of unconditional predestination. The following year divinity professor Peter Baro questioned the doctrine of limited atonement, the Calvinist teaching that Christ's sacrifice atoned only for the sins of those already chosen by God to be saved.[1] Questioning of such beliefs had continued into the seventeenth century, with much of the focus shifting to the teachings of the Dutch theologian and University of Leiden professor Jacobus Arminius, who offered his own modification of what had become mainline Calvinist teachings.[2]

While some churchmen revisited Calvinist theology, others on this conservative end of the spectrum lamented the "stripping of the altars," a term used to refer to the English Reformation's abolition of some of the ceremonial grandeur of Roman Catholicism.[3] They sought to restore "the beauty of holiness" and the authority of the clergy by emphasizing the importance of clerical vestments, restoring altars to their previous elevated positions in church buildings, requiring that parishioners kneel to receive the Lord's Supper, and advocating similar steps that many saw as a retreat to Catholic practice. Historians have found it difficult to define those on this end of the religious spectrum, many settling for "Laudianism" in discussing its seventeenth-century manifestation, because it seemed most of the clergy who took this stand supported Archbishop William Laud. But not all who advocated ceremonial renewal agreed on which ceremonies were to be restored, and not all who sought ceremonial renewal questioned Calvinist doctrine. And not all who sought revisions of predestinarian doctrine, called Arminians by their enemies, were interested in the "beauty of holiness." The unity of this presumed faction was more in the eyes of its opponents than a matter of fact.[4]

Similarly, the identification of those at the other end of the spectrum as "puritans" is misleading. While many clergy and laypeople believed that the reform of the church had not gone far enough, they were far from an organized faction with a single plan of action. Starting in the 1570s some reformers had sought a presbyterian restructuring of the church through parliamentary action. William Brewster and others followed the debate by reading the call for reform in the *Admonition to Parliament* written by the London clergymen Thomas Wilcox and John Field as well as the competing treatises by John Whitgift and Thomas Cartwright that it prompted. Efforts to effect such reforms were halted when the queen denied parliamentary jurisdiction over the church. Clergy in various regions organized themselves into an unofficial presbyterian movement, with regional conferences of clergy that met to discuss religious matters, but this effort was detected and suppressed by the authorities in the late 1580s.[5]

The reform end of the religious spectrum was broader than the presbyterian effort, however. Some believed that individual congregations of believers should be free of any superior authority, whether episcopal or presbyterian. But among these "Congregationalists" there were differences over the relative authority of the clergy and the laity. Still others were less concerned with structural issues and more concerned with matters that presented themselves in local churches every Sabbath day, such as what the minister was wearing, how well he could preach, and what ceremonies he employed in administering the sacraments. Lay believers as well as clergy met informally to discuss such issues, though they did not all agree on a single platform of reform.[6] Just as with Laudians and Arminians, the unity of puritanism is a polemical and rhetorical fiction.

The men and women who would eventually settle Plymouth emerged from the more radical end of the puritan spectrum. While most reformers struggled to advance their positions within the established national church and were willing to make some compromises to do so, as early as the 1560s some had prioritized the pursuit of purity over their membership in the Church of England. Drawing on the example of underground churches that had preserved Protestantism during the reign of Mary Tudor, some zealous believers in London met to listen to preachers who did not wear the Catholic-style vestments or perform ceremonies identified with Rome. At that time, relatively few believers were willing to give up on the hope of reform within the church, and they suffered from prosecution by the church authorities and disapproval by prominent reformers such as Thomas Cartwright, who accepted the ideas of these radicals but rejected their separation from the Church.[7] Five radicals in particular would have a significant role in shaping separatism at this time.

Robert Browne was one such figure. A Cambridge graduate, Browne had associated as an undergraduate with other students who were supporters of reform, and following his graduation in 1572 his commitment to that cause became more pronounced. He lived for a time with the puritan minister Richard Greenham in nearby Dry Drayton and possibly preached there. It was there that he began to develop strong feelings against episcopal rule.[8] By the early 1580s he had become disillusioned with the episcopal structure of the national church. He expressed his views in sermons at St. Benet's Church in Cambridge and started holding conventicles of like-minded believers. When the authorities forbade him to preach, he moved to Norwich, where he lodged with Robert Harrison, who shared his religious outlook. Harrison had demonstrated his nonconformist sentiments when he urged the vicar of his local parish to not use the sign of the cross in baptism.[9] The two men gathered a group of followers in Norwich to whom they preached and ministered.[10]

In 1580 Browne and Harrison signed a "Supplication of Norwich Men to the queen's majesty," a petition urging Elizabeth to remove nonpreaching ministers and institute a presbyterian style for the Church of England in which the ministers would be chosen by the members of their congregations. Around this time Browne and

Harrison formally separated from the national church, agreeing with their followers to "join themselves to the Lord, in one covenant and fellowship together, and to keep and seek agreement under his laws and government." They promised to avoid "disorders and wickedness" and to obey those whom they chose as ministers. Separation from the Church was illegal and led to persecution and imprisonment, so in 1582 the congregation emigrated to Middelburg. There Browne published his most famous work, *A Treatise of Reformation without Tarrying for Any* (1582). Disagreements soon split the congregation and Browne left, soon returning to England, where he ended up submitting to the Church of England and spending the rest of his career as a conforming reformist. Despite this, he had offered the clearest articulation to date of the justification for separation and those who later followed in his path were designated "Brownists."[11] Harrison attempted to merge the remnants of his congregation with the puritan-oriented church of English merchants in the same city led by Thomas Cartwright, but was unsuccessful.[12]

Among those who may have been attracted to Browne's preaching at St. Benet's church in Cambridge was Francis Johnson, who matriculated at the university in 1579. Elected a fellow of Christ's College in 1584, Johnson supported the reform position of Thomas Cartwright and other proponents of a Presbyterian discipline. In 1589 he was imprisoned for a sermon he preached at the university church, in which he was critical of imperfections in the church. He was expelled from the university and traveled to Middelburg, where he accepted the ministry of the English Merchant congregation. He adopted a separatist position after reading some works of Henry Barrow. Returning to England in 1592, he met with Barrow and John Greenwood, both of whom were in prison at the time, and then accepted election as pastor of a separatist congregation recently formed in London. He wrote a number of tracts defending separatism and attacking the established ministry of the Church of England. He was arrested for his activities and, on release in 1597, he became the first separatist leader to attempt a New World refuge. His effort to establish a colony on the Magdalen Islands in the Gulf of St. Lawrence failed, following which he settled in Amsterdam.[13]

John Greenwood was also a student at Cambridge when Browne preached in the town. Following graduation, he accepted ministerial posts in Lincolnshire and then Norfolk. But in 1585 he resigned his position, became a separatist, and moved to London. There he attended conventicles with other separatists. In 1587 he was arrested with twenty-one others in such a gathering in a private home. He remained in jail until 1592. On his release he was chosen to join Francis Johnson in the ministry of the newly established London separatist congregation. But later in the same year he was arrested again.[14]

Henry Barrow was a layman from a prosperous Norfolk family who graduated from Cambridge in 1570 and then studied law for a time. Having read Robert Browne's writings, he sought out Thomas Wolsey, a clergyman who, along with Browne and Robert Harrison, was recognized as a leader of the separatist movement in Norfolk. Having been persuaded of that position, Barrow journeyed to London, where, following a visit to John Greenwood, he found himself imprisoned alongside him. The two men developed a strong connection and were able to smuggle their own writings out of prison. Barrow was particularly prolific, and future separatists credited him with helping them come to see the national church and its ministry as antichristian. He was especially critical of the presence of ungodly people within the church. Barrow had remained in prison during the brief time when Greenwood was free. The movement they represented had continued to grow, fueled by active lay engagement. Bishop Edmund Freke had complained of "the vulgar sort of people" gathering to "the number of a hundred at a time in private houses and conventicles."[15] During a government attempt to crack down on the growing movement in 1593, Barrow and Greenwood were prosecuted and condemned to death for writing and publishing seditious literature. Executed in April, the two men became martyrs to the cause.[16]

The execution of Barrow and Greenwood was indicative of a restricting of all forms of puritanism that had been led by John Whitgift. Elevated to archbishop of Canterbury in 1583, Whitgift had dedicated himself to opposing all deviations from the doctrines and practices of the national church. While he was increasingly successful, as Elizabeth's reign ended the religious situation was still in flux. Laymen of some substance such as William Brewster were able to further the puritan cause in local communities, and there was hope that more substantial changes in the church might be possible under Elizabeth's successor, when he assumed the throne as James I in 1603. The new king would have passed through Scrooby on his progress south from Scotland to London along the Great North Road. Puritans hoped that the new monarch, coming from a country whose church was staunchly Calvinist in doctrine and Presbyterian in form, might agree to many of the reforms that they had long sought. But such was not the case. At the Hampton Court Conference in 1604 the king listened to calls for reforms that had been submitted to him in a petition signed by over a thousand of his subjects. The so-called Millenary Petition sought changes in the forms of worship, including doing away with the clerical surplice, the use of signing with the cross in baptism, and the practice of confirmation; demands for better observation of the Sabbath; an end to "popish" practices such as bowing at the name of Jesus; the admission of only those able to preach to the ministry; and the preparation of a new translation of the Bible.[17]

James supported Whitgift's position on the need for conformity, telling the puritan spokesman that he would have "one Doctrine, one Discipline, one religion in substance and in ceremony." As for those who were unwilling to accept this, he stated, "I will make them conform themselves, or else I will harry them out of the land, or else do worse."[18]

Archbishop Whitgift and other establishment leaders believed that they knew God's will, refused to entertain suggestions that they might be in error, and were preoccupied with efforts to impose their views as a required orthodoxy. That same sense of certainty was to be found among many of the puritans, including some separatists. But there were other reformers, including William Brewster, who believed that the search for truth was ongoing. This position is captured in a contemporary recollection of the teachings of John Robinson, who would be the spiritual leader of the congregation formed at Scrooby. Robinson "was very confident the Lord hath more truth and light yet to break forth out of his holy Word." He bemoaned "the state and condition of the Reformed Churches, who would come to a period in Religion, and would go no further." Thus, "for example the Lutherans

Fig. 2.1 The Old Vicarage in Scrooby. Photo by Jeremy D. Bangs.

they could not be drawn to go beyond what Luther saw, for whatever part of God's will he had further imparted and revealed to Calvin, they will rather die than embrace it. And so also," Robinson lamented, "you see the Calvinists, they stick where he left them, a misery much to be lamented; for though they were precious shining lights in their times, yea God had not revealed his whole will to them." He exhorted his own congregation "to take heed what we received for truth, and well to examine and compare, and weigh it with other Scriptures of truth, before we received it. For, saith he, It is not possible the Christian world should come so lately out of such thick Antichristian darkness, and that full perfection of knowledge should break forth at once."[19] Robinson was firm in defending his understanding of Calvinist predestinarian teachings against Arminian challenges. But on issues such as the relationship that "separatists" should have with godly Christians who had not followed that path he was willing to engage those who thought differently in order to achieve further light.[20]

Brewster sought greater understanding through introspection, but also through his reading. During these years Brewster read widely in the controversies of the time. He continued to express an interest in the types of issues that he would have been exposed to at the court, obtaining works such as Francis Bacon on the union of England and Scotland and on the treason of the Earl of Essex, and Thomas Lodge's translation of the works of Seneca. He continued to learn from leading Continental theologians and enhanced his understanding of the Bible through various commentaries. He showed an increased interest in the works of numerous puritan authors, including the complete works of Richard Greenham, and writings by John Udall, who was arrested for complicity in anti-episcopal publications; Robert Cleaver, who had been silenced for nonconformity in 1571; Henoch Clapham, who ministered to an English church in Amsterdam; and Dudley Fenner, a disciple of Thomas Cartwright. He familiarized himself with the extreme nonconformist and Separatist positions through Francis Johnson's *A treatise of the ministry of the Church of England* (ca. 1595–1597), works by Henry Barrow, including *Discovery of False Churches* (1590), Henry Ainsworth's *Apology or Defense of Brownists* (1604), and Henry Jacob's *Necessity of Reforming Churches* (1604).

Brewster also engaged in and encouraged discussions of these matters. There were a number of individuals with strong views on such matters within easy traveling distance. In 1586 Richard Clifton had been inducted as rector of the village of Babworth, seven miles away.[21] William Bradford was living in the village of Austerfield, three miles from Scrooby, and had long been interested in religious reform. When he was about twelve years old in 1602, a friend persuaded him to travel to hear Richard Clifton, a reformist whom he later remembered as "a grave and reverend preacher, who by his pains and diligence had done much good and under God had been a means of the conversion of many."[22] Through Clifton, Bradford soon became a protégé of Brewster. Another supporter of reform was Richard Bernard, the vicar of Worksop, ten miles from Scrooby. After the London merchant and supporter of reform William Hickman acquired Gainsborough Old Hall in 1596, he allowed John Smyth, another reformist Cambridge graduate, to preach there.[23]

In the 1590s the clerical and lay reformers in the region around Scrooby, while debating the extent to which they should conform to debatable church practices, had not yet followed Browne and Harrison down the road to separatism. The clergy held paid positions (church livings) and the lay believers attended their parish churches while supplementing that worship with private religious gatherings, and they benefited from lax enforcement of prescribed practices.

This changed in 1593, when Archbishop Whitgift obtained a statute banning "unlawful assemblies, conventicles, or meetings under pretense of any exercise of religion."[24] One result of this was stricter scrutiny of gatherings such as those that took place under Brewster's roof. At Easter 1598 the Scrooby churchwardens filed a report to the archdeacon in which they stated that Brewster, his family, and others were attending religious services somewhere other than their parish church of St. Wilfrid, which was a violation of the law. They also reported that William Brewster was "repeating sermons publicly in the church without authority." This was a type of exercise common among puritans, in which an individual took notes on a sermon, shared them with those who had not been at the service, and likely led a discussion of the key points.[25] Appearing before the court, Brewster responded to the charge of being absent from his parish by pointing out that "Bawtry and Scrooby do maintain one preacher between them who preaches one Sunday at the one town, and at the other the next Sunday by continual course, so that if the preacher preach at Bawtry he with other of the parish of Scrooby go thither to hear him, and otherwise he does not absent himself from his parish church on the Sabbath Day."[26]

As for the charge that he was repeating sermons, Brewster admitted that "he with others do note the sermons delivered by the preacher and in the afternoon they that have noted do confer with one another."[27] It is likely that Brewster had been leading such discussions ever since his return to Scrooby, a type of lay preaching that was referred to as prophesying.[28] The term "prophesying" as used by puritans at this time did not mean to foretell future events as had many of the Old Testament prophets. Rather it referred to a believer sharing an interpretation of a scriptural passage or any other religious viewpoint that he or she had learned from the inspiration of the holy spirit. While some clergy believed this was a gift bestowed only on ministers, other reformers believed that any believer could be so empowered by the Spirit. John Robinson defined it as "a kind of preaching" not to be limited to the ministry, "but that others having received a gift thereunto, may and ought to stir up the same, and to use it in the Church for edification, exhortation, and comfort."[29]

Prophesying as such became a critical means by which the laity helped shape the understanding of fellow believers. It could take the form of an individual preaching "by way of prophesying" to a gathered congregation, as many laity would do in England and later in New England, particularly when a Christian group lacked the services of a clergyman. The term was also used to describe sessions in which various members of a religious community meeting privately would share their understanding of an issue before them in a form of inspired dialogue. Such sessions might also involve believers sharing their experience of grace or their understanding of their spiritual state by providing accounts that might help others in their struggles to come to God.[30]

One of the questions that the records leave unanswered was the extent to which women participated in such gatherings. There is no doubt that women were expected to read so that they could access the scriptures directly, but less clear is how they were expected to use the knowledge and insight they thus gained. Looking at the broad picture of female participation in various religious exercises among puritans in the seventeenth century there are ample signs of women playing a role, though, as with so much of puritan doctrine and practice, there is no uniformity. Women were generally expected to lead family prayers when the head of the household was absent, but some also allowed this in cases where the female was more knowledgeable or pious. Various women of different social status—including Margaret Hoby, Jane Radcliffe, Brigit Cooke, Anne Fenwick, and Mary Simpson—were recorded as having led discussions of religious topics. Anne Hutchinson shared her views with fellow believers in Alford, Lincolnshire, and later in New England. Every collection of shared lay professions of faith includes contributions by women.[31]

Most clergy who wrote on the subject rejected the idea that women be allowed to prophesy, citing Saint Paul's injunction to the Corinthians that women be silent in church, and Timothy's instruction to "not allow a woman to teach or exercise authority over a man, but to remain quiet."[32] John Robinson, however, denied that Paul was urging a universal and absolute restraint of women prophesying, arguing that the apostle was rejecting this as an ordinary practice, but implicitly allowing women who were "immediately, and extraordinarily, and miraculously inspired" to "speak without restraining." To support this, he cited the fact that "Philip the Evangelist had four daughters . . . which did prophesy, and that in the presence of the Apostle," so that in biblical times "the spirit of prophesy kept his course upon their daughters as sons."[33]

In the Scrooby congregation and other churches following Congregational practices women took a leading role in the organization of the churches. Furthermore, they were admitted on the basis of their own qualifications, regardless of the position or faith of their fathers, husbands, or other relatives.[34] In the 1630s, members of the English Reformed Church in Amsterdam who had sought to secure Thomas Hooker and then John Davenport to join the congregation's ministry had been by thwarted the pastor, John Paget. They reacted by petitioning Paget to make changes in the church governance that would have enhanced the lay role. Women were among the signers of the petition, which among the other changes proposed would have allowed women to vote in ministerial elections.[35]

A fascinating example of female empowerment came in the reformation of the English church in Rotterdam by Hugh Peter in 1633. After the members of the congregation had subscribed to a new covenant, John Forbes, from a neighboring church, presided over the election of the church officers. Calling on a show of hands for the election of Peter as pastor, Forbes said, " 'I see the men choose him, but what do the women do?' . . . Hereupon," it was reported, "the women lift up their hands too."[36] The women obviously had not expected to have their votes counted, but Forbes and Peter evidently expected them to vote.[37] There was no hard and fast rule among puritans that prohibited female church members from participating in the choice of their officers or voting on censuring or excommunicating fellow members, as indicated by the petition in the English Reformed Church in Amsterdam. What happened in Rotterdam may have been unusual, but how unusual there is no way of knowing.[38] Nonetheless, the female members of the churches discussed in this book played a role even if its nature is unrecoverable.

Richard Bancroft, who succeeded John Whitgift as archbishop of Canterbury, undertook to further his predecessor's policy, formulating new church laws in 1604 and launching a zealous campaign to enforce them.[39] The effects were soon felt in Scrooby and the surrounding region. According to a report filed with the bishop of Norwich, John Robinson had delivered a controversial sermon in the parish of St. Andrews in Norwich in August 1603. While expressing hope that the new king might institute reforms, Robinson vehemently attacked the corruption of church courts and criticized the "dumb dogs" of the unlearned ministry.[40] He was consequently forced from his position.

Closer to Scrooby, Richard Clifton was deprived of his church living at Babworth, as was Richard Bernard at Worksop. John Smyth was deprived of his lectureship at Lincoln. John Robinson was removed from his position for having preached against the church establishment in Norwich. Initially some of those deprived continued to preach in parish churches. Robert Southworth, who had been in trouble with the authorities for refusing to wear the surplice, was finally deprived of his living in 1605, but subsequently preached at Scrooby as an unlicensed preacher. Two years later he was excommunicated. Henry Gray was deprived of his position as curate of Bawtry in 1605. Richard Clifton served briefly as curate there after his removal from Babworth.[41] These men supported their families with the income from their church livings so when they were deprived of their livings they lost their income. The price they and their families paid for their ideas was substantial.

While there was a continuing effort to reform the church from within, some of these men and many others began to question anew how far they could go in accepting the church's authority. When he lost his living, John Robinson continued to meet in a conventicle of laity in Norwich.[42] In 1605 he traveled to Cambridge to seek guidance from leading puritans there on some of the contested issues. In the morning he attended a lecture in which Laurence Chaderton argued that the power of church discipline rested in the individual congregation of believers. In the afternoon of the same day he listened to Paul Baynes argue for the importance of the godly to separate from the ungodly.[43]

In 1606 a meeting to discuss these issues was held in the Coventry home of Lady Isabel Bowes, a powerful puritan patroness. Robinson, along with Smyth, Bernard, and Clifton attended, as did the prominent clergymen Arthur Hildersham and John Dod. The focus of the discussion was "about withdrawing from true Churches, Ministers, and Worship corrupted." Smyth admitted that he had been vacillating about continuing to conform for nine months and had decided to leave the church. Robinson, Clifton, and Bernard agreed with him, though Bernard later changed his mind.[44] Hildersham and Dod urged patience.

At this point some of these individuals were becoming separatists, though Bernard's action demonstrated, as had Robert Browne's earlier, how fine the line between separatism and principled nonconformity remained, and how easy it was to cross that line. Brewster knew most of those who had met in Coventry. In addition to talking with them he began to read additional works that made the argument for separation. William and his wife had christened their first son Jonathan, which means "God has given" in Hebrew. As the religious situation evolved, the names they gave to some of their later children perhaps signified Brewster's concerns about what God had in store for him—Patience in 1603, when he hoped James I would bring change; Fear in 1605, when the repression of separatist groups was underway; Love in 1607, as he committed to seeking religious freedom abroad; and Wrestling (with God) in 1611, as he settled in the city of Leiden.[45]

In 1669 Nathaniel Morton, drawing on his uncle William Bradford's papers, wrote a history of the Plymouth colony in which he asserted that "In the year 1602 divers godly Christians of our English nation in the North of England, being studious of Reformation, and therefore not only witnessing against humane inventions, and additions in the Worship of God, but minding most the positive and practical part of divine institutions, they entered into covenant to walk with God, and one with another, in the enjoyment of the ordinances of God, according to the primitive pattern in the word of God."[46] It is much more likely that this actually occurred a few years later, after the new episcopal pressure for conformity and the deprivation of clergy such as Clifton and Robinson. In any case those who subscribed to the covenant proclaimed themselves members of a single visible body of saints committed to exemplifying the true Christian life. Another gathering of believers formed a similar congregation at Gainsborough under John Smyth.[47]

The core of the Scrooby congregation was likely the group of lay believers who had met regularly with Brewster to discuss sermons and examine the scriptures. According to William Bradford, who was one of those laymen, "they ordinarily met at his [Brewster's] house on the Lord's day . . . and with great love he entertained them when they came, making provision for them to his great charge."[48] Men and women would have shared their religious experiences. They organized themselves as a congregation by preparing and swearing to a covenant, a religious contract in which they committed themselves to a course of action. In later years John Murton, a disciple of Smyth, recalled the congregation's formation: "Do we not know the beginnings" of the Scrooby church, he wrote. "That there was first one stood up and made a covenant, and then another, and these two joined together, and then a third, and these became a church, say they, etc."[49] Bradford conveyed the essence of the covenant when he wrote that they threw off the "yoke of antichristian bondage, and as the Lord's free people joined themselves (by a covenant of the Lord) into a church estate, in the fellowship of the gospel, to walk in all his ways made known, or to be made known unto them, whatsoever it should cost them, the Lord assisting them."[50] The telling phrase "all his ways made known, or to be made known to them" indicates the openness of the believers to further light.[51]

The seventeenth-century historian Thomas Fuller identified "two grand ground-work" principles of the Scrooby covenant. The first was to "only take what was held forth in God's word," meaning they drew their beliefs about doctrine and practice from the scripture, rejecting traditions. The second was "not to make their present judgment binding unto them in the future." Fuller observed that this was a position their opponents found frustrating, since it enabled them to shift their positions, so that, for example, "they will not be tied on Tuesday morning to maintain their tenets on Monday night, if a new discovery intervene."[52]

Each of those who became a member of the congregation was an individual who believed him- or herself to be a recipient of God's saving grace and was perceived as such by the others who joined in the covenant. Those who had known each other for a while believed they could recognize the spark of grace in one another. When someone not so well known presented him- or herself the members were concerned, as the clergyman Henry Jacob expressed it, that they were neither "ignorant in religion, nor scandalous in their life."[53] Jacob applied ecclesiastical liberty to such individuals, regardless of whether they were men or women, masters or servants.[54] Such a candidate might be asked to profess his faith, and the congregants believed that they could judge whether the narration was inspired by grace. As one puritan writer expressed it, "A man that hath the spirit may know the spirit in another by the spirit."[55]

The covenant ceremony made the group a church of God. As John Robinson explained, "a company consisting though but of two or three separated from the world . . . and gathered into the name of Christ by a covenant made, to walk in all the ways of God made known to them, is a church, and so hath the whole power of Christ."[56] Having formed itself, the church chose the recently deprived Richard Clifton as their pastor.[57] He was, according to Bradford, "a grave and fatherly old man [who] . . . converted many to God by his faithful and painful ministry both in preaching and catechizing. Sound and orthodox he always was and so continued to his end."[58] It is believed that Brewster provided rooms for Clifton in the Scrooby manor house. It is likely that William Bradford also came to live with the Brewsters at this time.[59] At some point John Robinson joined the congregation, and he and his wife took up residence at the manor house.[60] Robinson was valued as a member of the church, but the fact that one of his children was baptized in Norwich in January 1607 suggests that he did not play a leading role with the Scrooby congregation until later that year.[61] Bradford's recollection was that he was "a famous and worthy man . . . who afterwards was their pastor for many years."[62]

A letter written by Thomas Helwys, who for a time was part of Smyth's Gainsborough congregation and became one of the leaders of the Baptist movement, provides insight into how these two groups worshipped. The believers began their Sabbath worship at eight in the morning, combining psalm singing with preaching and scripture reading. Members of the congregation discussed the reading by way of prophesying. After a mid-day break, the congregation reassembled for a similar afternoon session that would end at five or six.[63] Such gatherings were illegal and likely the cause of establishment suspicion. There is no indication in this letter or elsewhere that the congregations celebrated the Lord's Supper or administered baptism, which suggests that at the time Helwys was referring to, the members of the two churches were still wrestling with their relation to local parishes and parishioners and may have received the sacraments in their parishes.[64]

The best guide to the beliefs of the Scrooby congregation is to be found in the recollections of William Bradford, who tried to capture and explain them to the next generation in a series of "conferences" with those young men. These survive in manuscript as "dialogues between those born in New England and the ancient men who had come over from England." The third of these begins with an assault on Catholicism not unusual for a "hot Protestant." Perhaps most fundamental to the puritan critique of Catholicism was that "the Papists hold, and boldly affirm, that the church is not known by the word of God; but the word of God is known by the church." He further complained that the Catholic Church "teach[es] them [the laity] to worship images and fall down before stocks and stones." Bradford asserted that Catholics encourage worship of the saints and believe that relics of the saints have power to help those who pray to them. He called out the "doctrines of purgatory, penance, pilgrimages," use of the sign of the cross, use of incense in worship, "praying upon beads for the living and the dead," and others, "a number too tedious to relate."[65]

Their criticism of the Church of England rested in part on the retention of Catholic "vain ceremonies, profitable for nothing, . . . such as the cross in baptism, kneeling at the Lord's Supper, wearing the surplice, keeping of holy days, [and] bishoping of children, etc." Bradford also lamented that the English authorities were guilty of putting more emphasis on "strict conformity to the common [Prayer Book] service than either the powerful preaching of the word of God and sound doctrine, or holiness of life and conversation."[66]

Reformers such as had gathered in Scrooby recognized that bishops existed in the earliest Christian communities, but they denied that those men wielded authority over believers. "Lord Bishops," such as existed in the Church of England, "invested with sole spiritual power and government, and exercising sole authority, power, and government over the churches, without their choice or consent, is strange from the scriptures, no institution of Christ, but a human device and intrusion." For Bradford, Brewster, and those who gathered in Brewster's Scrooby manor house, the "church is not to be taken for certain of the worshipful clergymen alone, but for a whole assembly and congregation of God's people."[67] The believers were the church.

It is not clear how far the Scrooby believers had embraced the Congregational principles Brewster had read about by 1607, but Bradford in 1652 could clearly articulate the position toward which they had at least been moving. A "church," he wrote, "is a company of the faithful which agree together in following the word of God and embracing pure religion." The keys that Christ bestowed on the church were given to each individual congregation, meaning its members and not just its officers. And those officers were to be chosen by the members and not by "the king alone, or queen, or the patrons, or bishops, or archbishop, etc. as it is used in England."[68]

It was their hostility to Roman Catholicism and their criticisms of the governance and ceremonial practices of the Church of England that made this and other puritan groups distinctive. But the sermons they listened to and discussed had little to do with these issues. Indeed, it was "the preaching in England and hearing the same [that] doth beget men to the faith."[69]

The starting point of all doctrinal beliefs was accepting that the almighty God was unknowable. As John Robinson expressed it, "The essence of God is known only to himself, but is undiscernible to all men, and angels, partly by reason of its infiniteness, which therefore no finite understanding can comprehend, and partly for that no voice, sign, or form can sufficiently express it either to sense or reason." Those striving to understand God and his will could only know that which God revealed to them, and even with grace comprehending God and his will would be imperfect. This is why, through prayer and meditation, believers reminded themselves of their frailty even as they tried to find further light.[70] Aspects of God were revealed in the world, the creation revealing aspects of the creator. History suggested aspects of God's providential design. But the most important source of understanding God was what was revealed in the scriptures. This was why the ability to read and discuss the Bible was central to the Protestant mission in general and that of the puritans in particular.[71]

Their God was a single godhead consisting of three distinct and co-equal persons—Father, Son (Jesus Christ), and Holy Spirit. How this could be true was, like so much else, a mystery accepted by faith but incomprehensible to natural reason. God was immutable, eternal, and infinite, with attributes that included goodness, power, love, and wisdom, among others. They tried to convey some of what they believed about God by using analogies drawn from human experience—for example, God was a loving father, a just judge, a good shepherd. But while such images might enlighten believers about certain divine attributes, they carried with them a danger of confusing the image with the reality. This was why the puritans rejected the use of painted, carved, or sculpted images of God in their churches—God might behave like a father but he was not simply masculine. The true God also had maternal attributes, which some puritans focused on in their writings.

There was no such hesitancy among puritan preachers when it came to discussing mankind, though here too most warned about trying to reach hard and fast conclusions about the matter. For the most part they followed the understanding of human nature and destiny explicated by the French Protestant reformer John Calvin. Man was originally good, created in God's image, and offered eternal happiness in return for perfect obedience to God's will, a bargain some referred to as a Covenant of Works. But the parents of humankind, Adam and Eve, violated that covenant, losing their innocence through the original sin, corrupting their natures by that offense, and passing on that taint to all who came after them. As the *New England Primer* would put it, "In Adam's Fall, We Sinned All," though how that corruption was inherited was a matter of contention among theologians.

Following the Fall, God set forth commandments to lay out the path of righteousness. But the corruption of original sin led all men and women who followed the first parents to commit their own actual sins, choosing forms of self-gratification rather than obeying the law of God. Sin required punishment, and the penalty was damnation. One of the key points in puritan self-understanding was recognition that one was a sinner, in thrall to sin, and deserving of damnation. Nothing an individual could do on his or her own could break this addiction to sin or earn God's favor. But because God was loving as well as just, there was hope, for God chose some individuals to be saved despite their unworthiness. God had become man in the person of Jesus Christ, who atoned for the sins of the elect by his own suffering and death, and who offered renewed lessons of hope and love. There were nuances that were not clear. Calvin himself had urged that his followers not delve too deeply into the mysteries surrounding this doctrine of predestination, but many did so anyway. Did God explicitly select some to be damned as well as those to be saved? On what basis did God choose? Was there anything a person could do to influence that choice? Were those saved required to participate in the process in some way?

Saving grace could come in a moment of blinding revelation, comparable to the experience of Paul on the road to Damascus, or it could make itself felt in a slow, often unclear, progression with the individual alternately experiencing doubts and reassurance. But the elect, those who were chosen to be saints, received not only saving grace but also the sustaining graces that helped them to better comprehend and do God's will. Evidence of such comprehension and action were among the signs looked for as an individual examined his or her own spiritual progress, and by a gathered congregation in assessing a potential candidate. But while good behavior could be seen as evidence of a person having been saved, it could never be a cause of salvation.

What did the men and women of Scrooby, and their fellow puritans, believe constituted good behavior? Contrary to popular notions, the puritans were not killjoys opposed to drink, sex, or other activities. The starting point for understanding their views was the belief that all of the creation was good because the creator was good. "Evil," wrote John Robinson, "stands in the abuse of good." Drinking wine, beer, or ale was acceptable. But, wrote Robinson, sin occurs when things that are good are "unmeasurably used, as is said of wine, that the first cup quencheth thirst, the second procures cheerfulness, the third drunkenness, and the fourth madness." In cases such as this it was immoderate use that led to sin.

In other cases, such as in expressions of sexuality, sin resulted from applying God's gift "unaptly, or to wrong ends, or persons."[72] Many puritans actually viewed intercourse as a joyous expression of love bestowed upon mankind by God to bind a couple together. Preachers urged upon their congregations the "duty to desire." The English puritan minister William Gouge wrote that intercourse between a husband and wife should occur often, willingly, and cheerfully. In Massachusetts the Boston church on one occasion excommunicated a man for withholding sexual favors from his wife. But while intercourse between husband and wife was viewed as the proper use of the sexuality that God had bestowed upon man, any other use of that gift was an abuse. Thus, puritans condemned and punished fornication, adultery, homosexuality, bestiality, and other sexual indulgences outside of marriage.

The images of somber-looking figures dressed in black, so typical of nineteenth-century depictions of Pilgrims and puritans, are fundamentally misleading. Estate inventories reveal clothing of expensive fabric and vibrant colors. It was not uncommon for a gentleman such as William Davison or William Brewster to wear a suit of yellow canary silk or cardinal red satin. The heart of puritan views about dress was to wear what was appropriate to one's station in life. Laborers and farmers had limited wardrobes, often consisting of woolen outfits that were dyed in earth tones, colors that were less likely to reveal dirt. At the other end of the social spectrum the wealthier members of society might very well wear the types of garments worn by courtiers at the royal court, some of whom were, in fact, puritans. Magistrates and ministers (among those most likely to have their portraits painted) were likely to own clothing that was dyed black, but this was not a sign of somberness but of distinction, since black was the most expensive fabric dye and a sign of high status.

Of course, there were differences among puritans as to where to draw the line between use and abuse, proper and improper behavior. But it was not their understanding of God, salvation, and proper behavior that caused trouble for William Brewster and his fellow believers in Scrooby. It was their decision that membership in the Church of England required practices that led them away from the truth and inhibited them from properly pursuing it.

The situation of the Scrooby believers was made more dangerous when Tobias Matthew was transferred from the diocese of Durham to the archdiocese of York in 1606. His predecessor in the post, Matthew Hutton, had treated puritan dissidents with relative moderation and even suggested to the government a lenient policy. In contrast, Matthew was determined to curry favor with Archbishop Bancroft and the king by rooting out the reformers. On a visitation of his parishes in 1607 he preached a sermon, "Contra Brownists," at Bawtry. He struck at both the dissident clergy and their lay patrons. Gervase Neville of Scrooby was seized for "disobedience and schismatical obstinacy" in early November 1607, tried before the archbishop and High Commission as a "very dangerous schismatical separatist Brownist and irreligious subject," and jailed in York Castle. The following month orders were given (perhaps as a result of Neville's testimony) to arrest William Brewster and other Scrooby residents on charges of "disobedience in matters of religion" and separatism. When church officials came to get them, Brewster and his fellow believers had disappeared.[73]

Bradford described the situation they found themselves in: "They could not long continue in any peaceable condition," he remembered, "but were hunted & persecuted on every side, so as their former afflictions were but as flea-bitings by comparison." "Some were taken & clapped up in prison," he wrote, "others had their houses beset & watched night and day, . . . and the most were fain to fly & leave their houses & habitations, and the means of their livelihood."[74] Brewster, who had resigned his position as postmaster in September 1607, was fined £20 by the High Commission when he did not appear before them, and the body issued new orders for his apprehension.[75] Bradford remembered that after the first attacks on them the members of the congregation had "continued together about a year, and kept their meetings every Sabbath in one place or other, exercising their worship of God amongst themselves, notwithstanding all the diligence & malice of their adversaries."[76] But continuing to do so was impractical. So they decided to emigrate to the Netherlands, which was noted for its policy of religious freedom and where they knew that other English religious dissidents had found refuge.

3

Refugees

At the Hampton Court Conference, James I had asserted his intent to enforce conformity to the beliefs and practices of the church and to chase from the land all who resisted. In subsequent years steps were taken to achieve that goal in the Scrooby area, with leaders of the congregation brought before church authorities. But James had threatened further actions, saying that he would "harry them out of the land, or else do worse." What was meant by "worse" was no doubt of concern to those who remembered the executions of Barrow and Greenwood in 1593. But having decided to leave their homes, the members of the congregation found, according to Bradford, that "though they could not stay, yet were they not suffered to go, but the ports, & havens were shut against them."[1]

Why were there difficulties in their leaving? Since the 1540s, restrictions had been placed on those traveling overseas, many of them designed to curtail the journeys of Catholics.[2] Those who sought to leave were required to have a license, and the customs officials stationed in each port to check on the passage of goods would also have been on the lookout as well for those seeking to leave without authorization. These procedures would have raised difficulties for the separatist emigrants, though, as would become evident, local officials were not always aware of what was expected of them and how to handle offenders.

Faced with these legal barriers, the congregation decided to seek passage from Boston, a port in Lincolnshire where many residents had reform sympathies and where there could well have been puritans. Still, they were forced "to seek secret means of conveyance, and to bribe . . . the mariners, and give extraordinary rates for their passages."[3] Their first attempt, in the fall of 1607, failed. How many were involved in this effort is unknown, but after they had embarked the captain of the ship betrayed them to the authorities. The officials who boarded the vessel forced the passengers off, "rifled and ransacked them, searching to their shirts for money, yea even the women further than became modesty; and then carried them back into the town." "Stripped of their money, books and much other goods," the congregants were handed over to the Boston magistrates.[4] The various proclamations regarding emigration had not specified penalties. Since the local authorities seemed unsure of how to charge the prisoners, they wrote to the Privy Council for advice. These were likely not the types of emigrants the royal government had been targeting, but they were Separatists.

According to William Bradford's later recollection, after a month in confinement most of the prisoners were released to return to their homes, but the Council ordered that seven of the leading men were to be kept under guard in Boston until being transferred to Lincoln Castle for the Assizes, the periodic court sessions where judges from the national courts sat with local magistrates to hear serious cases. According to Bradford, William Brewster was the "chief of those that were taken at Boston and suffered the greatest loss; and of the seven that were kept longest in prison and after bound over to the assizes."[5] Meanwhile, Mary Brewster, deprived of her home and many of the family possessions, was forced to depend on the goodwill of fellow believers as she cared for the couple's three children.[6]

There are no surviving records of the local assizes at this time, but it would appear that the Boston seven appeared before the court and were released on bond for future trial. In a separate matter, in April 1608 the archbishop of York informed the Exchequer (the national treasury) that Brewster, Richard Jackson, and Robert Rochester, all of Scrooby, had been fined £20 each as separatists for not having appeared when previously summoned before the ecclesiastical authorities.[7]

The congregation made another attempt to depart in May 1608, but again they were thwarted. On the earlier occasion they had engaged an English ship captain; this time they found a Dutch captain who owned his own ship. They explained their situation and "he bade them not fear, for he would do well enough." He planned to take them on board at a point along the Humber River near Grimsby. But when only a small number of the men had boarded, armed militia were seen approaching. The captain quickly sailed away, leaving behind the women, some of the men, and most of their possessions.[8]

Those who were on the ship soon found themselves on a treacherous voyage across the North Sea. Bradford, whose account makes it likely that he was aboard, wrote of them having experienced "a fearful storm at sea" on a voyage that lasted "fourteen days or more," during which "they neither saw sun, moon nor stars, and were driven near the coast of Norway, the mariners themselves often despairing of life; and once with shrieks and cries, gave over all, as if the ship had been foundered in the sea, and they sinking without recovery." At one point the waves crashed over the ship and "the water ran into their mouths and ears, and the mariners cried out we sink, we sink." But eventually "the ship did not only recover, but shortly after the violence of the storm began to abate, and the lord filled their afflicted minds with such comforts as everyone cannot understand."[9] Many, Bradford included, would have remembered this experience when they later considered the far more dangerous voyage to America.

Meanwhile members of the congregation who had been left behind were taken up by the authorities, subjected to intrusive searches, had their possessions seized, and were hauled before the magistrates. Again, they were soon released. Over the following months, many of them gradually made their way across the North Sea, individually or

Fig. 3.1 Pilgrim locations in England and the Netherlands. Map created by Matthew Spak for the Geography Department's Geo-Graphics Laboratory at Millersville University, Millersville, PA, USA.

in small groups, and were able to reunite in Amsterdam, having used most of what remained of their resources.[10] According to Bradford, Robinson and Brewster were among the last to leave, having stayed behind to assist other members of the congregation.[11]

Amsterdam was familiar to William Brewster, but the city's scale and culture were a shock to the other English refugees from the Scrooby region. The Netherlands was a republic rather than a monarchy, its autonomy only recently achieved after a revolt against Spanish control. Independence had fostered growth, with newcomers arriving from all over Europe to take advantage of economic opportunities and greater religious freedom than was to be found elsewhere on the Continent. Amsterdam itself was the international trading center of a vigorously expanding Dutch economy, its port crowded with ships from the Baltic, southern Europe, and even the Far East, the sea air carrying the smells of fish and exotic spices. The Amstel River divided Amsterdam; the East Side was the older section. Passage through the city was facilitated by an expanding system of canals.[12]

These English immigrants faced challenges common to most refugee communities at all times. Few, if any, spoke the language of their hosts. They were unfamiliar with many of the customs of the new land, some of which challenged their own values. They were entering into an economy that called for skills that differed from those they had employed at home, and adapting to new work was made difficult by the language barrier.

The Dutch revolt against Spain had begun in 1568. The northern, mostly Protestant, provinces of the Low Countries formed a union in 1579. Two years later they declared their independence from Spanish rule, but not until 1648 did Spain recognize that independence. England under Elizabeth had supported the Dutch Protestant cause, sending troops and envoys such as William Davison as expressions of that support. When the Scrooby Englishmen arrived, open conflict had stopped, and in 1609 the Dutch and Spanish signed a formal truce that was not due to expire until 1619. The 1579 Union of Utrecht had called for freedom of conscience in the Netherlands, and though the official church was the Dutch Calvinist Reformed, other faiths were tolerated. Among them were Lutherans, Mennonites, and French-speaking Walloon Calvinists. There was a major influx of Jews from the Iberian Peninsula, with a Jewish quarter that grew from about two hundred residents to over a thousand between 1610 and 1642.

English merchants who did business in the country were allowed to organize their own churches, and many of those were ministered to by ordained English clergymen who had left England because of their puritan beliefs. For example, William Davison served as an elder to the English merchant church in Antwerp and solicited Walter Travers as the congregation's pastor. But the Dutch also tolerated religious dissenters who rejected the Church of England and fled England to put into practice a purer faith than they were used to.[13]

The most famous of these separate congregations was the "Ancient Church" in Amsterdam.[14] Its roots went back to the London separatist congregation that had been ministered to by Francis Johnson. Members had first arrived in the Netherlands in 1593 following Johnson's arrest in England. After a brief stay in the city of Kampen, they returned to Amsterdam, where they worshipped in the private home of Jean de l'Ecluse, formerly a member of the French Walloon church. Johnson, following his release and his failed attempt to establish a New World colony, joined them as pastor in 1597. Around the same time Henry Ainsworth joined the church and was chosen for the ministerial post of Teacher.[15] John Smyth had left Gainsborough, and by the time Brewster and Robinson arrived he was worshipping with the Ancient Church.

Henry Ainsworth, a former Cambridge student, had adopted a separatist position and been arrested by the English authorities. Upon release, he went to Ireland, where he was again arrested as a separatist.[16] The Scrooby puritans had no previous contact with Ainsworth but soon came to respect him for his knowledge and skillful preaching. William Bradford wrote that some of the "most eminent" language scholars at the University of Leiden believed that Ainsworth excelled all of them and most in Europe in his knowledge of Hebrew. In his sermons Ainsworth "had an excellent gift of teaching and opening the Scriptures and things did flow from him with that facility, plainness, and sweetness as did much affect the hearers." He was "most ready and pregnant in the Scriptures as if the book of God had been written in his heart." John Robinson consulted with Ainsworth on a wide range of subjects.[17]

Arriving in Amsterdam over a period of months, the Scrooby refugees made their way to the Ancient Church, where they joined in worship while maintaining their own identity as a covenanted congregation. They found the Ancient Church wracked by controversy. The greatest challenge for all Congregationalists was how to deal with differences of opinion within a particular church. This was especially difficult in the case of a congregation such as that of the Ancient Church, with a membership that was constantly changing due to new arrivals. Ideally, when a church could not agree on a particular matter of doctrine or practice its members would pray for and wait for further light. The danger was that someone who claimed inspiration from the spirit for an extreme viewpoint might not be willing to concede that there might be further light.

But nondoctrinal differences could be disruptive as well, and such clashes had divided the Ancient Church. One led to the excommunication of Francis Johnson's brother George over his wife's proper dress and deportment. In 1601 a group of members sought to remove Henry Ainsworth as teacher because he had previously submitted to the bishops and worshipped in the Church of England. A zealous minority not only rejected any interaction with the English national church as apostasy but also believed that anyone who had been guilty of such behavior in the past should be barred from office in the congregation. The faction attacking Ainsworth was unsuccessful, but considerable acrimony remained. In 1606 the congregation was thrown further into turmoil over charges that one of the deacons, Daniel Studley, had molested his stepdaughter and beaten his wife.[18]

Doctrinal controversy erupted in 1608, when John Smyth published a tract titled *Differences of the Churches of the Separation*, in which he took issue with some of the positions of the Ancient Brethren regarding governance and the sacrament. In later years William Bradford recalled that he had heard Smyth warn that those who had arrived in the Netherlands, "having now come into a place of liberty are in great danger if we look not well to our ways, for we are like men set upon the ice, and therefore may easily slide and fall." But, as Bradford concluded, "it appears it is an easier matter to give good counsel than to follow it," because Smyth himself soon disrupted the Ancient Church by espousing controversial views.[19]

Smyth argued that the congregation should reject donations from well-wishers in England because a church should be solely supported by its members. He did not explicitly reject lay prophesying but asserted that anyone who preached should be able to read the scriptures in the original languages and explain their meaning to his listeners. Smyth claimed that no true church existed. Because he believed that baptism was essential for salvation, with no true church to administer the sacrament he baptized himself and then offered to baptize all those who followed him. Early in 1609 Richard Clifton challenged these views.

Troubled by such disputes, the likelihood that the divisions in the Ancient Church would deepen, and the desire to avoid being tarred by the sexual scandals and anabaptist controversies in that church, John Robinson, William Brewster, and other leaders of the Scrooby group decided to seek a different Dutch refuge.[20] In January 1609 Robinson and Brewster journeyed the twenty-two miles to Leiden, where they met with Jan van Hout, the town secretary, whom Brewster knew from visiting the city with William Davison in the mid-1580s. Robinson, "Minister of God's Word, together with some members of the Christian Reformed Religion, born in the kingdom of Great Britain, and numbering one hundred persons or thereabouts, men and women," petitioned the Leiden authorities for permission "to come to live in this city."[21] The petition was granted and entered into the records on February 12, 1609.

The congregation's new home had figured prominently in the war for Dutch independence. In 1574 Leiden withstood a lengthy siege by the Spanish forces during which thousands died of starvation and thousands more of the plague. In the following year the Dutch leader William of Orange commemorated that victory by establishing a university there. Surrounded by town walls and defensive towers, the city was one of brick houses and large stone churches. It was a textile center that depended largely on refugee labor, particularly after its growth had been stunted by a significant loss of lives during an epidemic in the early seventeenth century. There was a substantial population of French-speaking Reformed Protestants known as Huguenots or Walloons.[22] The fact that only a truce with Spain preserved the peace was a reason why the city was also crowded with British mercenaries, one of whom was Myles Standish.[23]

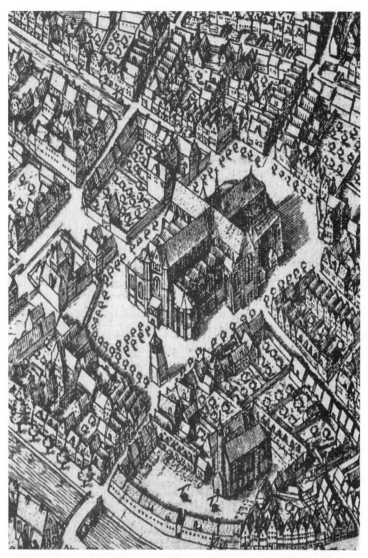

Fig. 3.2 Pilgrim neighborhood in Leiden. Detail of Pieter Bast's Map of Leiden (1600). Photo courtesy of the Leiden American Pilgrim Museum.

The move from Amsterdam was largely completed by May 1609, though some of the old Scrooby group, including their pastor, Richard Clifton, chose to remain in Amsterdam. In keeping with congregational principles whereby the departure of a covenanted member to another church required the approval of those he had originally covenanted with, the Scrooby-Leiden congregation officially dismissed Clifton to the Ancient Church.[24] For those who did make the move the first task was finding places to live, a challenge made difficult by a housing shortage that would only be alleviated with an extension of the city walls on the north side of the city in 1612. Some new arrivals squatted in former Roman Catholic convents that had been abandoned with the Reformation, while others found shelter in rows of little dwellings erected in gardens behind some of the substantial houses.[25] Brewster found a relatively large house, undoubtedly with the assistance of one of his Dutch friends. But life in Leiden was nevertheless a struggle. He had spent considerable sums on helping to finance the emigration, he had many children, and "in regard to his former breeding and course of life [was] not so fit for many employments."[26] The house he acquired was a corner property, a story and a half tall with stairs leading upstairs. The family lived on the ground floor, eating, sleeping, and praying in a confined space. The house did have an indoor privy. For a man who had lived in a manor house for much of his life, the lack of comforts and the most basic privacy must have been striking.[27]

By 1611, members of the church had acquired a house referred to as the Green Close, fifteen yards from the large Leiden church called the Pieterskerk. Green Close served both as John Robinson's home and a place for the congregation to worship. The property had an attached plot on which twelve small houses were built, with twelve families of church members accommodated there.[28]

Equally important to finding housing was finding employment. Some took advantage of opportunities in the textile trade. William Bradford worked as a weaver of fustian, a high-quality cloth that was a mixture of wool and linen.[29] The congregation member Robert Cushman, who had been a grocer in Canterbury, became a wool carder in Leiden. Other newcomers became glovers, hatters, wool carders, and twine makers.[30] After a number of years of struggle without a regular income, William Brewster "fell into a way (by reason he had the

Latin tongue) to teach many students who had a desire to learn the English tongue, to teach them English, and by his method they quickly attained it with great facility, for he drew rules to learn it by, after the Latin manner."[31] Danes, Germans, and presumably Dutchmen "resorted to him, . . . some of them being great men's sons."[32]

But many of the English whose search for freedom to worship God properly brought them to the Netherlands found themselves in poverty. This was not only a problem for the English in Leiden. One report of the "hardness in the Low Countries" was that in Amsterdam Henry Ainsworth had to "live on 9 pence a week" and that if his "people suffered him to live on 9 pence a week with roots boiled" for his diet, "either the people were grown extreme low in estate or the growth of their godliness was come to a very low ebb."[33]

In the decade following their arrival in Leiden members of the congregation would come to appreciate and adopt some of the practices of the Dutch, such as civil rather than church marriages, but they would also be confronted with cultural norms that forced them to think about and justify some of their own positions. Perhaps most important, in their search for further religious light they would encounter different views both in books that were more readily available in the Netherlands and in discussions with the men and women whom they met in the streets and academic halls.

At the time he left England, John Robinson had agreed with the extreme separatist position that condemned engagement in any form of religious activity with members of the Church of England. This viewpoint was clearly expressed in his 1610 work, *A Justification of Separation*. In it he lashed out at the "Church of England, wherein the greatest part of the parishes by far have dark midnight for vision." The ministry of the church was unlawful and ungodly, where "preaching is but an accident, and no way essential or necessary." The bishops were "accursed" for insisting on the use of ceremonies and requirements that "blind the eyes and stop the mouths of the best seers and painful preachers."[34] He was critical of the administration of baptism to children whose parents demonstrated neither "faith nor holiness."[35] He attacked admission to the Lord's Supper of individuals whom Christ himself "disdains all communion and fellowship" with.[36] A true church was that formed by two or more individuals who, as "lively stones couple themselves together by voluntary profession and covenants," becoming "a spiritual building, the Lord's Temple."[37] With or without a minister, such a covenanted community was a true church and not subject to the judgment of the national church or any other churches. In this work Robinson also set forth his belief in prophesying, not only by the ministry but by all who have "received a gift thereunto, [who] may and ought to . . . use it in the church, for edification, exhortation, and comfort."[38]

Because Clifton had remained in Amsterdam, the Leiden congregation elected Robinson their pastor. In that office he was responsible for overseeing the congregation's affairs, teaching, and administering the sacraments. He was expected to devote his time to studying the scriptures in order to understand them better and be the primary teacher of the congregation. He was also to exercise a pastoral role in tending to the spiritual welfare of his congregants.[39] Brewster was elected elder. Robinson and Brewster rejected the model of Presbyterians and others that gave elders a governing power in matters of discipline. They believed that governing authority rested in the congregation as a whole. Brewster's function was to lead the people rather than command them.[40] In addition to Robinson as pastor and Brewster as elder, the congregation elected three deacons—Samuel Fuller was one; it is likely that Robert Cushman and John Carver were the others.[41] The responsibilities of the deacons was to oversee the secular aspects of the church—collecting donations from the faithful for the support of the pastor, maintaining their place of worship, and caring for the poor, which could include visiting them and providing for their physical needs.[42] Deacons may have been responsible for supervising the children during worship. In a 1618 statement in which the church identified with most of the beliefs and practices of the French Reformed Church, they specified that, while that church chose its elders and deacons annually, the Leiden English church elected them for life.[43]

Central to the life of the church was religious worship in individual homes and that conducted as a congregation. Initially group services were in private homes. After Robinson took up residence in the Green Close, they assembled on the ground floor of that structure. Religious freedom was not absolute in the Netherlands. When religious controversies led the authorities to crack down on services in private homes, the University of Leiden allowed the congregation to use the Begijnhof Chapel on campus.[44]

Various sources suggest how they conducted communal worship. There were two services every Sunday. The four-hour morning service would begin with Pastor Robinson offering an extempore prayer, followed by a reading from scripture and an explanation of the text. Those gathered then joined in the singing of psalms without musical accompaniment; early on they used the Sternhold and Hopkins translation of the psalms, but after its publication in 1612 most likely they used the translation by their friend Henry Ainsworth.[45] Robinson, or perhaps another member of the congregation, would then preach, explaining a passage from scripture and applying its message to those gathered before him. The morning service ended with the singing of additional psalms. They baptized infants after the morning service. They then came together for Holy Communion, which Bradford says was celebrated weekly. The afternoon service, which could last three to four hours, featured lay prophesying, with a text being offered and then discussed by the congregation.[46]

Although female members of the congregation played a role in its affairs, the exact nature of that role is difficult to determine. There was no consistency in the positions taken by various leaders known to Robinson and Brewster. The separatist John Smyth believed that women should participate in the choice of new members and other church business but should not be allowed to preach. Henry Ainsworth and Francis Johnson rejected the idea of female voting, as did Robinson himself.[47] But women likely had a larger role in the Leiden church than in most puritan congregations. John Robinson believed women "may make profession of faith, or confession of sin, say amen to the churches prayers, sing psalms vocally, accuse a brother of sin, witness an accusation, or defend themselves being accused."[48] He went further, writing that "one faithful man, yea, or woman either, may as truly and effectually loose and bind, both in heaven and earth, as all the ministers in the world." On another occasion he stated that "in a case extraordinary, namely when no man will, I see not but a woman may reprove the church, rather than suffer it to go on in apparent wickedness."[49] Even if limited to certain circumstances, this authorization for women to criticize men in public was a striking departure from the norms of the time.[50]

Contrary to some scholarly opinion, joining the congregation did not require a narrative of how saving grace came into a person's life, but simply a statement of the principles of faith and a willingness to swear to the covenant. The doctrinal faith asserted had to be true, but the deciding factor in whether an individual was admitted to the church or not was how the existing members assessed the quality of the candidate's profession. While acknowledging that no one could be totally confident of judging whether someone had received the transforming grace of salvation, puritans believed that a saint would know another saint when he met him or her. Thomas Hooker wrote that the saints could "tell how to judge" those who were truly sanctified, and another puritan divine, Walter Craddock, stated that "a man that hath the spirit may know the spirit in another by the spirit."[51] In Scrooby and in Leiden the fact that an individual was willing to suffer persecution and economic hardship to join the congregation was likely seen as strong evidence that they were being moved by the spirit.

Not only did candidates not have to provide a narrative of how they were saved but also they did not have to explicitly reject the Church of England. Edward Winslow, who joined the congregation in Leiden, later wrote that "if any joining to us . . . , either when we lived at Leiden in Holland or since we came to New England, have with the manifestation of their faith and profession of holiness held forth therewith separation from the Church of England, I have divers times, both in the one place and the other, heard either Mr. Robinson our pastor, or Mr. Brewster our Elder stop them forthwith, showing them that we required no such things at their hands." All that was required was that a candidate "hold forth faith in Christ Jesus, holiness in the fear of God, and submission to every ordinance and appointment of God, leaving the Church of England to themselves, and to the Lord before whom they should stand or fall, and to whom we ought to pray to reform what was amiss amongst them."[52]

Though they had decided to leave the Ancient Church, the congregation tried to maintain ties with that church, interaction that would inform Robinson and Brewster in their search for better understanding of God's will. Shortly after the Scrooby group had left for Leiden a new dispute had broken out in the Ancient Church when Francis Johnson rejected a fundamental principle of congregationalism by asserting that in principle and practice governing authority over the church rested with the eldership. A faction led by Henry Ainsworth challenged this and appealed to the Leiden congregation for assistance. Robinson and Brewster agreed it was their duty to respond to this "request of the brethren . . . to come unto you [the Ancient Church], not to oppose any person, or to maintain any charge of error, but by all other brotherly means to help forward your holy peace." Despite their efforts, Johnson's supporters voted to remove Ainsworth as the congregation's Teacher.[53]

Brewster and Robinson traveled to Amsterdam to further discuss the issues with the church there. At one point in the meeting, according to a contemporary, the disruptions caused by Ainsworth's supporters was such that Robinson told them that "he had rather walk in peace with five godly persons, than to live with five hundred or five thousand such unquiet persons as these were." Ainsworth was temporarily restored to his office and various proposals made to bridge the gap between the two sides. But the resolution that the Leiden messengers thought they had achieved was broken. Johnson proposed allowing Ainsworth and the other dissidents to be dismissed to the Leiden church. But uprooting their families and abandoning their means of livelihood was unacceptable to Ainsworth and his supporters, who simply seceded from the Ancient Church.[54]

Robinson, Brewster, and their fellow believers were committed to the search for further understanding of God's truth. Their efforts to do so are a significant part of the story of their stay in Leiden and are critical to understanding the beliefs they brought to the New World. Robinson believed that "for things left dark in Scripture, they must be unto us [a] matter of humiliation in our natural blindness, and of more earnest meditation and prayer with all good conscience."[55] He sought to learn through interaction with other churches and individuals, including those who were not separatist. In Amsterdam and then in Leiden, the members of the congregation came into contact with representatives of various different faiths, including Dutch Reformed, Portuguese Jews, Scandinavian and Dutch Lutherans, and Dutch Mennonites. In 1617 the entire congregation participated in a two-day conference with Pieter Twisck, a Mennonite who had written a history of opinions advocating religious toleration.[56]

Robinson became particularly interested in breaking down the barriers among English puritans. Antonius Walaeus, a professor of theology at the University of Leiden, attested in 1628, after Robinson's death, that he and Robinson had spoken often "concerning the separation between their congregation and other English congregations in this country, and that he [Robinson] has at divers times testified that he was disposed to do his utmost to remove this schism."[57] Brewster, who had engaged with such churches during his travels with Davison, undoubtedly helped in this process. Robinson acknowledged that having met with others, he "through my vehement desire of peace" did "remit and loose of my former resolution & did (to speak as the truth is) forget some of my former grounds."[58]

In Leiden itself a group of English puritans had come together three years before the arrival of the Scrooby refugees to form what became known as the English Reformed Church in Leiden. That church was recognized as part of the Dutch Reformed Church, which meant it was a state church, receiving funds and a chapel for worship from the municipal authorities. In 1610 Robert Durie became their preacher. A Scottish Presbyterian, Durie had been banished after being convicted of treason for attending a church general assembly that had been condemned by the king. His son, John Durie (or Dury), was a student at the University of Leiden when the Scrooby congregation arrived, and he likely knew Brewster, Robinson, and other members of that church. In later years the younger Durie became one of the leading crusaders for Protestant unification, urging the various groups to overlook what distinguished them so as to focus on the essentials of faith, a position strikingly similar to that embraced by Brewster.[59] When the elder Durie died in 1616 he was replaced by Hugh Goodyear, an English puritan who was a friend and correspondent of various figures who would play a key role in the history of puritanism in the Atlantic world.[60] Goodyear was a friend of the English puritan John Cotton and sent promising students to reside with Cotton and learn from him in his household academy. Goodyear also corresponded with William Ames, Hugh Peter, and Ralph Smith, a longtime friend and later pastor at Plymouth.[61] Another church that Brewster and Robinson engaged with was the English merchant congregation in Middelburg, whose pastors had included separatists and nonseparatists.

While Robinson's beliefs evolved from his readings and discussions with William Brewster and other members of the congregation, it was discussion with three other English exiles—Henry Jacob, William Ames, and Robert Parker—that were most significant. It was later recalled that some of the Leiden congregation "knew Mr. Parker, Doctor Ames, and Mr. Jacobs in Holland when they sojourned for a time in Leiden, and all three boarded together and had their victuals dressed by one of our acquaintance."[62] The nature of these interactions is important to understand both the history of the Leiden congregation in the Netherlands and its later influence.

Henry Jacob was a graduate of Oxford University whose first publication, *A Defence of the Churches and Ministery of Englande* (1599), had been an attack on the separatist views of Francis Johnson. It is possible that at this time Jacob was ministering to the nonseparatist puritan church of the Merchant Adventurers in Middelburg. He was back in England by 1603 and played a prominent role in the campaign to get signatures on the Millenary Petition, being singled out by Archbishop Whitgift for his efforts in this regard. Frustrated by the outcome of the Hampton Court Conference, Jacob published a demand for a new hearing on the grounds that the puritan spokesmen at the conference had not properly represented the cause. He then criticized various aspects of the national church without going so far as to separate from it.[63]

While rejecting separatism, Jacob focused on the independence of individual congregations of believers. A recently discovered manuscript contains a series of exchanges in which his radical views on congregational independence were countered by moderate puritan voices.[64] By 1610 Jacob was living in Leiden, and if, as is believed, these exchanges were written in the early years of that decade, then he was likely testing his ideas against the views of Robinson, Brewster, and other members of the Leiden congregation. His belief in the independence of each congregation and his rejection of all forms of interference by superior authorities meshed well with their views. It is possible that all of these men were also familiar with the ideas of Hugo Grotius, the Dutch jurist whose views included the belief that natural rights had a theological foundation. Jacob argued that the right of individuals to associate and form an independent church was an expression of God-given Christian freedom.[65]

In 1616 Jacob returned to England. After further consultation with puritan leaders, Jacob, Sabine Staresmore, and several others observed a day of fast and prayer, after which they joined hands and stood in a ring, Jacob and each of the others making a profession of faith. "Then they covenanted together to walk in God's ways as he had revealed or should make known to them." In many respects this replicated the organization of the Scrooby congregation, but the Jacob church did not reject ties with the Church of England, and its members were free to attend services in parish churches and even to participate in the sacraments. Jacob sent news of this both to the separatist church in London that Barrow, Greenwood, and Johnson had been affiliated with, and to the Ancient Church in Amsterdam. Both of those congregations would reject communion with the Jacob congregation, referring to its members as "idolators" because of their acceptance of contacts with the parishes of the Church of England."[66]

Based on his interaction with the Leiden congregation, Jacob came to believe that the separatists were "very far off from being so evil as commonly they are held to be," though "in some matters they are stricter than I wish they were."[67] Robinson, in turn, was led to revise his views on contact with godly believers who refused to separate, a revision also prompted by discussions with William Ames. Ames was one of the key architects of what was seen as puritan theology. A graduate of Cambridge and a fellow of Christ's College, he was suspended from the university for nonconformity in 1609. He relocated in the Netherlands, initially spending time in Leiden, where he engaged Robinson and Jacob in discussions, with Ames challenging the rigid separatism that Robinson originally advocated. When Ames moved on in 1611 to accept a post as chaplain to English forces in the Netherlands, the two continued their exchanges in correspondence and then in print.[68] Ames influenced Robinson so far that he initially accepted that it was appropriate to have private exchanges with nonseparating believers such as Jacob and Ames. By the end of the decade, Robinson had come to accept the validity of listening to sermons and joining in prayer in parish assemblies, a position that rigid separatists such as those in the

Ancient Church and other separatist churches continued to reject. Years later, a member of the Ancient Church called Robinson out for this, stating that he did "with smooth words darken the truth, which formerly he had maintained."[69]

The third notable puritan with whom Robinson and Brewster engaged with in Leiden was Robert Parker, an English minister whose nonconformity was largely beneath the surface until he published a strong attack on the ceremonial use of the sign of the cross in baptism. Suspended from his ministry in 1607, he ended up in Leiden by 1610, where he was supported by members of Robinson's congregation.[70] Within a year he had moved on to Amsterdam, where he joined the English merchant congregation. Parker's *De politeia ecclesiastica Christi*, written in Latin, was printed by William Brewster and his Pilgrim Press at Leiden in 1616. Like Jacob and Robinson, Parker maintained the primacy of the individual congregation, though he restrained the democratic implications of that belief by asserting that authority was allocated to the church elders by the congregants, a position rejected by Robinson.[71]

Robinson and Brewster also had contacts with Willem Teellinck. Teellinck was a Dutch minister who had studied law and theology in Scotland and France before spending some time in England between 1603 and 1605, including at least eight months at Banbury, where William Whately was the local puritan minister.[72] Teellinck's stay in England convinced him to pursue a ministerial career. He was strongly influenced by puritan pietism and admired both William Ames and William Perkins. After returning to the Netherlands, he pursued his studies for the ministry at the University of Leiden. Though he left Leiden shortly before the Robinson congregation settled there, he continued to have contacts in the city. Teellinck ministered to different Dutch Reformed parishes, including Middelburg from 1613 to 1629. He translated works of English divinity and contributed many works of his own to what became known as the "Nadere Reformatie," or "Further Reformation." Like Robinson, Brewster, and John Durie, he was committed to breaking down barriers between godly believers.[73] Toward the end of his life, Robinson encouraged his son to prepare for ministry in the Dutch Reformed Church and called on his friend Teellinck for assistance.[74]

Early on, individuals who were not members of Robinson's congregation were not allowed to attend its services. But during the Leiden years Robinson came to believe that contacts in all forms but the sacraments were to be allowed. This meant that Leiden residents could have prayed with the congregation, joined in singing psalms, and listened to the preaching. During the decade of the 1610s the church grew to over four hundred members, some of them new arrivals from England, but others local converts. Defending the church at a later date, Edward Winslow wrote that Godbert Godbertson and Moses Symonson of the Dutch Reformed Church and members of the Walloon Congregation had been welcomed into the Leiden congregation and wrote that the Leiden church "made no schism or separation from the Reformed Churches, but held communion with them occasionally."[75]

The three deacons were among those drawn to the congregation after it settled in Leiden. Samuel Fuller had been born in Redenhall, Norfolk, and may have been a serge weaver before his arrival in the Netherlands, where he seems to have pursued that same vocation. He had been elected a deacon by 1610, when he was part of the delegation led by Robinson and Brewster that traveled to Amsterdam to intervene in a dispute in the Ancient Church. Christopher Lawne of the Ancient Church referred to Fuller as at that time being a deacon of Robinson's church.[76] Lawne also quoted a letter by Daniel Studley, the controversial deacon of the Ancient Church, in which Studley referred to Fuller and his "friends" as "ignorant idiots, noddy Nabalites, dogged dogs, fainfaced Pharisees, shameless Shimeites, [and] malicious Machiavellians."[77]

In America, Fuller would become valued as a physician as well as someone well versed in religious matters. A deacon would be asked to help members of the congregation suffering from disease, and it is possible that Fuller acquired medical knowledge in Leiden. Anatomy lessons at the university were open to the public, and the university had a botanical garden where different plants had labels referring to their medicinal values. A book by the university botanist would be among those brought to America. There is evidence that on the journey to America, Fuller would also learn about medical practices from Giles Heal, the ship surgeon on the *Mayflower*.[78]

Robert Cushman joined the congregation from Canterbury, England, where he first came to the attention of the church authorities for his support of reform. He was likely attending a conventicle of like-minded puritans in Canterbury as early as 1591. In 1603 he was prosecuted by the Court of High Commission for posting religious notices on church doors and spent a night in the Westgate prison. Three years later, he was involved in further controversy when he was accused of holding views contrary to those of the national church.[79] He left England and joined the Robinson congregation in 1609.[80] He served as deacon, prophesied, and wrote a description of congregational practice.

John Carver's English background is unknown, but he was on the continent prior to 1609 and received letters of transfer from a Walloon church near the Belgium-Netherlands border to the Walloon congregation in Leiden in that year.[81] He then attended services in the Robinson church and soon joined it. He too was chosen a deacon.

The congregation was a community of individuals committed to following what they perceived as a godly path and forged through a series of hardships in England and on their journey to Leiden. In addition to their espousal of Calvinist theological positions, this entailed upholding a social outlook that demanded that each individual make what sacrifices were necessary for the common good, and "such was the true piety, the humble zeal, and fervent Loue, of this people (while they thus lived together) towards God and his ways, and the singleheartedness and sincere affection one towards another, that they came as near the primitive pattern of the first Churches as any other church of these later times have done." Indeed, what most offended Robinson and the church leaders was individuals who were "cleaving to themselves and retired from the common good."[82]

While Robinson's views on church polity evolved during his years in Leiden, his commitment to Calvinist orthodoxy did not. Through his involvement with professors at the University of Leiden, he became caught up in the controversy between the teachings of those who asserted traditional Calvinism and those who supported a less rigid understanding of Calvin's teaching that had been offered by Jacobus Arminius. Leiden was the center of that storm, with Simon Episcopius, a professor at the university, defending the views of Arminius. In

1610, followers of Arminius met in Gouda and issued a Remonstrance signed by forty-six ministers. The document asserted five articles arguing that Christ's death was sufficient for the salvation of all men, that men had a role to play in acquiring salvation, that men could resist saving grace, and that those who received it could subsequently forfeit that grace by their sins and be damned. The following year Calvinists responded with a Counter-Remonstrance in which they asserted man's total dependence on God for salvation. In seven articles, the Counter-Remonstrants restated the Reformed confessions concerning the doctrines of grace. Because the support of the Reformed Church was essential for the leaders of the Dutch state, the controversy within the church spilled into politics. A national synod was called to meet to resolve the issues, and invitations were sent to the other Reformed Churches in Europe, including England, inviting their participation. Ultimately, the Synod meeting in Dort in 1618–1619 codified what it claimed to be the traditional Calvinist positions.

The conflict was particularly intense in Leiden. Arminius had been a professor at the university, and many of the city officials took the side

Fig. 3.3 Anti-Arminian riots of 1618 in Leiden. Jans Luyken after Claes Jansz Visscher. Photo courtesy of the Leiden American Pilgrim Museum.

of the Remonstrants.[83] Brewster and Robinson, who had witnessed similar attempts to weaken Calvinism in Cambridge, sided with the Counter-Remonstrants. Edward Winslow remembered that "our pastor Mr. Robinson in the time when Arminianism prevailed so much, at the request of the most Orthodox Divines" was urged to speak out against the Arminian threat.[84] Bradford also described Robinson's intervention, calling him "an acute and exact disputant, very quick and ready, and had much bickering with the Arminians who stood more in fear of him than of any of the university."[85]

There were battles in the streets as well as in the university lecture halls. Riots broke out in 1617 and 1618 around the Leiden town hall, where the Arminians constructed a defensive barricade topped with iron spikes.[86] The sympathies of Robinson and his congregation were well known, but there were suspicions of the English outsiders. On Sunday, April 28, 1619, a mob of twenty young men attacked eighty-three-year-old James Chilton, a member of Robinson's congregation, stoning him and leaving him bleeding and unconscious on the street. They believed that Arminians were meeting in his house, something that was very unlikely. They also threw stones at the Chiltons, injuring James in the head.[87]

In 1616 Brewster also took steps to influence the religious debates of the time, engaging with Thomas Brewer in the formation of what has become known as the Pilgrim Press.[88] Brewer was another puritan exile from England, and a member of Robinson's congregation. The goal of the enterprise was to publish books that set forth arguments for various reform proposals that would then be smuggled into England, where press censorship prevented their publication.[89] The actual typesetting and correcting was done by John Reynolds and Edward Winslow.[90] Over the next few years, the press published close to two dozen books and became what has been called "the main purveyor of radical Puritan books in the Netherlands."[91]

A few volumes, such as John Dod and Robert Cleaver's *Exposition of the Ten Commandments*, were noncontroversial. Others were reprints of popular puritan works. But some were more contentious, including two books by David Calderwood, *De Regimine Ecclesiae Scoticanae Brevis Relatio* and *Perth Assembly*, that would excite the ire of King James.[92] Brewster might not have anticipated the king's reaction, but it would prove fatal to the press. Calderwood was a Scottish divine who had opposed the efforts of the king to introduce episcopacy to Scotland and personally challenged the king in a meeting at St. Andrew's in 1617. When *De Regimine Ecclesiae Scoticanae* was published in 1618, King James, infuriated by the work, ordered his ambassador in the Netherlands Dudley Carleton to find and punish those responsible for it. When the *Perth Assembly* (rejecting Christmas and other holy days) was published the following year, Carleton was finally able to identify the Pilgrim Press as the source of both publications and lobbied the Dutch authorities to close it. Both Brewster and Brewer were initially placed in custody in the Leiden town hall, but Brewster, reportedly ill, was allowed to leave through the collusion of friends in town government. While a few more publications, including one by John Robinson, subsequently appeared (presumably they were already in press), the publishing endeavor came to an end.[93]

Due to this, there were concerns about the continuing viability of Leiden as a place of refuge. The split in the Dutch Reformed Church had led to riots, persecution, and curtailment of the toleration for which the Netherlands had been known. In 1619, shortly after the conclusion of the Synod of Dort, the States General largely prohibited religious gatherings outside of the Reformed Church. Brewster, Robinson, and other leaders of the Leiden congregation began to consider yet another move.

4

Setting a New Course

At some point in 1617 John Robinson and William Brewster shared concerns about the congregation's future and presented their views to their fellow believers.[1] Over the following months the Leiden congregation debated whether they should leave the Netherlands and, if so, where to go. As with all matters, the congregation was expected to debate the issues and decide. The members would have engaged in days of fasting and prayer as they sought God's will. Years later, William Bradford and Edward Winslow each identified the arguments that led some members to advocate leaving.

These considerations, Bradford explained, were not expressions of "newfangledness" or "giddy humors," but "weighty & solid reasons." In their accounts, both he and Winslow agreed that life in the Netherlands had proven challenging for the English refugees. In the Netherlands "they found both worse air and diet than that they came from."[2] The work the Englishmen could find was hard, and the experience of living in cramped conditions in a manufacturing city far different from life in the rural homes they had left. The circumstances the congregants found themselves in led some to return to England and discouraged others who sympathized with them from coming. Cultural differences were also troubling. The Dutch allowed behavior that offended the English puritans, particularly in the observance of the Sabbath. Some labored on what was supposed to be a day of rest and prayer; others played games or engaged in entertainment. These Englishmen had made little headway persuading their hosts about how the Lord's Day should be kept. Members of the congregation were especially concerned for their children, who in many cases were "drawn away by evil examples into extravagant and dangerous courses" and rejected their parents' efforts to raise them according to proper values.[3] Some children assimilated to their new culture to the point where they seemed to lose what made them English.

Recent developments in the Netherlands added to the congregation's concerns. The disputes between the Arminian and anti-Arminian factions in the Dutch church had broken into violence in the streets of Leiden and elsewhere. The attack on the Chiltons foreshadowed future threats to the English. Steps taken by the Dutch authorities to limit toleration put their religious freedom in jeopardy, and an edict that forbade special collections for independent churches jeopardized their ability to take care of their aged and infirm members.[4]

The threat that the Netherlands might soon be engulfed in war was perhaps the most troubling cloud on the immediate horizon. "The 12 years of truce" between Spain and the Netherlands "were now out," Bradford later recalled, "& there was nothing but beating of drums, and preparing for war."[5] Furthermore, in 1618 a conflict began in Bohemia that quickly evolved into the major European clash between Catholic and Protestant forces that became known as the Thirty Years' War. It took little imagination to see that the Netherlands would be drawn into that struggle. Brewster followed these events and undoubtedly shared his observations and concerns with his fellow congregants. His diplomatic service with Davison in the 1580s and the contacts he had made at that time likely gave him insights into the international situation that his fellow congregants would have valued.[6]

Years later, recalling the reasons for leaving Leiden, Bradford wrote that there was also "a great hope and inward zeal they had of laying some good foundation . . . for the propagating and advancement of the Gospel of the Kingdom of Christ in those remote parts of the world."[7] Such an assertion is commonly found in European goals for colonization, though efforts to achieve that goal were rarely initiated, and when attempted were rarely successful.

If these and other reasons suggested to some that the congregation should seek a new refuge, the question remained as to where they should go. They debated a variety of options. The Dutch New Netherland Company had established a trading post along the Hudson River near the future city of Albany in 1614. In February 1620 a company of Dutch traders, now known as the Van Tweenhuijsen Company, proposed to Prince Maurits that the Robinson congregation should be supported in an effort to establish a colony in Dutch territory in America. They explained that "It is the case that a certain English minister is living at Leiden, well versed in the Dutch language, . . . who would be well inclined to move his residence" to the Dutch colony. They told the prince that Robinson "knows means to obtain more than four hundred families both from these lands and from England, if they would be protected and preserved in those same lands from all violence from other potentates, by the authority and under the protection of your Princely Excellency and their High Mightinesses the Lords Estates General, to plant there the true, pure Christian religion, and to instruct the wild [Natives] of those same lands in the true teaching and to bring them to belief."[8] The proposition was rejected by the Dutch government. It is likely that this opportunity would have been discussed earlier within the congregation, but the decision by the government closed off any such possibility. Of course, the same religious and political developments that made their situation in the Netherlands precarious would have extended to the Dutch colony as well.

Given the concerns those wanting to move expressed over a loss of their English identity and that of their children, attention focused on settling in domains that were claimed by England. Just as Brewster's familiarity with some Dutch leaders had facilitated the Scrooby congregation's settlement in the Netherlands, similar contacts with colonial promoters would play a role in the group's next move. Brewster had followed the progress of England's overseas ventures and was familiar with the works of Richard Hakluyt, a principal promoter of English colonization. Among the works that found their way into his library at this time were Hakluyt's *The Principall Navigations, Voyages, and Discoveries of the English Nation* (1589) and the earlier *Discourse Concerning Western Planting* (1584). At the time when Brewster was in Davison's service, Hakluyt was in London and it is likely that the two knew each other.[9] Another book Brewster owned was John Smith's 1616 *A Description of New England*, a call for English planting in the New World that advertised the richness of the land and the abundance of resources.

Smith, best known for his role in the settlement of Virginia, had subsequently become a promoter of the region to the north, whose coastline he had surveyed. He designated the area "New England." It is possible that Smith contacted the Leiden congregation when he heard they were considering settling in America. In two of his later works Smith complained that though he had offered to assist them, the colonists had declined, "saying my books and maps were much better cheap to teach them, than myself" and that the Leiden colonists "having my books and maps, presumed they knew as much as they desired."[10] Since he had been in charge of the military defense of early Jamestown, he believed that this, coupled with his geographical knowledge, made him an ideal leader for the proposed colony. The congregation's decision not to employ him was likely due less to his financial demands and more to a combination of his controversial past and the fact that Myles Standish, who was likely a member of the Leiden congregation and whom John Robinson approved as "a man humble and meek," was available to serve as military leader of the expedition.[11]

Francis Johnson, the separatist clergyman whom Brewster had known in England, was another source on information on the challenges of colonization in America. In 1597 Johnson had participated in an effort to establish a refuge in Newfoundland. He and his supporters founded a colony called Ramea on an island in the St. Lawrence River.[12] After the effort failed, Johnson moved to the Netherlands, settling with the Ancient Church in Amsterdam. There were many contacts over the years between Johnson and the Leiden congregation.[13]

Some congregation members suggested Guiana, on the coast of South America, as a possible destination. Sir Walter Ralegh had explored the region in the 1590s and published a book praising the region that included a map showing the location of the fabled city of gold, El Dorado.[14] But this was an area of America claimed by the Spanish and there was a fear that "if they should there live [there] and do well, the jealous Spaniard would never suffer them long; but would displant or overthrow them, as he did the French in Florida."[15]

Discussion quickly focused on the possibilities offered in the vast domain from Canada to Florida then known as Virginia. The Virginia Company was a joint stock company chartered by King James I in 1606 with what were in effect two subsidiary groups. The London group had the right to establish settlements roughly between what is now

Cape Fear, North Carolina, and the Long Island Sound. The Plymouth group was permitted to colonize between the upper reaches of the Chesapeake Bay and the current United States border with Canada. There was an overlap in these territories, and the two groups were prohibited from establishing settlements within one hundred miles of each other. The Plymouth investment group never really accomplished anything, but the London branch established Jamestown and the surrounding settlements. At the time when the Leiden congregation approached the leadership of the London group in 1617 the governing council had determined to give patents for "particular plantations" as a means of encouraging greater migration. These settlements were to be under the jurisdiction of the official governing body but with a limited amount of autonomy. The patentees were free to choose any location to settle within the colony's jurisdiction, provided it was not within five miles of any existing settlement. The internal affairs of the plantation would be in the hands of the proprietors.[16] It was just such a patent that the Leiden group would seek.

In contrast to failures such as that experienced by Johnson, the Virginia Company had seemingly overcome the challenges of the previous decade, particularly the "Starving Time" of 1609–1610, and had established a viable settlement centered on Jamestown. But the company was divided, with two factions vying for its control; one promoted more economic and mercantile goals, while the other, sympathetic to puritanism, promoted a more humanistic and republican version of settlement. Those stressing the importance of civic virtue commonly drew on examples from the classical world, as when in 1610 William Crashaw preached a sermon to the company in which he drew on the writings of Cicero to argue for the importance of civic virtues, including the subordination of the desire for individual profit to common goals.[17] This outlook would have been attractive to Brewster and Robinson, who likewise drew on classical writings to complement their Christian social philosophy.[18] The mercantile faction, led by Sir Thomas Smythe, controlled the company in the early years of the 1610s.

Sir Edwin Sandys led the faction of the Virginia Company promoting a republican polity. Sandys was the second son of Archbishop of York Edwin Sandys, whom Brewster's father had served as bailiff and receiver of Scrooby Manor. The younger Brewster and Sir Edwin may have become acquainted as a result of that connection, but they certainly interacted during Brewster's service with William Davison. Two other members of the congregation, Thomas Brewer and Edward Winslow, also had connections with Sandys.[19]

Within the Virginia Company, Sandys was supported by a number of men who had puritan sympathies, including Sir Maurice Abbott and Sir Thomas Wroth, both members of the parish of St. Stephen's Coleman Street, and William Cavendish, first Earl of Devonshire. At the time when the Leiden congregation was exploring their options the Sandys faction's influence was growing within the Virginia Company. Indeed, Sandys's more active involvement in the company was initially welcomed by Smythe, the company treasurer (chief officer) as the colony had been reduced to around four hundred settlers and had a questionable future. But this cooperation proved short-lived, and the factional disputes, combined with the 1622 massacre, would eventually lead to the revocation of the charter and the transfer of the colony to the crown.[20]

Sandys had a reputation for strongly supporting international Protestantism, which raised suspicions of puritan inclinations. He hoped that the success of the Virginia colony would help undermine the Spanish Empire in the New World. His general religious sympathies and his desire to establish a "free popular state" in Virginia led to his being accused by some of trying to establish a "Brownist Republic" there.[21] But while he may have had sympathies with the reformed Protestant cause, his primary motivation in seeking to get puritans (even those seen as separatists) to settle in Virginia was a desire to boost its population.[22]

Just as Brewster's contacts from his diplomatic career eased the congregation's settlement in the Netherlands, so too his relationship with Sandys and others at court proved useful in seeking English authorization for the Leiden congregation's planned migration. In 1617 Brewster, along with Robert Cushman, traveled to England to explore the possibilities. Over the following months another member of the congregation, Robinson's brother-in-law John Carver, along with Sabine Staresmore, a member of Henry Jacob's congregation, also represented the congregation in London. Staresmore, though a layman, published a defense of separatist practices in 1619. He regularly visited the Netherlands and in later years joined Robinson's congregation. In order to make their argument to the Virginia Company, Brewster and John Robinson wrote a letter to Sir Edwin Sandys in December 1617 presenting the case for the congregation. They asserted their belief that the Lord was with them and would favor their venture. They were men and women already "weaned from the delicate milk of our mother country and . . . inured to the difficulties of a strange and hard land." They were as "industrious and frugal . . . as any company of people in the world." Brewster and Robinson stressed the communal values of the men and women they spoke for—"We are knit together, as a body, in a most strict and sacred bond and covenant of the Lord, of the violation whereof we make great conscience, and by virtue whereof we do hold ourselves straitly tied to all care of each other's good, and of the whole, by every one, and so mutually." The communal values expressed were likely to resonate strongly with Sandys as he tried to find colonists who would advance his own plans for the colony. The Leiden leaders closed by asking Sandys to bring their letter to "other worshipful friends of the Council."[23]

Anticipating questions that would be asked by those whose help they were soliciting, Brewster and Robinson also prepared seven articles explaining their religious position. Carver and Cushman presented these to "great persons of good rank and quality," who were key figures in the Virginia Company. The document has been categorized as "a severely toned down and misleading version of their separatist church convictions," but is more properly seen as an effort to express the congregation's openness to different Protestant insights.[24] Since their arguments with the Church of England concerned polity not doctrine, the first of the seven articles stated that the congregation "wholly assented" to the "confession of faith published in the name of the Church of England," as did the reformed churches in the Netherlands. Second, reflecting the fact that they had abandoned a strict separatist position, Brewster and Robinson wrote that they desired to keep spiritual communion with "the thousands in the land (conformist & reformists) as they are called" who had received saving faith. The remaining articles addressed the authority of the king. They acknowledged the king's authority in all matters that were "not against

God's word." They accepted the king's authority to "appoint bishops, civil overseers, or officers in authority under him" to govern in civil matters. They recognized the authority of the current bishops insofar as those officials had civil powers derived from the king. "No synod, classes, convocations or assembly of Ecclesiastical Officers" had any authority but the civil authority granted by the nation's magistrates. Finally, Brewster and Robinson expressed a desire "to give unto all superiors due honor to preserve the unity of the spirit with all that fear God, [and] to have peace with all men what in us lieth, & wherein we err, to be instructed by any."[25]

The critical issue was whether the Company leadership, the king, and his Privy Council would approve such a venture given the separatist religious commitments of the congregation. Late in November 1617, Sandys wrote to Robinson and Brewster indicating the seven articles had been presented to "divers select gentlemen of his Majesty's Council for Virginia," who had received the statement well. The Council was inclined to "set you forward" in the enterprise.[26]

The separatist reputation of the Leiden congregation would not necessarily have precluded permission to emigrate, since other separatist groups had emigrated without any specific assurances. It was at this time that an Essex clergyman, Thomas Draxe, writing from Harwich, published *Ten counter-demaunds propounded to those of the separation, (or English Donatists) to be directly, and distinctly answered* (1617). Draxe attacked separation from the Church of England and urged separatists to either return to the English church or to leave the country and create a plantation in America where they could work to "convert the Infidel." William Euring responded to this with *An answer to the ten counter demands propounded by T. Draxe* (1619), which was one of the last publications of Brewster's Pilgrim Press. Euring asserted that Draxe's work was designed as a response to Robinson and Brewster's seven articles, but it may have been intended more widely, as they were not the only separatist group attempting to emigrate to America at this time. In a strange way, Draxe's attack on separatism was also a justification for letting such groups leave England.

Sandys's plans for Virginia required a vast expansion of population, which explains why other separatist settlers were sent to the colony in 1618, while negotiations with Brewster continued. Christopher Lawne, who had served as one of the elders of Amsterdam's Ancient Church, received a "particular patent" and emigrated to the Isle of Wight region of Virginia with a few dozen other puritans in May 1618.[27] Edward Bennett, another elder of the Ancient Church, began sending colonists to Virginia and then joined them. His nephew, Richard Bennett, would become the leading puritan planter in Virginia in the mid-seventeenth century.[28]

By far the largest migration of separatists to Virginia facilitated by Sandys was organized by Francis Blackwell, who had served as an elder of the Ancient Church along with Bennett. Planning to emigrate to Virginia, Blackwell and other separatists, including some members of the Jacob congregation, were arrested in London as members of an unlawful conventicle during a fast they were conducting.[29] Blackwell obtained his freedom by betraying a fellow separatist, Sabine Staresmore, who was representing the Leiden congregation at the time. In the fall of 1618 Blackwell and approximately 180 others set sail for Virginia. Their crossing was horrendous, and Blackwell and 130 of the passengers died before they reached North America. Robert Cushman passed on news he had obtained from Samuel Argall. The passengers were, Cushman learned, "packed together [on the ship] as herrings. They had amongst them the flux [dysentery] and also want of fresh water; so . . . it is here rather wondered that so many are alive, than that so many are dead."[30]

Despite the fact that other separatists had been allowed to settle in Virginia, the leaders of the Leiden congregation clearly wanted a specific royal guarantee of their religious freedom. Brewster would have been aware of the factional struggle in the Virginia Company and might have feared that if Sandys lost influence a new regime could revoke freedoms that the Sandys faction had granted.[31] Representatives of the congregation reached out to Sir Robert Naunton, a contemporary of Brewster's at Cambridge who was one of the king's secretaries of state and a member of the Privy Council. Naunton was well regarded by puritan leaders in the Stour Valley.[32]

Naunton's sympathy for the reformed cause may have influenced him to present the Leiden congregation's case to the king and the Privy Council. But he likely was urged to do so by Sir Edwin Sandys, a close friend and ally who would name Naunton executor of his will.[33]

Naunton sought permission from James for the congregation to emigrate with "liberty of conscience under his gracious protection in America." The king reportedly said that this "was a good and honest motion" and asked how the colonists would support themselves. It "was answered fishing, to which he replied . . . *So God have my soul, 'tis an honest trade, 'twas the Apostles' own calling.*" But the king instructed those promoting the Leiden group to consult with the archbishop of Canterbury, George Abbot, and the bishop of London, John King.[34] According to one of Sandys's opponents in the Company, Sandys did approach Abbot to advance the case for the Leiden congregation, but if he did so he was unsuccessful.[35]

Sir John Wolstenholme, a prominent member of the Virginia Company, was sympathetic to the cause but had either raised questions himself about the congregation's religious practices or had heard that others had concerns. Brewster and Robinson prepared two statements in February 1618 and asked Sabine Staresmore to bring them to Wolstenholme for his reactions and opinion on which they should use. Both versions compared the Leiden congregation's positions to those of the French Reformed Church. Robinson and Brewster stated that their church agreed completely with the confession of faith of that church. As to polity, like the French they had "pastors for teaching, elders for ruling, & deacons for distributing the church's contributions" and administered two sacraments, baptism and the Lord's Supper. They pointed to a few differences. French ministers prayed with covered heads; they did not. The Leiden congregation elected elders for life terms, whereas the French chose them for a limited term. The Leiden elders were required to be able to teach, unlike the French. In Leiden discipline was administered by the entire congregation; the French dealt with disciplinary matters in a consistory of church officers.[36] Not addressed in the statements was the Leiden position on prophesying, which was an important part of their religious life. This would have been one of the more disturbing elements of the congregation's practice in the eyes of English authorities, and Robinson and Brewster would have been relieved that they had not been asked to address this.[37]

Staresmore waited while Wolstenholme read both versions and then questioned him. Wolstenholme wanted to know how ministers were chosen and was told that "the power of making was in the church, to be ordained by the imposition of hands, by the fittest instruments they had. It must either be in the church or from the pope, & the pope is Antichrist."[38] This was an answer that was not likely to advance the congregation's cause, and Wolstenholme suggested that the statements go no further. Besides, he pointed out that the king and bishops had already consented to the congregation's request, though it would not be committed to paper. The king had assured the advisors promoting the congregation's cause that he would not interfere with their church if they carried themselves peacefully but would not tolerate them officially.[39] The congregation had little choice but to settle for this.

Just when things seemed to be progressing well, the effort was "sidetracked by the dissensions and factions (as they term it) among the council and company of Virginia."[40] The Sandys faction's move to control the Virginia Company spurred resistance from the existing treasurer, Sir Thomas Smythe, and the more mercantile-oriented councilors. This may have caused problems for those supporting the Leiden group. William Bradford later recalled that "the Virginia Council was now so disturbed by factions and quarrels amongst themselves, as no business could well go forward."[41] The arrest of Sabine Staresmore on the revelations of Francis Blackwell removed one of the advocates of their cause, and his identification with the Leiden congregation may have caused difficulties.

The publication of Calderwood's *De Regimine Ecclesiae Scoticanae Brevis Relatio* by the Pilgrim Press in 1618 caused an uproar that could have had implications for the efforts to get approval for the migration. It was Sir Robert Naunton who was instructed to order Ambassador Boswell to seek out the press and publisher. If Naunton did not know or suspect that Brewster may have been involved, he certainly was aware that the work came from within the broad separatist community he had been speaking on behalf of. And when Boswell reported that Brewster was one of those responsible for the publication of both *De Regimine Ecclesiae Scoticanae* and then the *Perth Assembly* in 1619 one wonders how eager anyone on the Privy Council would have been to speak up for the Leiden congregation.

Despite this, a patent was granted in June 1619 by the Virginia Company and sent to Leiden for examination. The document has not survived, but would have authorized the group to establish a particular plantation anywhere south of the Hudson River. The grant was to "Mr. John Wincop (a religious gentleman then belonging to the countess of Lincoln) who intended to go with them."[42] It is possible that Wincop—who had been recommended to the Virginia Company in the previous month by the fourth Earl of Lincoln—was a tutor in the Earl's household. In later years the Earl would himself become known for his opposition to the policies of Charles I and for his promotion of the Massachusetts Bay Colony.[43] Wincop's years at Cambridge overlapped with Brewster's stay there, and the two may have known one another.

In February 1620, while the Leiden congregation was still arranging financing, the Council of the Virginia Company issued a new patent intended for them in the name of John Peirce, a London clothworker. Wincop may have died, necessitating a new patent, but this might also have been due to a new provision for particular plantations that the Council adopted at the same time.[44] This new policy gave greater governing authority to those heading such plantations, "to make orders, ordinances, and constitutions for the better ordering and directing of their servants and business, provided they be not repugnant to the laws of England."[45] Clearly Brewster and his fellow negotiators would have preferred this broader authority.

The fact that patents were issued in the name of someone who was not directly associated with the Leiden congregation is not surprising since this was a tactic used on other occasions to shield the actual identity of those organizing a colony. The fact that William Brewster was being hunted down for his publication of books that had infuriated the king would have provided further reason for deflecting attention away from the Leiden congregation. At the time of his escape from the Leiden Town Hall in May 1619, Ambassador Carleton reported that Brewster was in ill health, a fact confirmed by Robert Cushman. Nonetheless, Brewster had returned to London to work with Cushman in furthering the negotiations for a patent. Cushman indicated that "Mr. B. is not well at this time; whether he will come back to you or go into the north I yet know not."[46] In July, Carleton reported that Brewster was unlikely to return to Leiden, "having removed from thence both his family and goods," but there is some evidence suggesting that he may have returned to the Netherlands and stayed for a time in Leiderdorp, a small town on the outskirts of Leiden.[47] This would have both minimized the chances that he would be discovered and given him a chance to meet with the other members of the congregation as they continued to make their plans.[48]

At this point finances for the enterprise remained uncertain. Some of the money would be raised by selling the emigrants' property in Leiden, but more significant investment was needed. The Virginia Company was not prepared to finance the venture, and the crown never underwrote such costs. Early in the spring of 1620, Thomas Weston, an English merchant who had dealings with Edward Pickering of the Leiden congregation, arrived in the Netherlands and offered to form a joint stock venture that would provide the group with financing. The group struck a general agreement with Weston. Bradford, Cushman, and others planning to migrate sold their homes to raise funds for their share of the costs. Weston experienced more difficulties in attracting investors than he had anticipated, and in July 1620 Robert Cushman, then representing the emigrant group in London, felt compelled to renegotiate the agreement with Weston.[49]

Under the revised agreement the settlers would work for seven years for the investors, and all land, homes, and other assets would be divided at the end of that period. An understanding that the settlers would have two days a week to work in their own interests and have title to their own homes from the beginning was no longer part of the deal. Many became bitter over the changes but there was nothing they could do. Those planning the enterprise purchased a ship, the *Speedwell*, to transport some of the colonists and to remain in America for the use of the settlement. The investors hired another ship, the *Mayflower*, to transport the remainder of the emigrants and then return to England.

When Robinson and Brewster had raised the question of emigration in 1617, they had hoped that the entire congregation would join in the venture. But in subsequent years it became evident that many members were not willing to participate. Numerous factors would have played a part. Reports of disastrous voyages such as that experienced by Francis Blackwell's group must have been terrifying. Tales of Native attacks on colonists and Spanish assaults against settlements by other Europeans were disturbing. Most of those who had settled in Leiden had hoped that they would eventually be able to return to a reformed England. Moving to America would make the return to their homeland unlikely, if not impossible from a financial point of view. The last-minute changes in the contract with the investors angered many others because it essentially reduced those who settled in America to being indentured servants for seven years. A majority of the congregation opted to remain in Leiden for the time, with some expressing hopes of joining their fellow congregants later. Because the majority was remaining, it was decided that John Robinson would stay to minister to them. Elder Brewster would provide spiritual guidance for those going to America.

Members of the congregation who were emigrating planned to join the *Speedwell* in Delftshaven. The entire church observed a day of fasting and humiliation with prayers to seek God's blessing for the venture. Robinson preached on Ezra 8:21—"And there at the river, by Ahava, I proclaimed a fast, that we might humble ourselves before God, and seek of him a right way for us, and for our children, and for all our substance."[50] As remembered years later by Edward Winslow, Robinson told them that "We are now ere long to part asunder, and the Lord knoweth whether he should live to see our faces again." He urged them to be open to further light, expressing his belief that "the Lord hath more truth and light yet to break forth out of his holy Word." He reminded them of their "church covenant (at least that part of it) whereby we promise and covenant with God and one with another to receive whatsoever light or truth shall be made known to us from his written Word, and well to examine and compare, and weigh it with other Scriptures of truth, before we received it." He urged them to "use all means to avoid and shake off the name Brownist, being a mere nickname and brand to make religion odious, and the professors of it to the Christian world."[51] They then held a feast at Robinson's house, where everyone "refreshed ourselves after our tears with singing of Psalms, making joyful melody in our hearts as well as with the voice." Winslow remembered it as "the sweetest melody that ever mine ears heard."[52]

The following day the emigrants, accompanied by Robinson and many of their friends, journeyed by the canals the twenty-four miles to Delftshaven. Bradford would write that "they knew that they were pilgrims and strangers here below, and . . . lifted their eyes to heaven, their dearest country, where God had prepared for them a city, and therein quieted their spirits."[53] The reference to "pilgrims" and "strangers" has been interpreted by some to indicate a fundamental and significant division among the passengers, but this was not the case.[54] Bradford was more likely thinking of a biblical passage in Hebrews 11 where St. Paul refers to Christians as strangers to the world on a pilgrimage to heaven.[55] In Delftshaven few slept the night before their departure, most instead choosing to spend the time with supporters who had traveled from Leiden and from Amsterdam in "friendly entertainment and Christian discourse, and other real expressions of Christian love."

In the morning Robinson called the travelers to prayer and asked the Lord's blessing on their voyage. Men and women bade farewell to their friends and, in some cases, to children whom they were leaving behind. William and Dorothy Bradford decided to leave their young son John behind, fearing that the rigors of the voyage would be too much for him. William Brewster's two daughters also remained behind, entrusted to the care of the couple's oldest son, Jonathan. Their younger sons, Love and Wrestling, made the voyage. "Truly doleful was the sight of that sad and mournful parting, to hear what sighs and sobs, and prayers did sound amongst them."[56]

The *Speedwell* crossed the North Sea to Southampton, England, where the passengers united with others joining the enterprise, including William Brewster. Because not everyone had been in Leiden to hear John Robinson's parting sermon, the pastor had entrusted to John Carver a letter of advice to be read to the entire party once they were together in Southampton. In it Robinson expressed the importance of community, urging the aspiring colonists that in "your common employments you join common affections truly bent upon the general good, avoiding as a deadly plague of your both common and special comfort all retiredness of mind for proper advantage and all singularly affected any manner of way." "Let every man," he continued, "repress in himself and the whole body in each person, as so many rebels against the common good, all private respects of men's selves, not sorting with the general conveniency." He warned especially about not allowing rifts to develop in the early days of settlement, before the colony's foundations had hardened. "Lastly," he concluded, "whereas you are to become a body politic, using amongst yourselves civil government, and are not furnished with persons of special eminency above the rest, to be chosen by you into the office of government. Let your wisdom and godliness appear not only in choosing such persons as do entirely love, and will promote the Common Good, but also in yielding unto them all due honor and obedience for your good, not being like the foolish multitude, who more honor the gay coat than either the virtuous mind of the man or the glorious ordinance of the Lord."[57]

On August 5 the *Speedwell* and the larger *Mayflower* sailed west into the English Channel. After a week at sea the repairs to the *Speedwell* began to leak, so the two ships had to dock at the port of Dartmouth to effect further repairs. The journey resumed on August 21, but after about three hundred miles at sea the *Speedwell* again leaked dangerously. The ships turned back, this time to Plymouth, where the leaders of the expedition determined that the *Mayflower* would have to go on alone. Some of those originally on the larger ship, including Robert Cushman, remained behind, replaced by men and women from the *Speedwell*. Cargo had to be reallocated, and the addition of supplies from the *Speedwell* made the *Mayflower* even more crowded. Finally, on September 6, the *Mayflower* departed from Plymouth.

Crossing the Atlantic was a perilous undertaking in the seventeenth century. Ships were at the mercy of the winds. Lack of wind could leave a ship becalmed for days if not weeks. Storms could push a ship back along the course it had laboriously traveled. Food, fresh water, and beer (the preferred drink at a time when water was frequently contaminated) could not be replenished. The passengers on the *Mayflower* had used up many of their supplies during their false starts with the *Speedwell*, making shortages a serious concern. Leaving in the autumn could mean traveling in bitter cold, with the possibility that ocean spray would freeze on the sails and rigging, making the vessel unstable.

The *Mayflower* had more passengers than initially anticipated. Most spent their time in the deck between the hold (where their supplies were stored) and the upper deck that was open to the elements. There were no portholes, and the gloomy seventy-five-foot-long space was divided up by makeshift partitions. Erected to provide some sense of privacy, the partitions also hindered the flow of air. The passenger deck was cold, damp, and largely dark. Moving around required most men to stoop, since the headroom was likely no more than five feet. There

Fig. 4.1 The *Mayflower*. Drawing by Jeremy D. Bangs.

were no tables or benches, so meals were eaten while squatting on the floor. Rats and other pests plagued the passengers. Vomit and bowel movements were intended (not always successfully) for chamber pots, which periodically would be carried to the upper deck and emptied overboard. A passenger on another ship similar to the *Mayflower* graphically described "some spewing, some pissing, some shitting, some farting."[58] Lack of privacy made such matters especially difficult for the women. In the meantime, the stench added to the discomfort of life below decks. It was Elder William Brewster's task to uplift their spirits by leading them in daily prayer and psalm singing.[59]

The passage began smoothly, but in October the travelers experienced "cross winds and met with many fierce storms." During some of "these storms the winds were so fierce and the seas so high as they could not bear a knot of sail." The passengers were tossed about below decks. Water seeped into their quarters and their provisions, while vomit sloshed along their feet. During storms any lights below decks were extinguished for fear of fire, with the passengers left in total darkness. Winds shredded some of the sails. The crew and some passengers worked furiously at the pumps to rid the ship of the incoming water. Everyone knew of ships that had foundered and sunk crossing the Atlantic, and many despaired in the face of these storms. The colonists endured "a long imprisonment as it were in the ships at sea."[60] During a particularly violent storm, one of the main beams in the midships bent and cracked, jeopardizing the ship. Fortunately, the Leiden group had brought with them a "great iron screw," which was a house jack that was used to push the beam back into place.[61]

Finally, on November 9, after sixty-six days at sea, crew members sighted the towering sand dunes of Cape Cod. They had intended to settle in "some place about Hudson's River for their habitation"— the northernmost territory of the Virginia Company of London's domain—and with the wind and weather at the time being favorable they decided to switch course and head for that destination.[62] But in doing so they encountered dangerous shoals and breakers. After further deliberation, they decided to return to Cape Cod and find a place to settle.

5

Dawn Land

Before the region where the travelers settled became New England, it was Dawn Land. For many millennia prior to the arrival of the first Europeans off the northeast coast of America, tens of thousands of people inhabited this land. If the story of Plymouth requires understanding the English colonists' journey from Scrooby, via Leiden, to America, so too it requires understanding the culture they encountered in the New World. This is made difficult by the fact that Europeans who first encountered the Natives were either uninterested in their culture or failed to ask the questions of concern in the present day.[1] When they did make an effort they tried to find a link between something they saw and did not understand to something familiar to them; for example, they saw the authority of sachems as comparable to that of European monarchs.[2] This perspective often proved erroneous, and so sources written by the colonists must be used with caution. But new scholarship by Native scholars, combined with the findings of archaeology, make it possible to sketch the cultures of what the Natives called Dawn Land.[3]

In the early seventeenth century well over a dozen separate tribes of the Ninnimissinouk ("the People"), speaking forms of the root Algonquian language, occupied the region, with the boundaries between their homelands undefined and impossible to precisely recreate. While some clashed with one another, most lived in harmony with their neighbors. The population prior to substantial European contact may have been as high as two hundred thousand.[4]

In the northeast lived the Wabanaki, perhaps numbering as many as fifty thousand people. The Eastern Wabanaki consisted of semisedentary bands whose activities ranged across the coastal areas and internal woodlands from Newfoundland to the Kennebec River valley. They primarily depended on hunting, fishing, and gathering.

Between the Kennebec River and the Merrimac River lived the Western Abenaki, who survived not only by hunting and fishing but also by growing corn, beans, and squash; they resided in large villages. In the area of the Bay of Fundy, Natives mined copper, which they cold-hammered into sheets that they used in trade throughout their own region and farther to the south.[5]

A variety of other tribes lived south of the Merrimac River. Among these were the Massachusetts, centered on Massachusetts Bay, and the Nipmucs, slightly to the west of the Massachusetts. To the south of them the Wampanoag occupied the region that is now southeast Massachusetts and Rhode Island.[6] The Nauset inhabited the arm of Cape Cod. West of the Wampanoag lived the Narragansett, and farther west the Pequots. These people of southern New England were linguistically, politically, and culturally similar. More heavily dependent on agriculture than northern tribes, Native women tended a variety of crops that included beans, maize, squash, pumpkins, artichokes, cucumbers, and tobacco. Their diet was supplemented by seasonal hunting and fishing.[7] This meant that Native settlement was mobile, with hunting and fishing conducted from temporary camps in the fall and spring while the planting and harvesting of crops occupied the people in the summer.[8]

Europeans found the division of labor in Native communities difficult to understand because it was very different from European labor customs. Women were ordinarily in charge of moving and preparing homes. They also tended crops and made the pottery vessels in which they prepared and served meals. Roger Williams, writing a few decades after the settlement of New England, also found women engaging in other crafts. Men, on the other hand, took the lead in hunting and fishing, and in doing so they displayed a variety of skills that impressed European observers.[9] Occasionally they burned the forest undergrowth, which allowed fruit-bearing bushes to grow and game animals to move more freely.[10]

Exact forms of governance among the Native inhabitants varied, but revolved around deference to tribal elders, women as well as men.[11] The Wampanoag were a group of approximately seventy loosely federated villages, each led by a sachem, and connected by well-worn paths and kin networks.[12] The confederation as a whole was led by

Fig. 5.1 Map of Native tribes in southern New England. Map created by Matthew Spak for the Geography Department's Geo-Graphics Laboratory at Millersville University, Millersville, PA, USA.

a supreme sachem, who had the title of Massasoit.[13] In 1620 the supreme sachem was Ousamequin and he resided in Sowams, near present-day Barrington, Rhode Island.[14] The Massasoit visited the individual villages regularly to maintain unity, though villages sometimes switched allegiance to another leader.[15] Inheritance and lineage passed from a mother to her children. While the Natives did not keep written records, they had their own way of preserving their history. The Plymouth leader Edward Winslow reported that when "any remarkable act is done, in memory of it, either in the place or by some pathway near adjoining, they make a round hole in the ground, about a foot deep." When others passed by and inquired about the hole they were told the story of the event that it commemorated, "so that as a man travelleth . . . his journey will be the less tedious by reason of the historical discourses . . . related unto him."[16]

The difficulties encountered by Europeans in understanding Native culture were particularly acute when it came to abstract concepts such as those involved in religious beliefs.[17] Most Europeans failed to detect any religious beliefs in Native tribes, but the few who were interested soon discovered their mistake. Edward Winslow wrote that "whereas myself and others, in former letters . . . wrote that the Indians about us are a people without any religion, or knowledge of any God, therein I erred, . . . for . . . they conceive of many divine powers."[18] While some Englishmen were content to depict the Natives as savages and infidels, others—such as Winslow, Roger Williams, John Eliot, and the Mayhews—would seek to understand Native cosmology and use that knowledge as a bridge to teach them Christianity.[19]

As early as the late fifteenth century there had been English fisherman from the port of Bristol visiting the coast of North America. On one such voyage, perhaps in 1498, three Natives "taken in the New found land" were brought to England and displayed a few years later before King Henry VII, "clothed in beasts' skins."[20] The practice of bringing Natives to Europe had been started by Columbus in 1493. It brought Europeans—particularly those who had the ability to sponsor further voyages—face to face with the inhabitants of the New World and offered an opportunity for Europeans to learn the language of those with whom they wished to trade. But from the perspective of the Natives, this was the kidnapping of unsuspecting men who (even in cases when the explorers claimed the individual was willing) could have had no concept of what this would entail.

Returning from a 1530 sailing, Sir John Hawkins brought a Native "king" from South America back from a slave-trading voyage to Guinea, leaving behind one of his own men as surety for the king's return. After presenting the Native to King Henry VIII, Hawkins did bring him back to Guinea, though he died en route. The next documented case of Natives brought to England came when the explorer Martin Frobisher brought four captive Inuits in 1576.[21] The impact of these early "visitors" was minimal, but as Englishmen began to promote colonization as well as fishing ventures, interest in the Native populations increased. The promoter Richard Hakluyt stressed the need to "learn the language of the people," citing among the reasons to "distill in their purged minds the sweet and lively liquor of the gospel."[22] During the efforts to plant an outpost at Roanoke, Thomas Hariot, a member of Walter Ralegh's household and one of the leading scientists of his day, worked to teach rudimentary English to two Native men, Wanchese of Roanoke and Manteo of Croaton (brought to England in 1584), while compiling a guide to their Algonquian language. Wanchese and Manteo accompanied Ralegh's 1585 expedition to the Carolina coast. Wanchese encouraged his people to resist the English, while Manteo sought to help them, though his efforts were undermined by the actions against the Natives by Governor Ralph Lane. When that first English colony at Roanoke was abandoned, Manteo returned with the English and helped Ralegh make plans for another colonizing attempt, what would become the "Lost Colony."[23] While in England during the mid-1580s these Natives lived with Walter Ralegh in London and appeared at the royal court. This raises the possibility that William Brewster met or at least observed them during his service with William Davison, who knew Ralegh well.

English explorers continued to kidnap Natives from their coastal communities, including some along Cape Cod Bay. In 1603 the twenty-three-year-old Martin Pring was sent by Walter Ralegh to explore the region.[24] His expedition sailed along the coast of Maine and up the Piscataqua River. He then journeyed south and established a temporary outpost at the mouth of the Pamet River on Martha's Vineyard, erecting a small stockade there.[25] Supporting themselves with fish and game for two months, Pring and his crew harvested sassafras trees to carry to England. Pring's men had initially entertained the local Wanpanoags, but relations soon deteriorated. Following the departure of some of the expedition, over two hundred Natives attacked the stockade and burned the woods where the English had been gathering sassafras.

In the summer of 1605 Captain George Weymouth explored the coast of what is now the state of Maine. The account of this voyage by James Rosier, a member of the expedition, included detailed descriptions of the coast and offshore islands they visited, as well as the abundant opportunities for profit. Rosier's account also detailed the expedition's encounters with the local inhabitants. Initially the Natives appeared to wave them off, but they were attracted by the offer of copper kettles, knives, combs, and other items that induced them to board the ship, where Rosier reported they were "used with as much kindness as we could." He described the physical appearance of the Natives and praised their character, writing that they were "a people of exceeding good invention, quick understanding, and ready capacity."

He also admired their canoes, their bows and arrows, and their use of seines to catch fish. In all, Rosier marveled at "the kind civility we found in a people where we little expected any spark of humanity."[26]

Both the English and the Wabenaki saw value in exchanging goods. But Weymouth saw greater potential if the English could colonize the region. He believed a more thorough exploitation of the region's riches was justified by the fact that the Natives were a people "whose understanding it hath pleased God so to darken, as they can neither discern, use, or rightly esteem the invaluable riches . . . whereof they live." The more the English discovered the more they "found the land answerable to the intent of our discovery, viz. fit for any nation to inhabit."

To advance such future colonization, Weymouth broke the trust he had established with the local inhabitants by deciding to take some of the Natives. Inducing a group with trade goods, they seized "five savages, two canoes, with their bows and arrows." Weymouth hoped these would be hostages for the continued good behavior of the local tribes, but he also saw their value as interpreters and as sources from whom the English could learn more about the region. Rosier reported, "we have brought them to understand some English, and we understand much of their language, so as we are able to ask them many things." Native communication networks were extensive, and news of the English treachery spread quickly. The French explorer Samuel de Champlain, in southern Canada, heard news that after feigning friendship, an English expedition had killed five natives on the coast of Maine.

The five Abenaki were the first Natives from New England to be brought to England. Information derived from them contributed to the plans of Sir Ferdinando Gorges, who in 1607 sent an expedition to establish a colony at the mouth of the Kennebec River in modern Maine. Two of the Natives captured by Weymouth played a role in negotiations between these colonists and the local tribes, but the colony was abandoned after a year. A French observer in Canada wrote that during the colony's brief history the English "drove the savages away without ceremony; . . . beat, maltreated, and misused them outrageously, and without restraint." In response, deciding "to kill the whelp ere its teeth and claws became stronger," the Abenaki killed many of the English, leading to their departure.[27]

In 1611 an English expedition under Edward Harlow seized five Natives from the area around Cape Cod, including one, Epenow, from Martha's Vineyard. Gorges, still looking to use Natives to promote his colonial ambitions, acquired Epenow from Harlow. That Native leader appeared in London in 1612 and created a sensation, triggering speculation that he may have been the inspiration for the "strange Indian" whom Shakespeare mentioned in *Henry VIII* (1613). More importantly, Epenow's tales of New World wealth, such as gold to be found on Martha's Vineyard, led Gorges and the Earl of Southampton to organize another expedition to America. There was no gold on the Vineyard, but when the ship stopped there Epenow made his escape. In 1619 another Gorges expedition, this one captained by Thomas Dermer, stopped at the Vineyard. Epenow "speaking some English, laughed at his own escape and reported the story of it." When Dermer returned for trade a year later, Natives attacked and killed some of his men and severely wounded Dermer.[28]

Meanwhile, in 1614, John Smith, accompanied by at least two Natives who had spent time in England, led an expedition of several ships to further explore and map New England. One of the captains serving under him, Thomas Hunt, stopped at the Native community of Patuxet, where, Smith later reported, he "betrayed four and twenty of those poor savages aboard his ship," and another seven of the Nausets from farther along Cape Cod. Hunt, whom Gorges described as "more savage-like" than the Natives he abducted, was not interested in gaining future interpreters or in any other way advancing colonial interests. He carried the captives to the Spanish port of Malaga, where some Catholic friars intervened before he could sell them into slavery.[29] The fate of most of those captives is unknown, but one of them, Tisquantum (Squanto), ended up in England, perhaps carried there by some Bristol fishermen.

In London, Tisquantum ended up living with a London merchant, John Slany, who served as treasurer of a company that held a patent for exploration of Newfoundland. Tisquantum seized the opportunity to learn English and to explore the metropolis. It has been suggested that in 1616 he may well have met Pocahontas, the Virginian native who was then residing in the household of Sir Thomas Smyth.[30] Tisquantum was in Newfoundland briefly in 1618, presumably sent by the Newfoundland Company. In 1619 he boarded the ship commanded by Captain Thomas Dermer that was sent by Gorges to Cape Cod. He was likely with Dermer on Martha's Vineyard when Epenow told the captain how he had previously escaped from his English captors. On this occasion Tisquantum may have intervened to save Dermer's life.

Some of the English explorers, traders, and fishermen displayed a genuine interest in Native culture and sought to establish positive contacts with the inhabitants of Dawn Land, if only to further promote their own long-term interests. Gorges and Smith condemned in no uncertain terms the efforts of Thomas Hunt to sell the Natives he had seized into slavery in Spain. But the practice of abducting Natives for the purpose of making them interpreters was not generally challenged. Some argued that the Natives had agreed to come along, but clearly no Native could have imagined what sailing away on an English ship would mean. Some, such as Tisquantum, seemed to develop an affection for the English and would seek ways to turn their language skills to their own advantage. Despite rationalizations used by the English, engaging in this human trafficking alienated the Native population and

Fig. 5.2 Native wetu at Plimoth Plantation. Photo by Francis J. Bremer.

betrayed a cultural arrogance that would ultimately undermine relations between the two peoples.

Even more cataclysmic than the English seizure of Natives was the biological impact of continuing contact between the two peoples. In the years between Tisquantum's abduction and his return the tribes of coastal New England were ravaged by one or more virgin soil epidemics that contemporaries referred to as "a plague." When Tisquantum returned in 1619 to Patuxet, from which he had been kidnapped five years earlier, he found a deserted village with signs that the family and friends he had left were no longer alive. While he is often portrayed as the only survivor of Patuxet, it is likely that some other members of the community had survived and moved on to other villages.[31] Nevertheless, the scene that greeted him was devastating.

Accounts of the disease or diseases that had swept the land described symptoms that included headaches, lesions, bleeding from the nose, hemorrhaging, and changes in skin color. Disease spread so rapidly along the Native trade and communication networks and was so widespread that it was difficult to pay due respect to those who perished.[32] The exact nature of the affliction is still debated. Some historians once believed it might have been yellow fever but that has been largely discounted. More recent suggestions include smallpox, bubonic or pneumonic plague (there were many rats on the English ships and contemporaries spoke of fleas in Native huts), and Weil syndrome, a severe form of bacterial infection conveyed by contact with the urine, blood, or tissue of infected animals or rodents.[33] It is unlikely the cause or causes will ever be known.

The epidemics had their greatest impact on the coastal tribes, where Natives had the most contact with French and English traders and fishermen. While the Massachusetts suffered, the tribes to their west were relatively unaffected. In southeastern New England the Nauset and Wampanoag were afflicted, but the Narragansett to their west were relatively unscathed. In afflicted communities, mortality rates of over 50 percent were common, and some communities suffered losses of over 90 percent.[34] The fact that Native customs called for family and friends to gather around a sick person's bedside to offer prayers and perform healing ceremonies furthered the spread of the contagion. Villages indicated on maps drawn by the Frenchman Samuel de

Champlain and by John Smith had simply disappeared by 1620. Those that remained had inhabitants in the dozens rather than the hundreds or even thousands. In an account of his voyage in 1619, Thomas Dermer described "some ancient Plantations, not long since populous, now utterly void; in other places a remnant remains, but not free from sickness."[35] Based on reports from Natives, Robert Cushman reported that among the Wampanoag scarcely one in twenty Natives had survived.[36]

It was not uncommon for grandparents, parents, and children to all perish within days of each other.[37] Those who were still healthy could not provide their departed brethren with the customary treatment accorded the deceased. Consequently, social and cultural forms and norms collapsed in many areas. It was impossible to bury all of the dead in some communities, leaving some corpses to be defiled and eaten by scavengers.[38] When Edward Winslow visited Ousamequin, the chief sachem, or Massasoit of the Wampanoag people, in July 1621, he found on his forty-mile journey "the people not many, being dead and abundantly wasted in the great mortality . . . wherein thousands of them died. They not being able to bury one another, their skulls and bones were found in many places lying still upon the ground where their houses and dwellings had been, a very sad spectacle to behold."[39]

The impact that the plague had on different Native communities would significantly change the relations among the various tribes. In southern New England, the Narragansett sachem Canonicus, noting the impact of the plague on the Wampanoags, sought to use their misfortune to subordinate his neighbors.[40] To the north, where the mortality rate was likely 90 percent, Tarrantine raiders (Mi'kmaq and Eastern Etchemins) from the north, equipped with French firearms, asserted their influence over the Abenaki and captured the fur trade with the French for themselves.[41] One Native who had survived both Tarrantine attacks and the effects of the plagues was Samoset. He would play a key role in the early history of Plymouth but then return to the north. Living on Monhegan Island, Samoset had learned broken English from the various European fisherman and traders who frequented that island. He encountered Tisquantum there in 1619. Samoset perhaps accompanied Dermer and Tisquantum when the captain sailed to Cape Cod, which Samoset described as a day's sail from

Monhegan Island "with a great wind," or five days' journey by land. He was familiar with the coast because it was common for the Wabanaki to travel south from the Maine coast to fish and trade with the tribes of southern New England. In 1623, near Casco Bay, an Englishman named Christopher Levett encountered "Somerset [Samoset], a sagamore, one that has been found very faithful to the English, and hath saved the lives of many of our nation." Samoset visited Levett's trading post and told the English trader that their sons "should be brothers and that there should be mouchicke legamatch (that is friendship), betwixt them."[42]

When the *Mayflower* was spotted by the Natives off the coast of Cape Cod they had reason to be apprehensive about what the ship's arrival might portend. History gave them reason to be both fearful and angry at the new arrivals. Until the Massasoit Ousamequin could assess the possible threat posed to his people, the Natives would stand off and observe.

6

Small Beginnings

When the *Mayflower*, having failed to reach its intended destination on the Hudson River, turned back toward Cape Cod in November 1620, the devastation that had recently been inflicted on the land and its people was not evident. As the ship rounded Race Point and dropped anchor off what is now Provincetown the weary travelers "fell upon their knees." Elder Brewster led them in blessing "the God of Heaven who had brought them over the vast and furious ocean and delivered them from all the perils and miseries thereof." This was their first New England thanksgiving.[1] Reflecting on the occasion years later, William Bradford compared their joy to that of the Roman philosopher Seneca, who wrote in his *Moral Epistles* that he was greatly affected with joy on landing on the shore of the Bay of Naples after surviving a "tedious and dreadful" storm.[2] But their joy was tempered by concerns about what lay ahead. There were "no friends to welcome them, nor inns to refresh their weather-beaten bodies; no houses or much less towns to repair unto to seek for succor." Though accounts by John Smith and other explorers had extolled the possibilities of the region, for those who had endured the difficult crossing, what appeared before them seemed "a hideous and desolate wilderness, full of wild beasts and wild men."[3]

More than the wintry landscape worried them. The particular patent by which they claimed the right to settle and govern did not extend to the territory where they found themselves, and there was a concern that as a result some of the passengers might not submit to the authority of the colony's leaders. This was more than an abstract possibility. Bradford remembered that on the day before they came into Provincetown harbor, there were "some not well affected to unity and concord," giving "some appearance of faction."[4] He recalled that several settlers had made "discontented and mutinous speeches," asserting "that when they came ashore they would use their own liberty, for none had power to command them, the patent they had being for Virginia and not New England."[5]

Many historians have assumed that the discontented passengers on the *Mayflower* were those who had not been members of the Leiden congregation, assuming they were the "strangers" in William Bradford's reference to the colonists as "pilgrims and strangers." But Bradford was using the terms in the biblical context of Christians as strangers in an ungodly world.[6] Furthermore, the foremost student of the Leiden congregation has pointed out that "80 of the 102 passengers were either from Leiden or of uncertain origin but likely to have been from Leiden."[7] Some of the remainder, though not members of the Robinson church, also held strong puritan sympathies, such as Christopher Martin of Billerica, Essex, who had been cited by the English church authorities in 1612 for refusing to kneel to receive Holy Communion.[8]

Despite his evident puritan sympathies, Martin had been a divisive figure on the *Mayflower*. The merchant backers of the expedition had placed him in charge of the passengers during their voyage, and that power evidently went to his head. Robert Cushman noted that even before the *Mayflower* set sail, Martin had insulted "our poor people with such scorn and contempt, as if they were not good enough to wipe his shoes. It would break your heart to see his dealing, and the mourning of our people. They complain to me and, alas, I can do nothing for them. If I speak to him he flies in my face, as if I were mutinous, . . . and saith they are forward and waspish discontented people."[9] Concern over his arrogance likely increased over the course of the journey.

Another colonist, Stephen Hopkins, had experienced the consequences of such discontent during a previous expedition to America. Though not a member of the Leiden congregation, Hopkins had been a passenger on the *Venture* when that vessel shipwrecked on the coast of Bermuda while on a relief expedition to Virginia in 1609. The survivors had struggled for nine months before rebuilding a ship and resuming their voyage to Jamestown. Hopkins, who had a reputation as a pious and devout Christian, served as an assistant to the expedition's clergyman. His reading of the scriptures persuaded him that neither the captain of the *Venture*, Sir George Somers, nor future Virginia governor Sir Thomas Gates had any legitimate authority over the shipwrecked men. A resultant mutiny led to Hopkins being tried and convicted, though the death sentence delivered was not carried out.[10] Based on this experience, Hopkins likely warned his fellow passengers on the *Mayflower* of the danger of an unsettled government. The remedy chosen to avert any mutiny was to transform the colonists into a covenanted civil community.

John Robinson had anticipated such a situation in his parting letter to the colonists, enjoining them to avoid "as a deadly plague of your both common and special comfort all retiredness of mind for proper advantage and all singularly affected any manner of way." He urged them to "let every man repress in himself and the whole body in each person, as so many rebels against the common good, all private respects of men's selves, not sorting with the general conveniency. And as men are careful not to have a new house shaken with any violence before it be well settled, and the parts firmly knit, so be you, I beseech you brethren, much more careful, that the house of God which you are and are to be, be not shaken with unnecessary novelties or other oppositions at the first settling thereof."[11]

Fearful of the disruption that settling outside the geographic boundaries of their patent might cause, on November 11 the male passengers signed a document whereby they "solemnly and mutually in the presence of God, and one of another, covenant and combine ourselves together into a civil body politic, for our better ordering and preservation . . . , and by virtue hereof to enact, constitute, and frame such just and equal laws, ordinances, acts, constitutions, and offices, from time to time, as shall be thought mete and convenient for the general good of the colony."[12] This "Mayflower Compact" became the basis for the government of the colony. One of the first steps taken by those who had signed this covenant was to elect John Carver as their governor. Carver, a wealthy merchant in Leiden, may have originally been a member of the Walloon church. He was respected in the Leiden congregation he had joined, and the church had appointed him, along with Robert Cushman, to negotiate the agreement between the colonists and their London backers.[13] He was "a man godly and well approved" by his fellow colonists. Indeed, Bradford indicated that Carver's selection as governor was actually a confirmation of a previous plan for him to be in charge once the colonists landed.[14]

The form of the compact and its language is what would have been expected from a group that trusted in the judgment of individual saints. Those who had begun this journey in Scrooby had bound themselves together in a covenant more than a decade earlier under William Brewster's roof. Noting at that time they had "by the most wise and good providence of God [been] brought together in this place and desirous to unite ourselves into one congregation or church," they had promised and bound themselves "to walk in all our ways according to the Rule of the Gospel and in all sincere conformity to His holy ordinances and in mutual love to and watchfulness over one another, depending wholly & only upon the Lord our God to enable us by his grace hereunto."[15] Congregationalism in religious governance was a system of participatory democracy, reflecting a trust in the individual believer that expanded into the civil realm. Brewster, who had knowledge of forms of government both from his experience in the service of William Davison and from his extensive reading of political tracts, and who had also played a role in the original formation of the Scrooby congregation, is the most likely one to have drawn up the Mayflower Compact.

The fact that they were outside the boundaries of the patent that had been granted to them also raised questions about their right to the land. The patent itself rested on the idea that the North American continent was "vacant" and that the inhabitants who were there were "savage," thus justifying European claims to title of the lands they settled.[16] Like the French and the Spanish, the English monarchy granted land with no consideration of Native rights. But some Europeans dissented from this view. Of importance to the settlement of Plymouth are the views of the Dutch lawyer Hugo Grotius, whose ideas the Plymouth leaders would have been familiar with. In the anonymously published *Mare Liberum* (1608) Grotius expressed the view that there was no right to take possession of Native lands on the basis of the fact that the Natives were not Christians. This became the basis for the Dutch practice of purchasing Native lands that they desired. It also became the practice of English colonists at Plymouth and elsewhere in New England, though the value offered and the terms of the sale treaties are subject to question. However, the situation was different where there appeared to be no settled owners of the land. Purchase was not necessarily required when the land fitted the European concept of "vacuum domicilium," which identified some land as "vacant." Natives who did not have fenced fields and European-style permanent structures were considered to be free for the taking of anyone who would "improve" it by planting, fencing, building, and otherwise transforming it according to European standards. Due to the ravages of epidemic disease introduced by European fishermen and traders prior to 1620, much of the land along Cape Cod gave the appearance of being vacant. There was no recorded attempt to purchase the lands initially settled by the Plymouth colonists, though when they expanded into territory clearly occupied by Natives they did engage in purchase by treaty.[17]

The immediate challenge for the travelers on the *Mayflower* was where along Cape Cod to settle. On the same day that the Mayflower Compact was signed, fifteen or sixteen men landed on the shore to gather wood for the ship's cooking fires and to seek out the Native inhabitants. Meanwhile women went ashore to wash clothes and bed linens in the surf. They failed to contact the Natives but gathered large quantities of sweet-smelling juniper to burn. After spending the next day on the *Mayflower* in worship, on Monday, November 13, many of the passengers "went on shore to refresh themselves, and our women to wash, as they had great need."[18] Exploration of the land continued, with Myles Standish in charge and William Bradford, Stephen Hopkins, and Edward Tilley providing counsel. Two days later they spotted a small group of Natives, who evaded them. Over the next few days they pursued what they thought were Native paths, but "could meet with none of them, nor their houses, nor find any fresh water, which we greatly desired." Finally, they came upon a spring of fresh water "and sat us down and drunk our first New England water with as much delight as we ever drunk drink in all our lives."[19]

Natives of the region were likely concerned about the new arrivals' intentions, given their past experiences with Europeans. Were the new arrivals there to trade? Were they seeking to capture people? Europeans had not previously sought to establish footholds along the Cape, so it is unlikely that this was seen as a possibility. Clearly the Native response was to observe the English before contacting them. For their part the English were perplexed. Accounts of the region they had read described many villages and a large population. They had no knowledge of the devastation wrought by recent epidemics and likely did not fully comprehend the Native practice of shifting their habitations with the change of seasons. And they were fearful of Native attacks. Remembering these early days many years later, William Bradford would describe the Natives as "savage and brutish men, which range up and down little otherwise than the wild beasts of" the land.[20] They were "cruel, barbarous, and most treacherous, being most furious in their rage, and merciless when they overcome; not being content only to kill and take away life, but delight to torment men in the most bloody manner that may be, flaying some alive with the shells of fishes, cutting off the members and joints of others by piecemeal, and broiling on the coals, eat the collops of their flesh in their sight whilst they live, with other cruelties horrible to be related."[21]

In their explorations of the region the Englishmen traversed a landscape with well-worn paths, fields recently cultivated, and other signs of habitation—but no Natives.[22] On November 16 the exploratory party came upon "certain heaps of sand, one whereof was covered with old mats" with something like a mortar and an earthen pot on the top. When they left their summer villages the Natives of the region buried baskets of corn to retrieve on their seasonal return, covering the baskets with mats and topsoil to protect them against scavengers. They also buried their dead around the houses in which they had lived, placing in the graves bows, arrows, trinkets, and other tokens. The *Mayflower* exploratory party, after digging into the mound and finding a bow, concluded that they might have stumbled upon a grave, and so "put in the bow again and made it up as it was, and left the rest [of the heaps] untouched, because we thought it would be odious unto them to ransack their sepulchres."[23] This account, by Edward Winslow, reflected a greater interest in Native culture and greater sensitivity than was shared by many of the colonists, a reminder not to generalize about English attitudes.[24]

That same day, the English came upon another village, where they found a home site and a large European-manufactured kettle—a ship's kettle in Winslow's view—and a recently arranged heap of sand. Digging into it they "found a little old basket full of fair Indian corn, and digged further and found a great new basket full of very fair corn of this year." Not recognizing that this corn had been stored for the community's own spring planting, or simply prioritizing their own needs, they decided "to take the kettle and as much of the corn as we could carry away with us," planning if they later found some of the Natives they would return the kettle and "satisfy them for their corn."[25]

A few days later the shore party returned to the location where they had found the corn, which they named Cornhill, and discovered more corn (in all around ten bushels), some oil, and some beans. Winslow concluded that this was "God's good providence that we found this corn, for else we know not how we should have done." Nearby they discovered "a place like a grave" that was larger than the one previously examined. They dug this one up, the size evidently provoking a curiosity that overcame their previous scruples about disturbing sepulchers. In it they found "bowls, trays, dishes, and such like trinkets" and the bones of both a yellow-haired man and a child. They "brought sundry of the prettiest things away with us." Continuing on, they encountered two standing houses. Winslow carefully described the homes and their furnishings and reported that "some of the best things we took away with us." He indicated that they had planned to bring "some beads and other things to have left in the houses, in sign of peace and that we meant to truck [trade] with them," but they had forgotten to bring those goods.[26]

If, as the colonists believed, they were being watched from afar by the Natives, none of these actions would have been reassuring. Still looking for a place to settle, on December 6 an exploratory party including Standish, Carver, Winslow, and Bradford camped for the night on a sandy point. In the morning they were attacked by a number of Natives whose cries were "dreadful." Fighting off the attack, they gave "God thanks for our deliverance, . . . and called this place First Encounter."[27]

While William Bradford was returning from this expedition his wife, Dorothy, fell from the *Mayflower* and drowned. Dorothy, like many others, had remained in close and cold quarters aboard the ship at its Provincetown anchorage for almost a month. Her joy at having survived the Atlantic crossing was increasingly eclipsed by fear for the future as attempt after attempt had failed to find a viable site for settlement. Like other parents who had left children behind, she feared that she would never again see her son. Was her fall an accident or suicide?

No contemporary evidence for either verdict exists, though the puritan abhorrence of suicide makes the latter unlikely.[28] Whatever the cause, Dorothy's death cast a pall over the colonists and made the need to decide on a settlement site more urgent.

The exploration of the Cape had largely been conducted in a shallop (a light sailboat) that the colonists had carried on the *Mayflower*. But on December 15 the *Mayflower* was on the move and on the following day set down its anchor in Plymouth harbor. The settlers identified four or five brooks carrying fresh water and running down to the sea. The soil appeared "excellent black mould," suitable for planting. There were trees, including oak, birch, ash, cherry, and plum. They assessed that in season there would be ample supplies of fowl and fish. On December 18, after Brewster led them in prayers to "God for direction," they examined two specific sites, deciding to place their settlement "on

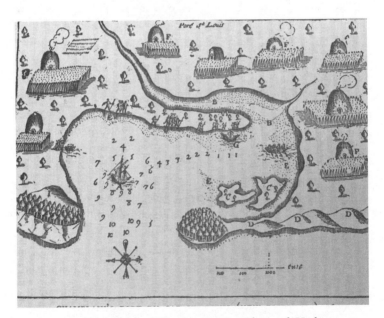

Fig. 6.1 Champlain's map of Port Saint Louis at Plymouth Harbor, 1605, which was the Native Patuxet. Note the wetus and the fields of corn. Samuel de Champlain, *Les voyages*. Paris, 1613. Photo courtesy of Beinecke Rare Book and Manuscript Library, Yale University.

a high ground, where there is a great deal of land cleared, and hath been planted with corn three or four years ago." There was "a great hill" where they planned to build a platform for the cannon they had brought.[29]

On December 23, many of the colonists went ashore to begin cutting down trees and carrying the timber the quarter mile to the settlement site. Two days later, on December 25, they began to erect a common house in which they could store their goods. Like other puritans, the Pilgrims viewed that date as no different than any other, rejecting Christmas as a pagan holiday with no scriptural justification, and so they turned to their work. Over the next few weeks they labored in snow, sleet, and wind on the common house and laid out where they would erect other structures and a palisade to surround the settlement. On January 9, with the common house almost finished, they began to build two rows of individual dwellings.[30]

The work was difficult, and the conditions took their toll. Eight had died by the end of December. Edward Winslow's account of the early months of 1621 are constantly interspersed with comments such as "rain . . . forced us to give over work"; "in the morning cold frost and sleet"; "cold frosty weather and sleet, that we could not work"; and "very wet and rainy, with the greatest gusts of wind that ever we had." On January 11, "William Bradford, being at work . . . was vehemently taken with a grief and pain" which shot to his hip-bone. He was carried to the common house, where he joined the others who had also fallen ill.[31] Three days later the common house caught fire. "The house was full of beds as they could lie one by another, and their muskets charged." Bradford and Carver, both of whom "then lay sick in bed, . . . if they had not risen with good speed," would have been "blown up" if the stored powder ignited, but it didn't and "through God's mercy, they had no harm." The thatched roof was burned, but the roof frame remained intact.[32] Eight colonists died in January, seventeen more in February, and thirteen in March.[33]

Those who were able continued to work on building shelters while also tending the sick. While these efforts continued, some of the colonists returned to the *Mayflower* every night. Through all this they were sustained by their faith. Every day started with a brief prayer.[34] Brewster continued to lead them in prayer and scripture lessons as he had during the voyage and their stay in Provincetown harbor. On January 14 all of the colonists were able to gather on land for the first religious service in Plymouth. Planned for the common house, it had to be held outdoors when that structure's roof burned on the same morning.

While there were still reverses—a heavy rain and wind on February 4 caused some of the daubing exterior of the structures to fall off, another small fire erupted in the common house on February 9—progress was slowly made. The colonists, aided by some of the *Mayflower*'s crew, unloaded hogsheads of supplies from the *Mayflower* and laboriously rolled them up the hill. On February 17 the community gathered and officially "chose Miles Standish our captain and gave him authority to command."[35] On February 21 the sailors unloaded the small cannons brought for the settlement's protection and helped the colonists bring them to the crest of the hill and place them on the platform they had built.

During their first months ashore there were sightings of the Natives, who were clearly observing the colonists. Some tools left in a field were taken by Natives. But efforts to make contact proved unsuccessful. Then, on March 16, an alarm was given as a Native approached and then walked into the settlement. As recorded in Winslow's contemporary account, "He very boldly came all alone and along the houses. . . . He saluted us in English and bade us welcome." He was "stark naked, only a leather about his waist, with a fringe about a span [nine inches] long, or little more. . . . He was a tall straight man, the hair of his head black, long behind, only short before, none on his face at all."[36]

This was Samoset, a Wabanaki from Monhegan Island in the Pemaquid area of modern Maine. He had journeyed to the Cape Cod region along with the Wampanoag Tisquantum in 1619. When they discovered that Tisquantum's village of Patuxet no longer existed, with most of Tisquantum's kin and neighbors dead and the survivors dispersed, the two Indians had been taken in by Ousamequin (who would be known to the English by his title, Massasoit) in the Wampanoag village of Pokamoket.[37]

It is likely that the exchange with Samoset involved the settlement's civil, military, and religious leaders (Carver, Standish, and Brewster) as well as Edward Winslow, who recorded the details of the encounter.

Samoset was able to inform the settlers of the peoples of eastern New England (primarily Maine) and the resources along the coast. He also told them of the epidemic that had wiped out Patuxet and many other villages and explained that the attack on the exploratory party at First Encounter Beach was by the Nausets, the tribe from which Captain Hunt had kidnapped seven men in 1614. The next day Samoset left, bearing some small gifts, but soon returned with other Natives, who "made semblance unto us [the colonists] of friendship and amity." They were entertained with food and drink and in return sang and danced.[38]

In encounters between Natives and Englishmen both sides were interested in how contact could benefit or threaten them.[39] The Wampanoag and Nauset certainly had reason to be hostile to the English, and, despite the ravages of disease, they were, as Robert Cushman observed, strong enough so that they "might in one hour have made dispatch of us."[40] While there were ample reasons for Natives to be suspicious of Europeans, there were also examples of Natives benefitting from contact by obtaining through trade steel knives, ships' kettles, woolen blankets, and other such useful items. The discussions between Samoset and Massasoit and the former's assessment of the Plymouth settlers were every bit as important as Samoset's conversations with Carver, Brewster, and Standish.

Having escaped the epidemic largely unscathed, the Narragansett had used that advantage to extend their influence to the east and southeast. They had raided their neighbors and in one such raid killed the Massachusetts sachem Nanapeshamet, possibly in 1619.[41] An alliance with the English at Plymouth might help Ousamequin stave off the Narragansett. On March 22 Samoset came again, accompanied by Tisquantum, whom the colonists were told was "the only survivor of Patuxet, where we now inhabit, who was one of the twenty captives that by Hunt were carried away." Soon Ousamequin appeared on a nearby hill with sixty of his men. Negotiations led to an exchange of hostages, following which the Native leader sat down with the colony's leaders to negotiate. Winslow's account identifies the English negotiators as himself, Standish, Carver, and Elder Brewster.[42]

The two sides negotiated a treaty that was more precisely a mutual defense pact. The first provision was a guarantee that neither Massasoit nor any of his people should injure or harm any of the settlers. Next,

Massasoit agreed that if any of his people should violate this pledge they would be sent to the English to be dealt with. The third provision called for tools taken from the English to be returned, but also pledged that if any English "did any harm to any of his, we would do the like to them." The fourth item was the most important, that "if any did unjustly war against him, we would aid him; if any did war against us, he should aid us." The fifth provision pledged Massasoit to send news of the treaty to the neighboring tribes so that they would not attack the English. By the same token, this would let the Narragansett and others know that the Wampanoag could call on the English for help. It was also agreed that when Natives came to Plymouth they would leave their weapons outside the palisade and Englishmen who visited Native communities would do the same. Finally, because he agreed to these terms, the English told Massasoit that "King James would esteem of him as his friend and ally."[43] Following their agreement, Governor Carver accompanied the Native leader to the town brook, where they embraced one another before Ousamequin departed.

It is likely that Brewster, with his experience of diplomatic negotiations, played a key role in shaping these terms.[44] Significantly, the treaty identified Massasoit as a "friend and ally" of King James and never demanded tribute, which is an important distinction from the identification of Natives as "subjects" of the king in other colonies such as Virginia. Over the following years the English would bring Massasoit gifts and refer to him as a "friend."[45] With this agreement the colonists had reason to feel more secure. It was an important turning point in Plymouth's history. In its aftermath another Wampanoag, Hobomok, along with his family, came to live with the English. Together with Tisquantum and another Native, Tokamahamon (about whom little is known) helped the English adapt to the New World. Early in the summer of 1621 Bradford, newly chosen governor after the death of John Carver, dispatched Edward Winslow and Stephen Hopkins to visit Pokamoket, where Ousamequin was residing, to further strengthen the treaty.[46]

There were still, however, the Nauset, the tribe that had attacked the exploratory party at First Encounter Beach. In July 1621 an English boy, John Billington, got lost in the woods. After wandering for five days he was found by some Natives and brought to a Nauset village. Ousamequin heard about this and provided a guide to bring a party of colonists there. The English had learned that this was the tribe that Hunt had captured Natives from, and when they arrived they were confronted by an old woman who had lost three sons to the English captain. The colonists acknowledged Hunt's crime and said that all Englishmen who had heard of it condemned it. They rewarded the Natives for having rescued Billington and compensated them for the corn they had seized from Nauset sites during their early explorations.[47] These actions secured peace with the tribes in the immediate vicinity.

But there were other Natives to the north and the west with whom relations were troubled. Not long after the settlers had made their treaty with Ousamequin they received word that he had been taken by the Narragansett, the tribe that had sought to exploit the losses the Wampanoag had suffered. The Narragansett had entered into an agreement with Corbitant, sachem of a Wampanoag band at Mattapoiset, who had disapproved of the treaty with the English. While the Narragansett detained Ousamequin, Corbitant seized Tisquantum, Hobomok, and Tokamahamon. But Hobomok escaped and carried word of these events to Plymouth. Recognizing the serious nature of the threat, Bradford dispatched Myles Standish with fourteen armed men to support Ousamequin as called for in their recent treaty.[48]

The English attacked Corbitant's village and freed Tisquantum, who they had feared was dead. News of the energetic response spread through the region. Ousamequin returned to his lands, and Native sachems who had opposed the treaty, including Corbitant, appeared in Plymouth in September and subscribed to an instrument of submission. Notably, the sachems who signed "acknowledge ourselves to be the loyal subjects of King James," an important distinction from the language of the treaty signed by Ousamequin and Carver.[49]

Nevertheless, threats to the colony continued, in part shaped by the actions of other Englishmen who arrived along the coast at this time. In 1622 Thomas Weston, one of the English investors in the Plymouth enterprise, sent a separate party of fifty or sixty Englishmen to establish a trading post along Massachusetts Bay. Friends of the Plymouth settlers back in England sent warnings about these new arrivals. John Pierce found Weston's men "so base in condition (for the most part) as in all appearance not fit for an honest man's company." Robert Cushman was particularly concerned that "these people will hardly deal so well with the savages as they should. I pray," he continued, "you therefor signify to Squanto that they are a distinct body from us, and we have nothing to do with them, neither must be blamed for their faults."[50]

After a brief stay at Plymouth, where their behavior validated the concerns of Pierce and Cushman, Weston's men set up a trading post at Wessagusset, along the southern shore of Massachusetts Bay.[51] The Plymouth authorities soon heard that the newcomers were stealing corn from the Massachusetts tribe and offending them in other ways. By the fall of 1623 there was a concern that the Massachusetts were plotting both against the Wessagusset settlement and perhaps the English at Plymouth, obviously not distinguishing between the groups as Cushman had hoped they would. As he tried to deal with this threat, Bradford was hindered by the death of Tisquantum from disease.[52] Ousamequin too fell ill. Edward Winslow, accompanied by Hobomok, journeyed to help the Massasoit as best they could and was successful in nursing Ousamequin back to health.[53] On their journey back to Plymouth, Hobomok passed on to Winslow the Massasoit's warning of the Massachusetts plot and the fact that Plymouth was to be one of the targets. Ousamequin had been solicited to join the attack but had rejected the overture.[54]

Fears of Native conspiracy were heightened by news of the June 1622 massacre of 347 English colonists in Virginia. The Plymouth colonists reinforced their stockade and, having decided that the threat to their colony was credible, the authorities dispatched an armed force under Myles Standish to make a preemptive strike against the Massachusetts tribe. Standish was specifically directed to execute "Witawamet, that bloody and bold villain ... whose head he [Standish] had order to bring [back] with him, that it might be a warning and terror to all of that disposition."[55] Standish and his small force surprised the Natives, killing Witawamet and half a dozen of his warriors. The sachem's eighteen-year-old brother was captured and hanged. Witawamet's head was cut off, brought to Plymouth, stuck on a pole, and raised above the stockade.

Standish would have believed his actions justified by the standards of European war, in which preemptive attacks and the displaying of an enemy's head were seen as legitimate tactics for sending a warning to potential enemies. His actions were endorsed if not ordered by Bradford, but not all of those connected with Plymouth approved. John Robinson wrote from Leiden in December 1623 that he was appalled by "the killing of those poor Indians" and expressed the view that "how happy had it been, if you had converted some before you had killed any." He feared, rightly as it would eventually prove, that "where blood is once begun to be shed, it is seldom staunched of a long time after." Robinson accepted that the colonists believed they were provoked but could not believe the actions—especially the number of Indians killed—were justified. As for Standish, Robinson expressed his love for the soldier and believed that he was "a man humble and meek . . . in ordinary course." But he feared that on occasions such as this Standish "may be wanting that tenderness of the life of man made after God's image which is mete."[56] There is no evidence as to whether any in the colony shared Robinson's reservations.[57]

While the attack on the Massachusetts effectively intimidated other Natives who may have been considering similar plots, it added to a history of English aggression that dated back to before 1620 and that would fuel future conflict. Eventually the expansion of the colony would undermine the long-peaceful relations with the Wampanoags.[58] But in 1623 Robinson's letter was a reminder to the colonists of the religious aspirations that had sent them to the New World. While they negotiated relations with the Natives they also had challenges to overcome in forging a godly society.

7

The Godly Community

Understanding Plymouth's religious history is difficult because the earliest published accounts of the colony—*Mourt's Relation* and Edward Winslow's *Good News from New England*—included little on the subject. The authors deliberately did not document their separatist practices for their financial backers, the king, and the bishops. Nevertheless, it is possible to tell much of the story from accounts of visitors to the colony, as well as letters between the colonists and their friends in England.

Until John Robinson died in 1625 the members of the Plymouth church thought of themselves as members of the Leiden congregation, with Robinson as their pastor. They had hoped that Robinson and other members of the congregation who had remained behind would soon join them in the New World. Some fellow congregants did come, including William Brewster's son Jonathan and others on the *Fortune* in November 1621. Yet Robinson never joined them, and as time passed the colonists (and Robinson himself) attributed this to the obstruction of their financial backers, some of whom were focused on financial profit and were not sympathetic toward the congregation's beliefs and practices. In the absence of Robinson, the congregation reverted to the type of lay leadership and control that had characterized the meetings of ordinary believers in the Scrooby manor house prior to the formal gathering of the congregation, and which remained at its core. Even after ministers were found later in the seventeenth century, the laity would dominate the affairs of the Plymouth church.[1]

The majority of those who successfully crossed the Atlantic on the *Mayflower* were members of the Leiden church, including the congregation's elder, William Brewster, and two of the church's deacons, John Carver and Samuel Fuller. Other settlers, such as the contentious Christopher Martin, had not been members of the congregation but were puritan in their outlook. Given both the fact that the Leiden church had allowed nonmembers to attend, listen to sermons, and participate in all nonsacramental ceremonies and that Robinson had emphasized the importance of binding all into a community, it is likely that all of the colonists were allowed to, and perhaps even required to, attend religious services. Any who were moved by this to seek membership would have come before the congregation to have their fitness evaluated. This would have entailed the existing members seeking to discern the existence of saving grace in the candidate according to the criteria previously discussed—a gracious life and comprehension of the principles of Christian faith. As Edward Winslow explained it, "All we require" of an individual is that they "render a reason of that faith and hope they have in Christ, which together with a good testimony of an honest life, we admit them."[2]

Without their pastor, religious services were conducted by Elder William Brewster, who had comforted the passengers on the *Mayflower* with prayers and psalm singing. During the first days of settlement, worship would have been conducted outdoors or in the common house. Like other puritans, the congregation did not believe in the sanctity of church buildings and were opposed to statues, pictures, and other decorations. They had worshipped in the Scrooby manor house, in John Robinson's Leiden home, and in 1622, they "built a fort with good timber, both strong and comely, which was of good defence, made with a flat roof, on which fort their ordnance was mounted, and where they kept constant watch, especially in time of danger. It served them also for a meetinghouse and was fitted accordingly for that use."[3] If they followed the examples they knew in Leiden, the ground level of the fort would have had a simple enclosed pulpit.[4] Not until 1648 did the colonists build a separate meetinghouse on the top of the hill.

As had been the case during the years in Scrooby and Leiden, the congregation's worship and belief were centered on their understanding of the scriptures, but influenced by books dealing with theology, ecclesiology, and history. The inventories of men and women who lived and died in the colony in the seventeenth century include collections of books that attest to their search for truth. Many of these private libraries—particularly those of Brewster, Ralph Partridge, and William Bradford—compare well with the libraries of the first generation that settled in Massachusetts in the 1630s. It was their grounding in such materials that gave Plymouth believers the confidence to speak out in prophesying sessions.[5]

The congregation devoted themselves to religious observances in both morning and afternoon on Sundays. A visitor to the colony around 1628 described the colonists gathering for worship: "They assemble by beat of drum, each with his musket or firelock, in front of the captain's door; they have their cloaks on and place themselves in order, three abreast, and are led by a sergeant without beat of drum," and proceeded "to the fort, the lower part [of which] they use for their church, where they preach on Sundays and the usual holidays." Next in the march to the fort came "the Governor, in a long robe; beside him, on the right hand, comes the preacher with his cloak on, and with a small cane in his hand—and so they march in good order, and each sets his arms down near him."[6] There they would sit on hard benches or stand for hours as the services demanded, in the freezing cold of winter and the sweltering heat of summer. The visitor did not record how the women and children joined in this procession to the meetinghouse nor where they sat once inside.

Brewster would open the morning service by leading the congregation in prayer. He preferred short, extemporaneous prayers. Like other puritans, he believed that reading a prayer composed by someone else would be a mockery of true prayer, which should arise from the heart.[7] At the conclusion, those present, eyes uplifted to God, would say, "Amen." Next Brewster offered readings from scripture and discussed the text. A sermon would be preceded and followed by singing psalms. This involved the entire assembled body—men, women, and children, congregants and noncongregants—lifting their voices in unison without any musical accompaniment. The sermon was the heart of the service and could easily last for two hours. As a preacher Brewster employed a plain style, but was "moving and stirring of affections," "ripping up the heart and conscience" of his listeners."[8]

The afternoon service offered an opportunity for members of the congregation to discuss matters of faith or practice, offering their views by way of prophesying.[9] Insight into how prophesying was conducted is provided by an account from John Winthrop, governor of Massachusetts, recorded in 1632, when he and Boston's pastor,

John Wilson, traveled to Plymouth. On the Sabbath they joined the Plymouth congregation in worship. At the time Ralph Smith was the pastor of the Plymouth congregation, Roger Williams was the teacher, and William Brewster served as elder. After attending the morning service, the visitors partook in communion, since the Boston church was recognized by the Plymouth congregation as a true covenanted church.[10]

In the afternoon the Boston visitors rejoined the congregation. "Roger Williams," Winthrop noted, "according to their custom, propounded a question, to which the pastor, Mr. Smith, spoke briefly. Then Mr. Williams prophesied." After this, Governor Bradford spoke to the question, followed by Brewster, "then some two or three more of the congregation. Then Brewster desired Winthrop and Wilson to speak to it, which they did." At the end of this session "the deacon, Mr. Fuller, put the congregation in mind of their duty of contribution." Winthrop and Wilson joined the others in going "down to the deacon's seat" and putting an offering into the box.[11]

The form of prophesying described by Winthrop was a formal exercise derived in large part from John Robinson's beliefs and the practices of the Leiden church. In such formal settings visitors from a true church could join, but the nonmembers of the community were not allowed to offer their views. But there was a related history of believers in England and abroad sharing their spiritual insights with one another in family settings, local conferences, and conventicles. In many of these settings those participating were not all members of a covenanted congregation, and there is evidence that in Plymouth noncongregants joined in private conferences as they tried to work out their religious identity.[12]

The purpose of all forms of prophesying was to lay open the truths of scripture and find further light. It could also be a means by which an individual's spiritual life was enriched by the story of how a fellow believer had experienced God's grace. The danger always was the risk that an individual might present false truths, mistaking the suggestions of the devil for the inspiration of the Holy Spirit. This was one reason why formal prophesying in a congregation was limited to those perceived by their peers to be godly recipients of grace. And testing ideas against the insights of fellow believers was a way of finding a way forward for all.[13] Robinson did not believe that a believer had to be well educated to be inspired by the Spirit. Common people were as likely to be blessed in this way as those of higher status and better schooling. He also had taken the position that under some circumstances women as well as men could prophesy in church. Their participation may have been greater in Plymouth, and they were free to share their insights in private settings.[14] Many women owned the Bible and various religious tracts, which suggests that they played a role in religious discussions, if a largely undocumented one.[15]

A few things hint at that role being larger than commonly assumed. In 1623 Bradford wrote to the colony's backers in England, responding to complaints that had been registered against the colony. He wrote, "touching our government, you are mistaken if you think we admit women and children to have to do in the same, for they are excluded, as both reason and nature teacheth they should be."[16] The question is where this claim came from. The most likely answer is that women were allowed to participate in church matters, which made some critics conclude that they also had a vote in civil matters. Also suggestive is that when government restraints on religion were largely abolished in England following the outbreak of the English Civil Wars, a large number of women took to the streets to preach to whomever would listen. These "street preachers" emerged from the more radical end of the puritan spectrum and they were likely acting in public much as they had in private.[17]

The nature of Plymouth prophesying was also a tempting target for the enemies of the colony and its puritans. Thomas Morton, a survivor of the Wessagausett outpost and a sharp critic, took particular relish in attacking the Plymouth church, claiming that every cow keeper was invited to "exercise his gifts." In the 1640s English Presbyterians such as William Rathband sought to use the Plymouth practice as a way of ridiculing the entire New England Way.[18]

The dialogue that went on in sessions such as described by Winthrop was a form of lay preaching. But more formal lay preaching also fell in the category of prophesying. According to Bradford, "when the church had no other minister," which was during most of the colony's first decade, Brewster "taught twice every sabbath, and that both powerfully and profitably, to the great contentment of his hearers and their comfortable edification." He also preached on Thursdays, which was the regular lecture day in the church. Bradford noted that Brewster's preaching was "very moving and stirring of affections" while "plain and distinct." He had a gift for extempore prayers, "ripping up the heart and conscience before God in the humble confession of sin and begging of God in Christ for the pardon of the same." While some ministers prayed at a considerable length, Brewster's practice of offering separate, shorter prayers was based on his belief that "the heart and spirits of all, especially the weak, could hardly continue and stand bent as it were so long towards God as they ought to do in that duty without flagging and falling off" in their attention. Bradford did note, however, that Brewster was more likely to offer longer, more piercing prayers on appointed days of fast and humiliation.[19]

There was no recorded legal requirement for colonists in Plymouth to attend religious services until 1650, when the colony's General Court passed a law punishing "whosoever shall profane the Lord's Day by doing any servile work or any such abuses." The following year the Court decreed that any "person or persons [that] shall neglect the frequenting of the public worship of God that is according to God in the places where they live" should be fined.[20] During the early years of the colony, however, men and women who were not members of the church were allowed and even expected to attend services, since the congregation had decided in Leiden that they could engage with nonmembers in prayer, listening to sermons, and singing psalms. Indeed, Bradford recorded that "every Lord's Day some are appointed to visit suspected places, and if any be found idling and neglect the hearing of the Word (through idleness or profaneness) they are punished for the same."[21] Nonmembers were forbidden to share in the administration of the sacraments, but since the sacraments were not administered in Plymouth until 1629 that was not an issue. Just as some Walloons and others had attended services in Leiden and been converted, so in Plymouth Bradford tells us that "many were brought to God by his [Brewster's] ministry. He did more in this behalf in a year than many that have their hundreds a year do in all their lives."[22]

While Brewster was the primary preacher, lay prophesying offered the opportunity for others to preach as well. Edward Winslow acknowledged to the English authorities that he had "spoken by way of exhortation to the people."[23] Samuel Fuller also preached, as did Robert

Cushman and likely others. Only one such sermon is known to have survived, one preached by Robert Cushman on Sunday, December 9, 1621.[24] Cushman preached to the congregation on *The Danger of Self-Love, and the Sweetness of True Friendship*.[25] Published in London the following year, the text provides excellent insight into the message that the congregation's leaders were offering to the colonists. The text Cushman took for his sermon was from 1 Corinthians 10:24: "Let no man seek his own, but every man another's wealth." Like Brewster, Robinson, and other puritans, Cushman opposed the growing individualistic ethic that was gaining strength. He urged his listeners that they "let this self-seeking be left off, and turn the stream another way, namely, seek the good of your brethren, please them, honor them, reverence them, for otherwise it will never go well amongst you." The temptation to seek one's own welfare regardless of the cost to others was particularly strong in colonial settings, where resources were limited. Cushman was familiar with the disorder that persisted in Jamestown and told the Pilgrim audience, "It is reported that there are many men gone to that other plantation in Virginia, which, whilst they lived in England, seemed very religious, zealous, and conscionable, and have now lost even the sap of grace and edge to all goodness, and are become mere worldlings. This testimony I believe to be partly true, and amongst the many causes of it this self-love is not the least."

Cushman feared that the hardships the Plymouth settlers faced in their first year had tempted many to focus on their personal welfare rather than the common good. It was this temptation that Cushman feared and addressed. He warned of "that bird of self-love which was hatched at home," saying that "if it be not looked to, will eat out the life of all grace and goodness. And though men have escaped the danger of the sea, and that cruel mortality which swept away so many of our loving friends and brethren, yet, except they purge out this self-love, a worse mischief is prepared for them."

Illustrating his argument with references to scripture, Cushman told them, "Great matters have been brought to pass where men have cheerfully, as with one heart, hand, and shoulder, gone about it, both in wars, buildings, and plantations; but where every man seeks himself, all cometh to nothing." Not surprisingly, the message was the same as that John Robinson had conveyed to the colonists in a letter written

Fig. 7.1 A scene in Plimoth Plantation, a living history museum representing the community in the 1620s. Photo by Francis J. Bremer.

at the time of their departure. Robinson had pointed out that because many of the settlers were from different locations and unknown to one another they should take special care to prevent factions from developing and should focus on their common needs and tasks and bend their efforts to the general good.

Cushman's words were similar to those John Winthrop would utter in 1630, which is not surprising since this was a central theme of the puritan social gospel. Indeed, most sermons in such communities focused not on the intricacies of doctrine but on how believers were to lead exemplary lives and contribute to shaping godly communities. Cushman exhorted the Plymouth colonists to "labor to be joined together [as one body] and knit by flesh and sinews. Away with envy at the good of others, and rejoice in his good, and sorrow for his evil. Let his joy be your joy, and his sorrow thy sorrow. Let his sickness be thy sickness, his hunger thy hunger, his poverty thy poverty. And if you profess friendship, be friends in adversities; for then a friend is known and tried, and not before." Putting this social gospel into practice, the role of the deacon was to collect offerings from the congregation and to distribute funds to those in need.[26] Reflecting an expansion of this impetus to the general community, Plymouth towns levied taxes to cover the cost of medical treatment and living expenses of townsmen, church members or not, who became incapacitated or ill.

While Cushman, Brewster, and others preached to all comers in Plymouth, Elder Brewster alone was responsible for supervision of congregation members. In regard to "the government of the church, which was most proper to his office," Bradford commended him for being "careful to preserve good order in the same, and to preserve purity both in doctrine and communion of the same, and to suppress any error or contention that might begin to rise up amongst them." He supervised monthly business meetings of the congregation, but much of his work was done in one-on-one encounters with members. He carried out these tasks with a grave demeanor combined with a cheerful spirit. Humble in assessing his own qualities, he sometimes, according to Bradford, overestimated those of others. In dealing with those in trouble, particularly those who had lost family or fortune, he was "tenderhearted and compassionate." Sympathetic to those who had suffered, he was offended by "such as would haughtily and proudly carry and lift up themselves, being risen from nothing and having little else in them to commend them but a few fine clothes or a little riches more than others."[27]

The Plymouth church order denied the clergy a role in marriage. While clergy in England were accustomed to presiding at weddings, the Plymouth colonists made marriage a civil ceremony. In doing so they followed the practice that had been introduced in Leiden in 1575 and that the members of the Leiden congregation followed for their own unions. Couples appeared before civil magistrates to exchange their vows. After the ceremony it was customary to celebrate with a feast and exchange of gifts.[28] The same practice was followed in Plymouth and would be adopted in Massachusetts, where the puritans followed the Plymouth example. In a 1623 letter Emmanuel Altham wrote to his kinsman, he described the wedding party that followed Governor William Bradford's second marriage—a feast that included "about twelve pasty venisons, besides others, pieces of roasted venison and such good cheer in such quantity that I could wish you some of our share."[29]

In the autumn of 1621, the foundations of the colony seemed to be secure. The members of the Leiden congregation had found a place to worship without fear. They had found a viable place to settle and had shaped a system of government that commanded the allegiance of all. Peace with the Native tribe that dominated their corner of New England had been achieved, and with the help of Natives such as Samoset, Tisquantum, and Hobomock, they had learned how to plant crops and harvest the sea. And so the Plymouth colonists observed what has come to be identified as the "First Thanksgiving." There are two sources for the event. One is the account given by William Bradford, the colony's governor, in his history *Of Plymouth Plantation*. Bradford wrote that the colonists began "to gather in the small harvest they had, and to fit up their homes and dwellings against winter, being all well recovered in health and strength and had all things in good plenty." Some colonists caught large quantities of cod, bass, and other fish, while others successfully hunted waterfowl, wild turkeys, and deer. Bradford did not write of an actual celebration but indicated that details were sent to England in letters that contained true reports.[30]

One such letter was written by Edward Winslow and included accounts of the colony published in 1622 as *A Relation or Journal of the beginning and proceedings of the English Plantation settled at Plimoth in New England*, commonly referred to as *Mourt's Relation*. Winslow reported that when the harvest had been gathered, Governor Bradford sent four men hunting "that so we might after a special manner rejoice together after we had gathered the fruit of our labors." The four men "killed as much fowl as, with a little help beside, served the company almost a week." They combined feasting with various recreations and military drills. During that week about ninety Natives, including Massasoit, joined them, bringing with them five deer and joining in the celebrations for three days.[31] All, including women and children, would have helped in butchering the deer, plucking the feathers of turkey and other fowl, grinding corn, gathering shellfish, and doing everything else necessary to feed the group over those days. Natives would have erected temporary shelters.[32]

In recent years the meaning of this event has become hotly contested, particularly whether it was the "first" thanksgiving in America and whether it was religious. This was a time when virtually all people believed that the events that affected them were shaped by supernatural forces. Clearly men and women of all faiths had a history of giving thanks to the God they believed had bestowed personal blessings upon them, such as the birth of a child or recovery from disease, and public blessings such as battlefield victories and abundant harvests. When Europeans came to America and got beyond the initial thanks they offered up for surviving the perilous journey, they recognized other reasons for offering thanksgiving. There were many such gatherings to give thanks in Spanish and English colonies in America from as early as 1541.[33]

Moreover, Native Americans everywhere, including New England, regularly attributed their good fortune to the creator and regularly offered thanks. They had a cosmology in which all people had a place in the cycle of life in the creation. They had rituals that included feasting and exchanges of goods at the time of the corn harvest. In cases, such as at Plymouth in 1621, when they were involved in European thanksgivings, the basic thrust of the effort would have been something they could recognize.

So what happened in Plymouth in the fall of 1621? That celebration was permeated, as were all other aspects of those colonists' lives, with their religious faith. But rather than look for specific models they may have drawn on, it makes more sense to review the broad traditions of giving thanks that the Scrooby-Leiden congregants were familiar with. Deeply familiar with the scriptures, the colonists were acquainted with the observations of bountiful harvests by the Jewish people described in Deuteronomy 16:13–14: "Thou shalt observe the feast of the tabernacle seven days, when thou hast gathered in thy corn, and thy wine. And you shalt rejoice in thy feast, thou and thy son, and thy daughter, and thy servant, and thy maid, and the Levite, and the stranger, and the fatherless, and the widow, that are within thy gates." In the context of the Plymouth thanksgiving, the injunction to include the stranger is notable. The gloss in the Geneva Bible, widely used by puritans, directed reader to the twenty-third and twenty-fourth chapters of the book of Leviticus, which detailed how the various Jewish feasts were to be observed and directed that the Feast of the Tabernacles be a multiday affair.[34]

There were numerous other examples in the scriptures of the peoples of the Bible offering thanks to God for the blessings they had received, including the feast of Purim, commemorating the deliverance of the Jewish people from an Persian plot to kill all the Jews. Offerings of thanks were part of Christian liturgies from the time of the early church through the Reformation and beyond. These included numerous prayers in the book of Psalms, which were regularly sung in puritan services.

On the level of domestic life, English men and women were familiar with the suggested "Thanksgiving after Meals" in the 1559 English *Book of Common Prayer* expressing gratitude to God for "the manifold benefits which we continually receive at thy bountiful hand, not only for that it hath pleased thee to feed us in this present life," but for all other blessings. Although puritans were critical of aspects of the *Prayer Book* and generally disdained set forms for extemporaneous prayer, when they gathered in their homes they offered comparable thanks. On a public level the men and women who eventually formed the Scrooby congregation were instructed by official proclamations to commemorate numerous blessings of God on the land. The *Book of Homilies* issued in 1571 had recommended both days of fast to ask God's favor and thanksgiving to thank him for favors received.[35] English authorities in Queen Elizabeth's reign instructed parishioners to gather and thank God for "withdrawing and ceasing the plague" (1563), for thwarting Catholic plots against the queen's life on three occasions, (1584, 1585, 1586), the general welfare of the realm (1587), the defeat of the Armada (1588), and at least five other occasions.[36] Similar instructions were issued by the authorities during the reigns of James I and Charles I. After they had relocated to Leiden, the congregation witnessed similar religious thanksgivings. The residents of Leiden annually celebrated the relief of the city from Spanish siege in 1574. On October 3 of each year the community gathered for a religious service of prayer and thanksgiving, followed by ten days of feasts, games, and a public fair.[37]

All of this was part of the cultural heritage that the colonists brought to New England. Whether the celebration in the fall of 1621 was modeled on any particular Jewish, English, or Dutch practice, it was certainly a celebration permeated by religious sentiments that would have been understood as a "thanksgiving." It should be noted that Winslow's account incorporated phrases derived from scripture—John 4:3 and Psalm 33—that would have been evident to his readers. The character of the event was likely to have been recognized by the Wampanoag, who had their own such rites and joined in the festivities. These were not somber events spent entirely in church, but also occasions for rejoicing. The fact that there were exercises of arms and games should not be surprising. Objections to the *Book of Sports*, a proclamation authorizing Englishmen to engage in athletic contests after Sunday services, issued by James I and then reenacted by Charles I was not to the sports so much as to allowing them on the Sabbath. Puritans believed in needful recreation. At Cambridge University in William Brewster's time, puritans such as John Wheelwright engaged in an early form of football; Laurence Chaderton was known to wrestle, and Thomas Hooker used wrestling imagery in his sermons; William Brewster himself named one of his sons Wrestling; Symonds D'Ewes wrote of "jumping, running, and pitching the bar"; and most of the colleges had tennis courts and bowling greens.[38] Puritans commonly incorporated the words of scripture into their writings, and when Winslow wrote about the colonists gathering "in a more special manner [to] rejoice together, after we had gathered the fruits of our labor," he was evoking the language of John 4:36—"and he that soweth, and he that reapeth, might rejoice together." His audience would have been familiar with the message of Psalm 33, calling on the righteous to bless God for his gifts unto them.[39] And the general understanding of how their trials and blessings were related to God's will emerged in 1623. Faced with a serious drought from the third week in May to the middle of June, with no rain and intense heat, Governor Bradford appointed "a solemn day of humiliation to seek the Lord by humble and fervent prayer." When this was followed by "seasonable showers . . . [that] caused a fruitful and liberal harvest," they "set apart a day of thanksgiving."[40] Codifying such events, the colony's General Court in 1636 gave the governor and those holding the office of assistants the authority "to command solemn days of humiliation by fasting, etc., and also for thanksgiving as occasion shall be offered."[41] Puritans would never stipulate an annual day of thanksgiving as it is celebrated today. The Sabbath was the only regularly recurring day for religious exercises. They would never presume God's blessing, but they regularly appointed days of fast when faced with trials and of thanksgiving when they received a positive answer to their prayers.

What made the Plymouth thanksgiving of 1621 different from many others was the presence of the Wampanoag visitors, regardless of whether they were specifically invited or if, as has been suggested, they came, having heard gunfire while hunting and were welcomed to join in the events. The biblical injunction for the Feast of the Tabernacles did call for the inclusion of the "stranger," and certainly the Natives qualified as such. In this case the Natives outnumbered the English almost two to one. It is striking in this context that immediately following his description of the event, Edward Winslow wrote, "We have found the Indians very faithful in their covenant of peace with us, very loving and ready to pleasure us. We often go to them, and they come to us."[42] There was little reason to doubt the strength of that covenant.

Further evidence of the strength of the covenant between Natives and Englishmen occurred in August 1623, when William Bradford married Alice Southworth. "Upon the occasion of the Governor's marriage," according to a letter by Emmanuel Altham, a visitor to the colony, "Massasoit was sent for to the wedding, where came with him his wife, the queen, . . . and he brought the Governor three or four bucks and a turkey. And so we had very good pastime in seeing them dance, which is in such a manner, with such a noise that you would wonder." The Massasoit was given a hat, coat, band, and a feather. While this account reinforces the sense of mutual celebration such as described in accounts of the 1621 thanksgiving, Altham also displayed the underlying misunderstanding of Native culture that would eventually undermine a true coexistence. Having described the wedding celebration to his uncle, Altham wrote that at the time when the Massasoit was given his gifts, Altham "craved a boy of him for you, but he would not part with him." Nevertheless, he reassured his uncle that he would "bring you one hereafter," it evidently never occurring to him that the English interest in acquiring Natives for their own purposes could rupture the trust established after earlier English kidnappings of Natives.[43]

In November 1621 the *Fortune* had brought thirty-six new settlers, most of them men who did not share puritan values, who were sent by the investors to bolster the colony.[44] Bradford referred to most of

Fig. 7.2 Plimoth Plantation. Drawing by Jeremy D. Bangs.

them as "lusty young men, and many of them wild enough."[45] Robert Cushman had traveled with these newcomers on the *Fortune*, and it is likely that his call for sacrificing for the common good in his early December sermon was in part directed at these new arrivals. A few months after the thanksgiving feast (the exact date of which is unknown), another event shed light on the religious culture of the infant colony. On Christmas Day, 1621, Governor Bradford led the colony's men to engage in tasks such as cutting down trees. But "most of this new company excused themselves and said it went against their consciences to work on that day." Though some puritans attended worship on the day, most objected to the celebration of Christmas, pointing out that the nativity had not occurred in December, but more importantly that the holiday was no more than a Christian veneer put over pagan revelries.[46] Bradford "informed them that if they made it a matter of conscience he could spare them until they were better informed."[47]

The governor's decision may have been simply an effort to avoid a confrontation that would disrupt the colony. Nevertheless, when the workers returned from the fields, the governor "found them in the street at play, openly; some pitching the bar, and some at stool-ball and like sports."[48] He took away their equipment and told them that if they abstained from work as a matter of conscience they should stay inside and engage in religious devotions, and that it "was against his conscience that they should play and others work."

8

Sustaining the Vision

The incident involving how Christmas would be observed suggested religious divisions that would persist. The English Merchant Adventurers who had provided the principal financial backing to the venture continued to send over settlers who were not committed to the puritan community. In fact, friends of the congregation in England reported that there was "a strong faction among the Adventurers against them, and especially against the coming of the rest [of the congregation] from Leiden."[1] John Robinson, still viewed by the congregation as their pastor, was convinced that the investors were "unwilling that I should be transported," referring to a faction among them as "adversaries" whose malice would "stop my course when they see it intended."[2] Increasingly, some of the new arrivals sent by the investors chafed at the religious order in the colony and complained to the Adventurers. In the spring of 1624 Governor Bradford received a letter from one of the investors sympathetic to the Leiden group that outlined twelve objections to how things were ordered in the colony, many made by settlers who had been in the colony but then returned.

Four of these were focused on religion. The first complaint concerned the colonists' divergence from English religious practices, to which Bradford responded (somewhat disingenuously) that he knew of no complaints or opposition that had been brought to the attention of the leaders of the church or government. The next complaint was that there was a "neglect of family duties on the Lord's Day." Bradford denied that the colony's leaders tolerated any such behavior, though he acknowledged that some of the newcomers might have provided a better example of proper devotions. The third complaint was that the sacraments were not administered. Bradford pointed out that when they were in Leiden they enjoyed the Lord's Supper every Sunday, and that baptism was administered there whenever an infant was presented.

The problem in the colony was that much to their grief their pastor was "kept from us." The final religious complaint was that children were neither "catechized nor taught to read." The governor defended the colonists, pointing out that children were taught by their parents and that they hoped to soon find and support someone capable of running a common school. There is no record of any such school being established at that point in time, though Brewster taught some in his home and Bridget Fuller, Samuel's wife, may have taught young children in her house in the early 1630s.[3] A William Wetherell or Witherell, whom some wanted to call to the ministry in Scituate in the mid-1640s, was evidently a schoolmaster at Duxbury.[4] Despite the lack of schools, the large number of books listed in colony inventories speaks to the literacy of many of the settlers.[5]

As for the complaint about the sacraments not being administered, Brewster had taken steps to attempt to correct the problem. In December 1623 he had written to Robinson to ask if he, as a church elder, might administer the sacraments. Robinson's reply was that only a minister, "a teaching elder," could do so. Robinson had all but abandoned hope that he would himself be able to journey to Plymouth. Perhaps some other "learned man," suitable to be called to the ministry, would go to the colony.[6] Most Christians accepted the concept of lay baptism in cases where there was no option, but it does not seem as if any children were being baptized by Brewster or other laymen.[7] If the congregation had elected Brewster as their pastor or teacher (a second ministerial post in many congregational churches), this problem would have been solved. It was certainly within the authority of the congregation to do so, and he must have been approached, for Bradford reported that Brewster "would never be persuaded to take higher office upon him."[8]

Meanwhile the Adventurers, many of whom had worked to prevent Robinson from joining his congregants in the colony, dispatched a clergyman of their own choosing, John Lyford, to Plymouth. Robert Cushman, who along with Edward Winslow was back in England at the time to represent the colonists' interests, wrote that Lyford was "(we hope) an honest plain man, though none of the most eminent and rare." Cushman told Bradford and Brewster to use their own judgment as to whether they would call him to ministerial office. Alluding to the fact that Lyford recognized that congregational practice made the choice of clergy the prerogative of the members, Cushman wrote that Lyford "knows he is no officer amongst you." But Lyford had been an ordained clergyman in the Church of England, and Cushman feared that "perhaps custom and universality may make him forget himself." With this caution, he indicated that "Mr. Winslow and myself gave way to his going, to give content to some here, and we see no hurt in it, but only his great charge of [Lyford's many] children."[9]

There is not much known about Lyford's background. He may have been the John Lyford who received degrees in 1597 and 1602 from Magdalen College, Oxford. This would fit with his being curate at Treddington, Worcestershire, as of 1603 and minister of the chapel at Shipston-upon-Stour, Treddington, Worcestershire, in 1609. Prior to his coming to Plymouth, he had served in the ministry at the parish of Levalleglish in county Armagh, Ireland. Given that Lyford had no previous connection with the Leiden congregation or any other puritans, Cushman's wariness was justified.[10]

When Lyford arrived in Plymouth in March 1624, he "saluted them with that reverence and humility as is seldom to be seen, and indeed made them ashamed, he so bowed and cringed unto them, and would have kissed their hands if they would have suffered him." He "wept and shed many tears, blessing God that had brought him to see their faces, and admiring the things they had done." Lyford made a statement of his faith and confessed to "disorderly walking" in his past while not specifying his offenses, and he was accordingly admitted to the congregation. He joined Brewster and others in preaching by way of prophesying, and Bradford consulted him on matters of concern to the colony. But he was not called and ordained to serve them as a clergyman. Thomas Morton claimed that before considering Lyford for the ministry the colonists demanded that he "renounce his calling to the office of the ministry received in England as heretical and papistical," something he refused to do.[11] Soon Lyford, along with John Oldham, a supporter who had come over on the same ship, were holding private meetings of those who were disaffected. Presumably these were colonists who were not members of the congregation, though perhaps the meetings also included some church members who were frustrated by the lack of sacraments.

Whether or not Lyford conducted services according to the *Book of Common Prayer* or whether he baptized children or celebrated Holy Communion is unknown. While the brotherhood of saints was the communion that mattered most to the puritans, Bradford himself had noted that members of the Plymouth church when in Europe had been accustomed to celebrating the Lord's Supper weekly. Infant baptism was a higher priority. Puritans rejected the idea that the sacrament sealed salvation, but nevertheless it was a tradition that they retained. William Hilton was not a member of the congregation, but initially was content with the colony's religious practice. Shortly after arriving in Plymouth in November 1621 he had written to his cousin, "Our company are for the most part very religious honest people, the word of God sincerely taught us every Sabbath."[12] But, according to the Reverend William Hubbard, who wrote a history of New England in the 1670s drawing on recollections of some who had been alive in Plymouth at the time, when William Hilton's wife gave birth to a son, John, in 1624, Lyford baptized the infant.[13]

There was clearly a serious rift in the colony. In June 1624, as a ship was prepared for the return voyage to England, Bradford learned that Lyford had been observed writing numerous letters. The governor secretly boarded the ship and, in collusion with the captain, made copies of letters penned by Lyford, Oldham, and one of their supporters. He also found letters written to Brewster and to Winslow that Lyford had intercepted and copied to send to John Pemberton, an antipuritan clergyman.[14] Bradford bided his time, even when Oldham refused to serve on the night watch, pulled a knife on Myles Standish, and called the colonists rebels and traitors. But when Lyford and his supporters held their own service one Sabbath and administered the sacraments by right of his "episcopal calling," the governor called Lyford and Oldham before the colony's General Court.

The accused men denied plotting against the civil and religious order of Plymouth until Bradford produced the copies of their letters. In his letters Lyford made some of the same charges the Adventurers had previously complained of, and in the trial the colony leaders, perhaps Bradford and Brewster, responded. And in one of those letters Lyford wrote to the Adventurers that "the Leiden Company (Mr. Robinson and the rest) must still be kept back, or else all will be spoiled." He further cautioned them to be careful that Captain William Pierce, who was sympathetic to the congregation and the captain who had allowed Bradford to copy Lyford's letters, should not be employed by the Adventurers lest he connive in bringing the pastor over secretly.[15]

The Court sentenced both Lyford and Oldham to exile, but Lyford was given a six-month respite to repent. When he later did so before the church, some were persuaded of his sincerity. Deacon Samuel Fuller was convinced, and he joined others in petitioning for the sentence of banishment to be lifted. But Lyford remained duplicitous and wrote again to the English investors seeking to justify himself. In this case he added to his charges that there was no "ordinary minister for the conversion of those that are without" the church.[16] Commenting on this in his history, Bradford pointed out that all were required to attend to Brewster's preaching and that some had been converted in Plymouth, just as some in Leiden had been converted by Robinson's preaching. He added that Brewster "had labored diligently in dispensing the Word of God" before Lyford came, and that the elder was "not inferior to Mr. Lyford (and some of his betters) either in gifts or learning."[17]

Again, Bradford discovered and copied Lyford's letters while allowing the originals to go to their destination. Edward Winslow, in England on the colony's business, was allowed to represent the colony. The Adventurers chose Thomas Hooker, at the time residing in John Davenport's St. Stephens Coleman Street parish, to assist in mediating the dispute.[18] Winslow discovered and revealed to the Adventurers information that Lyford's own wife had gone to the Plymouth deacons and told them that her husband had fathered a bastard while in a previous ministerial posting in Ireland. Winslow was able to get additional proof of this from Irish witnesses. Lyford's support collapsed. The disgraced clergyman left Plymouth for Nantasket, a settlement up the coast. Oldham and Roger Conant left at the same time and also settled there, while Hilton moved to what is now New Hampshire.[19]

Some elements of the controversy that had been highlighted by Lyford's ministry continued to linger. There was a split in the ranks of the Adventurers with some investors seeking to withdraw from the partnership on the basis that the Leiden congregation had deceived them and the king when they claimed to be in accord with the discipline of the French church, and also for accepting Lyford into their congregation when he denied "all universal, national, and diocesan churches." But the settlers rejected those arguments. Brewster, as the leader of the church and one of the authors of the earlier letter that asserted their agreement with the French church, would have prepared the response. The Plymouth church did "both hold and practice the discipline of the French and other reformed churches."[20] But this did not mean a perfect agreement, since "the French may err, we may err, and other churches may err, and doubtless do in many circumstances." This was in keeping with their openness to further light—"it is too great arrogance for any man or church to think that he or they have so sounded the Word of God to the bottom, as precisely to set down the church's discipline without error in substance or circumstance."[21]

John Robinson died on March 1, 1625, never having rejoined the congregation in America. In the years following the departure of Brewster and the others for America, differences over Robinson's form of moderate separatism had led to a quarrel with the Ancient Church in Amsterdam. That church had refused to admit Sabine Staresmore, who had helped the Leiden congregation in their negotiations with English authorities, because they regarded the London Jacob Church and Robinson's Leiden congregation as guilty of idolatry because they allowed interactions with godly members of the Church of England.[22] This produced tensions in the Leiden church, which may have contributed to the fact that the remaining members of the congregation failed to find someone to assume the pastorate. Some individuals continued to find the means to migrate to New England, and the congregation slowly diminished in size. Some individuals, including Robinson's wife, joined the Dutch Reformed Church, though she eventually journeyed to Plymouth. Those who remained in the original congregation continued on under lay leadership, much as the Plymouth group did, until eventually it merged with the English Reformed Church in Leiden led by Hugh Goodyear in 1644. Relations with the English Reformed Church had always been cooperative, and it is possible that Goodyear provided baptism for members of the Leiden congregation after Robinson's death.[23] Although he could no longer fall back on the hope that Robinson would join those in Plymouth, Brewster continued to reject suggestions that he assume the pastorate. According to Hubbard, this was because of what he considered "the weightiness of the ministerial work."[24] In 1628 Isaac Allerton, one of the members of the congregation who had arrived on the *Mayflower* and subsequently traveled often on trade missions, came to Plymouth with a minister in tow. Bradford, identifying the clergyman simply as Mr. Rogers, said that the church in essence gave him a trial before possibly calling him to the ministry, but that Rogers was found to be "crazed in his brain." They sent him back to England where he grew even more "distracted."[25] Plymouth continued on with preaching led by Brewster and other lay preachers.

Through all this Brewster struggled to maintain peace in the Plymouth church and heal the divisions caused by Lyford. In time some of those who had supported Lyford joined the congregation.[26] William Hubbard, who gathered information from those acquainted with Brewster, described him as "a grave and serious person [who] . . . acquired by his long experience and study no small degree of knowledge in the mysteries of faith and matters of religion."[27] Brewster continued to explore those mysteries, importing numerous theological works and Bible commentaries. His library of books published after 1620 included a number of works by Thomas Taylor, a prominent London puritan; Paul Baynes's *The Diocesan's Trial*; five works of Richard Sibbes; three volumes by his friend John Robinson; and Davenport's defense of congregational principles. He also kept track of the progress of fighting between Protestant and Catholic forces on the continent now known as the Thirty Years' War, soliciting and reading news sheets and books on the conflict.[28] John Cotton Jr., who later served as pastor of the Plymouth Church, noted Brewster's reputation as "a man of considerable parts and learning (being educated at the University of Cambridge) as well as of great piety."[29]

The participatory character of Plymouth's congregational church found a parallel in the civil government of the colony. The Mayflower Compact had bound the colonists to abide by the rules and leaders they had selected. The rebelliousness that had prompted the adoption of the compact recurred during the difficult first months of the settlement but had been quelled by the leadership. During those early months in the colony's history the signers of the Mayflower Compact gathered on a number of occasions to "conclude of laws and orders for ourselves" and also to consolidate the colony's military organization.[30]

When Governor John Carver died in April 1621, the colonists came together and elected William Bradford to replace him.

While there were still occasional meetings to address various crises, the pattern was set for annual meetings of the colonists. Initially this occurred in March and primarily involved the forty-one settlers who had signed the Mayflower Compact. Attendance expanded as the colony grew. The gathering came to be known as the General Court, and those who attended were called freemen (voters). In 1636, the first Tuesday in March was set by law for the election of colony officials and the deliberations of the General Court.[31] Such deliberations were at times contentious. In 1621 Bradford acknowledged to one of the leading English investors that there had been much "discoursing and consulting," largely because their backers had sent out too many "ill conditioned people, who will never do good, but corrupt and abuse others."[32] But the social compact held.

Though the forms of civil government paralleled those of the church, the two spheres were distinctly separate. This was clearly expressed in 1633. The government of Massachusetts, established three years earlier, was faced with the same issue. The Boston church wrote to the church at Plymouth for advice on "whether one person might be a civil magistrate and nominated to be a Ruling Elder at the same time." Plymouth responded that such a combination was not acceptable.[33] This became the policy in both colonies. Unlike Massachusetts, however, Plymouth never required church membership for citizenship.

While there was an institutional separation between church and state in the New England colonies, clergy and other religious leaders often called on each other for advice. From afar, John Robinson offered his views. In Plymouth, Brewster was frequently consulted. The elder had prepared himself by acquiring a variety of books that would help provide guidance for the colony leaders. His library, in addition to the many religious books, included works on surveying, medicine, government, and law. It is believed that he provided the colony leaders with a copy of the 1592 edition of William Lambard's *Eirenarcha*, which defined the functions of the justice of the peace.[34]

William Brewster and the congregation's pastor as of 1629, Ralph Smith, lent their expertise to the committee that in 1636 reaffirmed the Mayflower Compact and codified the colony's laws. That code identified far fewer capital offenses than English laws. The same awareness of human frailty and the possibility of errors in judgment that made the Pilgrims open to discussion of spiritual issues made them ambivalent about capital punishment. John Robinson had urged forbearance in this regard, believing in the importance of blending justice with mercy. He asserted that "The law which sayeth *Thou shalt not murder* forbids especially violence in judgment." "Punishments," he argued, "must be administered with sorrow, and commiseration, [just] as rewards with joy and gladness." Those clearly guilty must be punished, "but we are to pity them in their misery also."[35] In Peter Martyr's *Commonplaces*, read by both Brewster and Bradford, that Protestant theologian expressed reservations about executing criminals. Referring to St. Augustine, Martyr wrote, "We (saith he) do imitate God, when we would not have the guilty to be destroyed but to be kept unto repentance." Dictated in part by their theology, leniency may have been influenced by their stay in Leiden. While numerous capital crimes were committed during their time there, only ten executions were carried out between May 1614 and May 1619.[36]

There were a few notable cases in which the death penalty was imposed in the early decades of the colony's history. John Billington, who as a young man had been lost in the woods and redeemed from the Nauset, who found him, in the summer of 1630 "waylaid a young man, one John Newcomen," with whom he had previously quarreled, and shot him fatally. In addition to following the colony's own due process, Bradford consulted the recently arrived Massachusetts governor John Winthrop "and other ablest gentlemen" in that colony about the propriety of the death penalty in this case. Reassured, with "great sadness" the Plymouth authorities executed Billington in September.[37]

In 1638, when Thomas Prence was governor, three men—Arthur Peach, Thomas Jackson, and Richard Stinnings—were tried and executed for murdering a Native, while a fourth Englishman, Daniel Cross, escaped. Peach was a veteran of the 1636 war waged against the Pequot tribe.[38] Following the war he found himself "out of means and loath to work." He decided to move to the Dutch settlement on the Hudson River and persuaded the other three men to escape from their indentures and join him. What he did not tell them was that his decision to leave Plymouth was also influenced by wanting to escape possible punishment for having impregnated a female servant.[39]

On their way out of the colony the four encountered a Native named Penowanyanquis (as his name was given in the records of the subsequent trial), who was returning from a trading trip to Boston. The Native was carrying his profits and the Englishmen invited him to join them in smoking tobacco. Peach then proposed killing and robbing Penowanyanquis, arguing that he had likely killed many Englishmen. Peach then "took a rapier and ran him through the body once or twice," stole his wampum and other possessions, and left him for dead. Penowanyanquis survived long enough to return to his people, where he soon died. Roger Williams, then living in Providence, was summoned to offer medical assistance and to hear Penowanyanquis's story before he died. Williams believed him.

Members of the Narragansett tribe captured Peach, Jackson, and Stinnings. Because the crime had occurred within Plymouth's jurisdiction, all three were delivered for trial in that colony. Despite complaints by some that "any English should be put to death for the Indians," the three were put on trial, convicted, and executed on September 4. According to Bradford, "some of the Narragansett Indians and of the party's [Penowanyanquis's] friends were present when it was done, which gave them and all the country good satisfaction." There appears to have been no consideration given to allowing the guilty parties to be judged according to Native justice, but the colonists did demonstrate that a Native life was deemed as valuable as that of the English.[40]

William Brewster and his fellow believers had come to the New World to find the freedom to follow God's will in their religious practice, something that had not been possible in England or the Netherlands. They did not desire to establish a society in which all beliefs would be tolerated, and this was made clear when they stopped John Lyford's efforts to establish religious practices which they had condemned. But they did recognize that exposure to different ideas might lead them to a better understanding of the truths expounded in scriptures. This made them open to discussing various views in household and congregational prophesyings, though there would be limits to what they would consider, as would become evident.

9

Plymouth and the Bay

In the decade after the settlement of Plymouth, other Englishmen visited the region to fish, to trade, and in some cases to create outposts from which to further such activities. Some of them had an impact, directly or indirectly, on the religious history of New England. After the expedition led by Myles Standish eliminated the immediate physical threat to the remaining Englishmen of Thomas Weston's Wessagusset settlement, most of those settlers departed. Shortly thereafter, a new settlement was established nearby, in the present area of Quincy, Massachusetts, by a Captain Richard Wollaston. Wollaston and most of those whom he had brought abandoned the settlement in 1626, but some remained, including Thomas Morton, who became the leader of the outpost. Prior to coming to America, Morton had been a member of Clifford's Inn, one of the Inns of Chancery, a London institution that trained men for the law. It is unclear why he joined the Wollaston expedition, though some have speculated that he may have been seeking to flee a series of lawsuits filed against him by his new son-in-law.[1]

Morton was successful in trading with the Natives, and he would claim that it was his success that prompted the Plymouth authorities to take steps against him. Bradford complained that Morton traded guns and liquor to the Natives, which jeopardized all the colonists in the region.[2] In his own account of his stay in New England—*New England Canaan*, published in 1637—Morton described aspects of his settlement that were sure to have been offensive to the Plymouth puritans. He renamed the settlement Ma-re-Mount and "resolved to have . . . revels, & merriment after the old English custom." Morton and his followers "set up a maypole . . . & brewed a barrel of excellent beer, and provided a case of bottles to be spent, with other good cheer for all comers of that day."[3] He wrote and fixed to the maypole a poem in which he portrayed the land as a fertile woman whose virile husband, the Indians, had fulfilled her needs until he perished. The Plymouth puritans were not skilled enough to satisfy her and make her agriculturally fertile, while Morton and his supporters claimed they could be a productive husband to the land. On the day of the revels, his followers danced round the maypole singing a song that began "Drink and be merry, merry, merry, boys / Let all your delights be in hymen's joys," and ended, "Lasses in beaver coats come away / Yee shall be welcome to us night and day."[4] Bradford wrote of how "Morton became Lord of Misrule, and maintained a school (as it were), of Atheism." As for the Maypole celebrations, Morton's followers engaged in "drinking and dancing about it many days together, inviting the Indian women for their consorts, dancing and frisking together like so many fairies, or furies rather; and worse practices."[5]

Morton openly confessed to be "a man that endeavored to advance the dignity of the Church of England," which the Plymouth congregation rejected. Those puritans, he wrote, "inveighed against the Book of Common Prayer," while he "used it in a laudable manner amongst his family [the settlement's servants], as a practice of piety."[6] Plymouth wasn't alone in seeing Morton's activities as dangerous, and in 1628 a number of small New England settlements contributed to a fund to enable Plymouth to take action.[7] Myles Standish—"Captain Shrimp" in Morton's account—led a force that captured Morton, whom the Plymouth authorities sent to England. Some of his followers, and the maypole, remained.

Among the settlements that contributed to the expedition against Ma-re-Mount were some that had been established by dissidents who had left Plymouth in the aftermath of the Lyford affair. After departing Plymouth in 1624, John Oldham settled initially at Nantasket (now Hull) on the Massachusetts coast. The following year John Lyford himself joined Oldham. Some of Lyford's other supporters, including Roger Conant, joined him there. Conant and his broader family were well connected in English puritan circles. He was resident in the London parish of St. Lawrence Jewry in 1619, when the noted puritan John Davenport was curate. Conant had arrived in Plymouth on the same ship as Lyford in 1624 and likely had befriended the clergyman on the voyage. In England, Conant had been a member of the Salters Company, and the Adventurers had sent him to the colony to show the

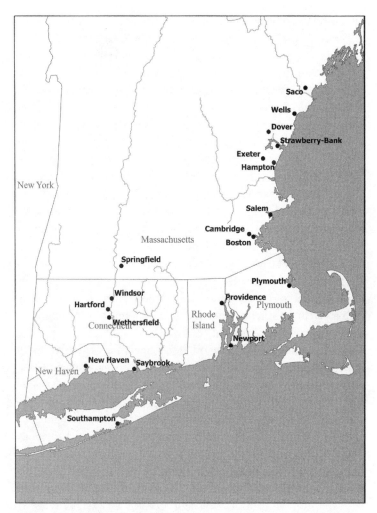

Fig. 9.1 New England, 1620–1650. Map created by Matthew Spak for the Geography Department's Geo-Graphics Laboratory at Millersville University, Millersville, PA, USA.

settlers how to process salt. Bradford judged him "an ignorant, foolish, selfwilled fellow," a judgment no doubt shaped by the support Conant had given to Lyford, because Conant was a puritan but not a separatist.[8]

Another settlement was Nantasket, a place where the Plymouth colonists had engaged in trade with the Natives around the Massachusetts Bay. It remained small because it offered little as a permanent settlement.[9] Meanwhile, in 1623 a group of investors in the West Country of England, led by the puritan clergyman John White, had formed the Dorchester Company, which was organized to develop the fishing industry along the New England coast with the goal of subsidizing social reform projects in Dorchester, England.[10] John Conant, a clerical friend of White's, proposed that his brother Roger be appointed to lead a settlement at Cape Anne, and Roger Conant accepted that charge in 1625.[11] Lyford accompanied him and ministered to the settlement.[12] Conant moved the settlement along the coast to the future site of Salem. The Dorchester Company folded, but White urged Conant to remain with his own followers and promised to secure a patent for the new settlement. Lyford, meanwhile, accepted a call to Virginia, where he would die in 1629.[13]

In the summer of 1628 yet another settlement was begun when John Endecott entered Salem harbor on the *Abigail*. The fifty or so colonists who sailed with him were the advance guard of the Great Migration, a movement of thousands of English puritans and those sympathetic to puritanism to New England over the next decade and a half. Some of the adventurers of the failed Dorchester Company had joined forces with investors from London and East Anglia to form the New England Company, which was chartered by King Charles I in 1628. It was this group that had dispatched Endecott to the region. Meanwhile, the Company reorganized itself and received a new charter as the Massachusetts Bay Company, with Endecott remaining in charge until the new governor, John Winthrop, arrived in 1630.

The new arrivals soon began to sicken, presumably suffering from scurvy like those who had sailed on the *Mayflower*. Endecott wrote to Governor Bradford in Plymouth asking for assistance, and the Plymouth governor dispatched Samuel Fuller, a deacon of the congregation who was also the colony's physician.[14] There is no evidence of how successful Fuller was in treating the bodies of the new arrivals, but he clearly played an important role in shaping the religious practices of the Endecott group. William Hubbard, who had access to materials that are no longer available, indicated that in the letter he sent on May 11, Endecott had identified Fuller as "well versed in the way of church discipline practiced by Mr. Robinson's church."[15]

Fuller was not only a deacon of the Plymouth congregation but also one of the members who had preached by way of prophesying. While in Salem he engaged in numerous discussions of religious matters with the community's leaders. The ships that had brought the new colonists to Salem had also carried some members of the Leiden congregation who were at long last going to reunite with their brethren in Plymouth.[16] Discussions between the passengers while crossing the Atlantic would have provided those who settled in Salem with some understanding of the Leiden-Plymouth congregation and, perhaps, of Samuel Fuller. Lacking a clergyman, the Salem puritans planned their religious future in conferences similar to prophesying sessions.

Endecott acknowledged such conversations with Fuller in a letter he sent Bradford in May 1629 that demonstrates the clear religious influence of Plymouth on the early settlement of the Bay. In it Endecott noted that he had found that he and the Plymouth faithful were "servants of one master and of the same household." "God's people," he explained, "are all marked with one and the same mark, and sealed with one and the same seal, and have for the main one and the same heart, guided by one and the same spirit of truth, and where this is there can be no discord, nay, here must be sweet harmony."[17]

It was to be expected that the puritans of the Bay and those of Plymouth would have been largely in agreement on matters of faith, but on issues of church practice puritans who had separated from the Church of England differed from those who remained in its parishes. But Endecott found that based on his conversations with Fuller he was "satisfied touching your judgments of the outward form of God's worship." Indeed, he had been convinced that "as far as I can yet gather, no other [such form] . . . is warranted by the evidence of truth." And so he expressed the hope that "we may, as Christian brethren, be united by a heavenly and unfeigned love, bending all our hearts and forces in furthering a work beyond our strength with reverence and fear, fastening our eyes always on him that only is able to direct and prosper all our ways."[18]

Fuller's visit to Salem was not the only contact between settlers of the two colonies at this time. In addition to the correspondence between Endecott and Bradford, there is also evidence of a visit by some of the Salem settlers to Plymouth, perhaps to learn more about the church there. Charles Gott, one of the passengers on the *Abigail*, became an early leader of the Salem church. In a 1629 letter to Bradford describing the formation of that church, he thanked the Plymouth governor for hospitality extended to him and his wife on a visit to Plymouth and asked that his best wishes be given to Brewster, Fuller, and other members of the Plymouth church. Gott and any other Salem visitors would have had the opportunity to personally witness the congregational practices employed at Plymouth, attend church services there, and perhaps, like John Winthrop and others in future years, been invited to share their views in a session of prophesying.[19]

There was no clergyman at Salem when the *Abigail* arrived, as Lyford had already departed. The puritan arrivals were reduced to the practice of joining together in conference style to read and discuss scripture, pray, and sing psalms. By the summer of 1629 some of these individuals were ready to organize themselves into a church, and the advice from Plymouth would have given them an understanding of how this could be done. They had, according to William Hubbard, "sufficient experience and acquaintance one with another" from their voyage together that they believed they could discern the godly among them, and so "they resolved to enter into a church fellowship together." They "consulted with one another about settling a reformed congregation according to the rules of the gospel, as they apprehended, and the pattern of the best reformed churches." Hubbard acknowledged that the first covenant and the manner in which they embraced it was known, although the Salem church of the 1670s was not wholly willing to "own that they had received their platform of church order from those of New Plymouth." Hubbard himself conflated the earliest actions of the godly in Salem with those that occurred later in that summer, following the arrival of clergymen from England, but the letters of Gott and Endecott make it clear that the congregation was formed prior to their arrival.[20]

In the spring of 1629 the Massachusetts Bay Company sent three approved ministers, Francis Higginson, Samuel Skelton, and Francis Bright, as well as another, Ralph Smith, whom the Company had not financed but allowed to journey to Massachusetts under certain conditions. Those approved had been vetted by John White and John Davenport, both of whom at the time held clerical livings in the Church of England. The clergyman not officially sent by the Company was Ralph Smith. His life in England is unknown, but from Company records it is clear he was a separatist who had run afoul of the church authorities. At the time the leaders of the Company strongly supported a nonseparatist stance. The officers noted "his [Smith's] difference of judgment in some things from our ministers." Smith had already arranged for passage before his views had become known to the Company. Despite the fact that they had "a very good opinion of his honesty," they feared the disruption that might develop from his "different judgments." Thus, they stipulated to Endecott that "unless he will be conformable to our government, you suffer him not to remain within the limits of our jurisdiction."[21] Smith arrived on the *Talbot*. Francis Higginson, who sailed on the same ship, recorded in his journal of the voyage at least one occasion when he and Smith joined in consecrating a "day as a solemn fasting and humiliation to Almighty God as a furtherance to our present work."[22] One can easily assume that they also discussed issues of faith and practice during the voyage. Arriving in Salem, Smith removed himself from what he anticipated would be a nonseparatist community and settled for the time at Nantasket.

Higginson and Samuel Skelton had shown no separatist inclinations in England, but on arrival in Salem they found a congregation that had already been formed along congregational principles that were generally viewed as separatist. The third of the ministers sent by the Company, Francis Bright, had served as a curate in Davenport's parish of St. Stephens Coleman Street, London.[23] When he discovered that the Salem church was organized in keeping with what he would have viewed as a separatist posture, he moved from Salem to the town of Charlestown. The following year he returned to England, where he evidently remained in good standing with the Church of England.[24]

The standard historical account of the formation of the Salem church identifies Higginson and Skelton as the driving forces, but a close reading of Charles Gott's letter to Governor Bradford makes it clear that the congregation had been formed before the arrival of the clergymen.[25] According to Hubbard, those intending to join "accepted of one another, according to some general profession of the gospel, and the honest and good intentions they had one towards another, and so by some kind of covenant soon molded themselves into a church."[26]

Gott reported that John Endecott had appointed July 20 as "a solemn day of humiliation for the choice of a pastor and teacher." Before such an election was held there had to be members to vote, which means that a congregation had already been formed. On that day, after the congregation had spent the morning in prayer, they questioned Skelton and Higginson about their calling. The two men expressed their understanding that the first calling a minister received was when "the Lord moved the heart of a man . . . and fitted him with gifts for the same," while a second calling was when chosen by "a company of believers . . . joined together in covenant to walk together in all the ways of God, every member (being men) are to have a free voice in the choice of their officers." After they heard from Skelton and Higginson each male member of the congregation "wrote, in a note," whom they wished to hold office. Skelton was chosen as pastor and Higginson as teacher, and three or four leading members of the congregation ordained the two by laying their hands on the heads of the ministers and praying that they be guided by God. The congregation then settled on August 6 for another day of fasting and prayer to be followed by election and ordination of the remaining church officers, completing the foundation of the church.[27]

While this was happening, a trading vessel from Plymouth had stopped at Nantasket, where Ralph Smith requested that they transport him to Plymouth, since he was "weary of being in that uncouth place and in a poor house that would neither keep him nor his goods dry." If some of the settlers at Nantasket were remnants of the Lyford supporters who had settled there in 1624, they would not have appreciated his separatist leanings. After arriving in Plymouth he "exercised his gifts" as a lay preacher and performed in such a way that he was chosen pastor of the congregation by the end of 1629.[28]

With a pastor finally in place, the congregation could at last enjoy the sacraments. Brewster, however, remained a key figure.

Smith was born in the parish of Gorton in Denton, Lancashire, not far from Manchester.[29] A letter he would write to Hugh Goodyear, the pastor of the English Reformed Church in Leiden who befriended the Plymouth puritans there, suggests that Smith and Goodyear knew one another from their Manchester youth.[30] They both went to Cambridge University, from which Smith graduated in 1613. In a later letter written to Goodyear from New England, Smith indicated that he had experienced "many sorrows in Europe." Much of his time before moving to America would have been "in a persecuted condition" involving (counting his time in America) "18 removals in 6 years."[31]

Smith's reputation has suffered because of William Hubbard, who, drawing on the memories of those who knew them both, asserted in his history of New England that Smith was chosen because of his separatist principles as opposed to "any fitness for the office he undertook." He was "much overmatched by him that he was joined with in the presbytery [William Brewster], both in point of discretion to rule, and aptness to teach."[32] But this is likely unduly critical. In contrast to Hubbard's characterization is that of Samuel Gorton, who knew Smith from their youth in Gorton, Lancashire, and stayed with the Smiths when he first arrived in Plymouth. Though he later quarreled with the Plymouth pastor, Gorton described Smith as "a godly man" and "as pure and precise in your [puritan] religion as any of you."[33]

In preparation for the official formation of the Salem church, that congregation extended an invitation to the Plymouth church to send representatives to the event. Bradford and others, likely Brewster and Fuller, and possibly Smith, set sail for Salem. "Hindered by cross winds, . . . they could not be there at the beginning of the day, but they came into the Assembly afterward, and gave them the right hand of fellowship, wishing all prosperity and a blessed success unto such good beginnings."[34]

Not all of Salem's residents approved of the formation of that church. It may have gone too far in the separatist direction for Roger Conant and those who had joined him in his support of Lyford, though Conant made no known public objections and did join the church. But the brothers John and Samuel Browne took exception to the new religious practices. John Browne was an important member of the Salem community, a stockholder in the New England Company, and a member of Endecott's council. He and his brother, a lawyer, complained that Skelton and Higginson administered the Lord's Supper and baptism without using the prescribed ceremonies; that good men and women were denied membership; and that the clergy were separatists and Anabaptists. They began to hold alternative services featuring readings from the *Book of Common Prayer*. Endecott viewed their actions as a threat to the settlement's order and shipped them back to England, where they promptly complained to the Company's leaders. The Company appointed a committee to evaluate their complaints, but rejected the Brownes' arguments, though reimbursing them for what they had invested in the Company.[35]

Cooperation between Plymouth and Salem continued. "Letters did pass between Mr. Higginson and Mr. Brewster, the reverend Elder of the Church of Plymouth" on the subject of infant baptism. The two agreed that infants should be baptized but that upon reaching adulthood "they being not scandalous, they were to be examined by the church officers, and upon their approbation of their fitness, and upon the children's public and personal owning of the covenant, they were to be received unto the Lord's Supper."[36]

In April 1630 John Winthrop arrived in Massachusetts on the *Arbella*, one of a fleet of vessels carrying many more people to the colony, which would rapidly expand over the next decade. Samuel Fuller was soon back in the Bay and offering advice to those who had come over with Winthrop. Plymouth's influence on the new arrivals was soon felt. Fuller wrote to Bradford that he had been having many conferences with the new arrivals. John Endecott remained his "dear friend, and a friend to all of us." He referred to Endecott as a "second Burrow," referring to the separatist martyr Henry Barrow.[37] Fuller found Winthrop, who had taken over from Endecott as governor of Massachusetts, "a godly, wise, and humble gentleman, and very discreet, and of a fine and good temper." He discovered that Plymouth Congregationalism had "some privy enemies in the Bay" but more friends. Winthrop, he wrote, had "had conference with me, both in private and before sundry others; opposers there is not wanting, and satan is busy, but if the Lord be on our side who can be against us?"

Interestingly, one of the new arrivals, William Coddington of Boston, Lincolnshire, told Fuller that it was "Mr. [John] Cotton's charge," when he preached a departure sermon for the Winthrop fleet at Southhampton, "that they should take advice of them at Plymouth and should do nothing to offend them."[38]

Fuller was still in Massachusetts in late July, visiting the Salem church along with Plymouth's Edward Winslow and Isaac Allerton, when they heard from Winthrop that the settlers at Charlestown were suffering illness and dying. The governor asked advice and indicated that "they would do nothing without our advice."[39] The Plymouth men recommended that the three new towns (Charlestown, Watertown, and Dorchester) hold a day of fasingt and humiliation on July 30 to ask for God's assistance and that at the conclusion of the exercise, "such godly persons that are amongst them and known to each other . . . make known their godly desire and practice the same, viz., solemnly to enter into covenant with the Lord to walk in his ways." Notably, the advice was to form the three churches but to avoid "intending rashly to proceed to the choice of officers," thus emphasizing the practice of believers forming a congregation prior to seeking ministers. Reporting this to Bradford, Brewster, and Smith, Fuller and Winslow requested that the Plymouth church offer their prayers for their friends in the Bay on the same day. The letter further elaborated how those churches would be formed, each proceeding in accordance with the congregational principles that had shaped the Scrooby-Leiden congregation and the recently formed Salem church.[40]

Further insight into Fuller's role (and thus that of Plymouth) in shaping the Bay churches is found in another letter he sent to Bradford. In it he described being at Mattapan (later Dorchester) "at the request of Mr. [John] Warham" and "had conference with them till I was weary." Warham believed that "the visible church" could consist of ungodly as well as godly people, upon which subject they conferred at length, Fuller concluding with the hope that "the Lord will give a blessing." He also conferred with another recently arrived clergyman, George Phillips, who accepted the idea that a clergyman had to be called and ordained by an individual congregation, and who confided to Fuller that if the Watertown church wished him to "stand minister by that calling which he received from the prelates in England, he will leave them."[41] There can be little doubt that Congregationalism in Massachusetts derived from the influence of Plymouth.

A week later Fuller wrote once again to Bradford, recounting the formation of the Charlestown church, which would shortly move to Boston, and the continuing ravages of disease. He soon ran out of drugs and could no longer help as a physician. Preparing to return to Plymouth, he indicated that Endecott and Isaac Johnson intended to accompany him. Winthrop wanted to come but was too busy and said he couldn't even spare two hours away from his duties. Other "honest Christians . . . are desirous to see us [Plymouth]; some out of love, which they bear to us, and the good persuasion they have of us; others to see whether we be so evil as they have heard of us."[42]

Puritans rejected the notion that a superior authority could create local parishes of a national church, which left few options for organizing themselves into churches.[43] They knew of the experiences of English reformed Christians who had sought refuge abroad during the reign of Mary Tudor, and the establishment of congregations in the Netherlands in the late sixteenth and early seventeenth centuries. They were familiar with the writings of fellow puritans who had advanced ideas on church governance. But there is little doubt that Plymouth, and particularly Samuel Fuller, played a key role in providing the puritans of the Massachusetts Bay colony with a model for forming their churches. As Plymouth's Edward Winslow later wrote of the Bay leaders, "some of the chief of them advised with us . . . how they should do to fall upon a right platform of worship."[44]

Committed as they were to searching for better understanding God's will in matters of practice as well as faith, many Massachusetts settlers had engaged in discussion of such matters with fellow laymen and with clergymen in conferences in England. They were not likely to blindly endorse the Plymouth model, and there is evidence that some of the new congregations modified that pattern while adopting the broad design. While the Plymouth church rejected the validity of Church of England ordination, the Charlestown/Boston congregation, after considerable debate, did not require John Wilson to denounce his English ordination. When the congregation chose him for office they agreed that this was "a sign of election and confirmation, not of any intent that Mr. Wilson should renounce his ministry he received in England."[45]

Prophesying, which was critical to sustaining the faith of the Plymouth colonists, also proved valuable in Massachusetts. In March 1631, when John Wilson left Boston to journey to England to bring his wife to the new colony, he spoke to the church and "commended to them the exercise of prophesy in his absence." He suggested John Winthrop, Thomas Dudley, and Isaac Nowell as individuals to provide such preaching.[46] Winthrop had been accustomed to this; his "Christian Charity" sermon was one of the most famous examples of lay preaching. Over the next few years Winthrop and other laymen would also preach to new communities without a clergyman. Prophesying in the Boston church continued after Wilson returned and John Cotton joined the congregation's ministry. William Hubbard wrote that the "eminent gifts [that] did abound in private brethren of that church . . . forwarded the edification and salvation of others."[47] In 1672, looking back on how things had changed in New England in his lifetime, William Coddington wrote to remind William Hathorne how when they sailed together for America in the 1630s Hathorne had given "testimony against persecution, and stinting or limiting the spirit of prophecy in any."[48]

John Cotton may have urged the emigrants to follow the lead of Plymouth, but he was shocked by what this meant. Still in England, he wrote to his friend Samuel Skelton in October 1630, rebuking the Salem pastor for having denied the Lord's Supper to Winthrop, Coddington, Johnson, Thomas Dudley, and others because they were not members of the congregation nor of any other recognized reformed church, a point underlined when the sacrament was administered to a member of the London church formed by Henry Jacob and recognized by the Leiden congregation. Additionally, baptism had been denied to Coddington's child. Cotton would later adopt those same practices, but he clearly objected to the Salem church having followed Plymouth in this regard.[49]

Meanwhile, the leaders of the Bay continued to seek guidance from the Plymouth church. On the occasion of the visit of John Winthrop and John Wilson to Plymouth in October 1632, two matters were discussed. In the prophesying session, Roger Williams propounded, and Ralph Smith supported, the scriptural "unlawfulness of calling any unregenerate man by the name of 'goodman such an one.'" Evidently this was dividing the congregation, and the "wiser people" in the Plymouth church, which would have included Brewster and Bradford, "took the opportunity of Governor Winthrop's being there to have the thing publicly propounded in the congregation." Offered the opportunity to share his view in the prophesying, Winthrop "distinguished between a theological and a moral goodness." He pointed out that "when juries were first used in England it was used for the crier" to address those called to serve as "good men and true," by which "it grew to be a civil custom . . . for neighbors living by one another to call one another 'good man such an one,' and it was a pity now to make a stir about a civil custom so innocently introduced."[50]

Brewster and Bradford both spoke in support of Winthrop's position, as did John Wilson. Two or three others also shared their insights. In the end, Winthrop's view was accepted by the congregation and the issue was settled. The incident is evidence of the puritan openness to different views in the search for further light. It points to how Williams was already advancing some views that were troubling to Brewster and would soon lead to the young radical's departure from Plymouth. But it also suggests that Ralph Smith may have been open to some of Williams's extreme separatist views.

The issue that had originally brought the Boston leaders to Plymouth concerned the puritan desire to maintain an institutional separation between church and state. Though civil magistrates in both colonies turned to church leaders for advice, those who held church office never held civil office. William Brewster was a prime example of this. But in Massachusetts, Increase Nowell, who was one of the colony's magistrates, had recently been selected as an elder of the Boston church. That congregation wrote a letter to the other churches in the region, including Plymouth, asking "whether one person might be a civil magistrate and a ruling elder at the same time?"[51]

John Winthrop indicated that the response from the churches was unanimous that this should not be allowed, but the visit to Plymouth allowed for further discussion. William Hubbard wrote that it was this "conference with the chief of Plymouth (in whose opinion those in Boston did much adhere in their church matters, as those at Salem had done before) that he [Nowell] could not conveniently or regularly hold the place of a rule in the church and Commonwealth at one and the same time."[52] Following the return of the Bostonians to the Bay, Roger Williams heard of the outcome of their discussions and wrote to Winthrop that it was "music to our ears when we heard [you] persuaded . . . our beloved Mr. Nowell to surrender up one sword."[53]

In 1646 Bradford injected an observation about English events into his narrative. At that time the congregational system that many referred to as the "New England Way" was being advocated by some of the English puritans in rebellion against King Charles I.[54] Referring to the influence Plymouth had on the Bay colony, and thus the shaping of the New England Way, Bradford claimed that "out of small beginnings greater things have been produced by His hand that made all things of nothing, and gives being to all things that are; and, as one small candle may light a thousand, so the light here kindled hath shone onto many, yea in some sort to our whole nation; let the glorious name of Jehovah have all the praise."[55] In discussing the reasons for having decided to settle in America, Bradford had written that those committing themselves to the enterprise had hoped that "they should be but even as stepping-stones unto others for the performing of so great a work."[56] He drew an analogy to the history of Rome, drawing on the writings of Pliny the Elder that recounted how a small settlement on the Tiber rose to greatness.[57] In 1646 that hope seemed to have been realized. While some in England and New England would dispute the value of Congregationalism, no one at the time seriously disputed the role of Plymouth in shaping that system.

10

Congregationalism Advanced

While the Plymouth church helped shape the religious practices of the Bay colony, neither the Massachusetts churches nor those formed in the towns of an expanding Plymouth colony slavishly followed Plymouth's advice. There was unity but not uniformity. That became evident following the arrival in Boston of Roger Williams on the ship *Lyon* in January 1631. John Winthrop referred to Williams as "a godly minister," and the Boston church unanimously invited him to join John Wilson in the ministry, as teacher of the congregation.[1] But he "conscientiously refused and withdrew to Plymouth because," he explained, "I durst not officiate to an unseparated people, as upon examination and conscience I found them to be."[2]

In his *Journal*, Winthrop explained that the reasons for Williams's departure from Boston were that the clergyman insisted that the Boston congregation "make a public declaration of their repentance for having communion with the Churches of England while they lived there." He also related that Williams had expressed views denying civil magistrates the authority to enforce breaches of the first table of the Ten Commandments, including violations of the Sabbath.[3] Williams found evidence of the imperfect separation of the Boston church in the fact that they had continued "communicating with the parishes in Old [England] by their members repairing on frequent occasions" with them on trips to England.[4]

After leaving Boston, Williams first went to Salem, where the church chose him as their teacher to replace the late Francis Higginson. The Bay colony's General Court wrote to John Endecott, chastising the Salem congregation for proceeding without the advice of the colony magistrates and asking that Williams's ordination be deferred. This played into the hands of Roger Conant and the faction of Salem "Old Planters" who were dissatisfied with the extent of the community's separatist impulses. Salem evidently bowed to these pressures, and Williams moved on to Plymouth.[5]

Late in 1631 Williams arrived in Plymouth. Bradford, writing years later, called him "a man godly and zealous, having many precious parts but very unsettled in judgment." Initially the young man's questionable views were not evident. The congregation welcomed him, and he "exercised his gifts amongst them and after some time was admitted [as] a member of the church." Williams later wrote that when in Plymouth he preached as a lay member of the congregation "on the Lord's Day and week days," and supported his family by working hard in the fields.[6] His teaching was "well approved," and Bradford personally benefited from his conversation and blessed God and was "thankful to him even for his sharpest admonitions and reproofs so far as they agreed with truth."[7] Williams was there in October 1632, when John Winthrop and others visited Plymouth, were entertained by Bradford and Brewster, and participated in a prophesying session where Williams posed the question for discussion.[8]

It was in 1633 that Williams "began to fall into some strange opinions," according to Bradford, "and from opinion into practice, which caused some controversy between the church and him." Williams requested and received his dismissal from the congregation as required in congregational practice, though "with some caution to them concerning him, and what care they ought to have of him."[9] Bradford felt that he did "not need to name particulars" concerning the dispute that led to Williams leaving the colony.[10] Nathaniel Morton, Bradford's nephew, provided more detail, indicating that some of the members of the congregation supported Williams, but that it was "through the prudent counsel of Mr. Brewster" that he was eventually dismissed, as were some of his followers. Brewster feared that his views would cause divisions in the church, in particular that "he would run the same course of rigid separatism and Anabaptistry which Mr. John Smyth, the Sebaptist at Amsterdam had done."[11] Williams had evidently succumbed to the danger that John Smyth had warned about (and then fallen prey to) regarding the risk of slipping on the ice in his use of liberty. He agreed with Smyth that there was no church with a true descent from the church of the original apostles, and he accepted the need for adult believer baptism. Despite sharing the concerns expressed by Brewster, Bradford believed that Williams was to be "pitied and prayed for" and offered the "desire the Lord . . . show him his errors, and reduce him into the way of truth, and give him a settled judgement and constancy in the same." Bradford hoped that Williams "belonged to the Lord, and that he will show him mercy."[12]

Returning to Salem, Williams initially assumed an unofficial position in that church, preaching by way of prophesying. Over the next few years his views divided that congregation. The Conant faction was critical of his views, while John Endecott was among his strongest supporters. Among his controversial positions, some of which he had shared with Bradford and Brewster, included the belief that Christian kings (including Charles I) had no right to grant Native lands to their subjects, that women must wear veils in church, that the civil magistrate could not engage in enforcement of the first four commandments nor require citizens to swear any oaths, that even informal meetings of clergy violated congregational autonomy, and that the red cross on the English ensign that was used by local trained bands (militia) was a papist emblem—the last of these prompting Endecott to cut the cross from the ensign used by the Salem trained band.[13] Perhaps his most extreme position was that it "was not lawful for a regenerate man to pray with his carnal family."[14] Efforts to get Williams to retract some of his views had limited success, but tolerating any of them was made impossible when Samuel Skelton died in August 1634 and the congregation sought to choose Williams as their new pastor. During the ensuing controversy Williams argued that the Salem church should cut itself off from the rest of the churches in the Bay. This was a step too far, and in October 1635 the Massachusetts General Court ordered that Williams be shipped back to England. John Winthrop, not governor at the time but a member of the court, warned Williams, who set off into the winter wilderness.[15]

A difficult journey through the snow brought him to Wampanoag territory, where the Massasoit Ousamequin allowed him to settle close to Narragansett Bay. When the Massachusetts authorities complained to Plymouth about their allowing Williams to settle in their jurisdiction, Governor Edward Winslow suggested that Williams cross to the nearby Narragansett territory, assuring him the Plymouth colonists would be his friends if he did.[16]

A few years after Williams left Plymouth, Samuel Gorton arrived. Gorton and Ralph Smith came from the same town in England and evidently knew one another. Gorton had moved to London, and it was there that he first began to explore radical ideas that were circulating on the fringes of the puritan underground, views that were beyond the pale for most of those who emigrated to New England.[17] Upon arriving in America, Gorton first settled in Boston at a time when Massachusetts was torn by a controversy that centered on the First Church in Boston.

Anne Hutchinson, wife of one of the town's foremost merchants, had continued a practice she had begun in England of gathering fellow believers in her home to discuss sermons and scripture. This was a form of conventicle that was familiar to many English puritans. Her skill in analyzing difficult passages of scripture drew many members of the Boston church, including then governor Henry Vane. Claiming the inspiration of the Spirit, she was soon developing a take on John Cotton's views on the nature of salvation that challenged the teachings of many of the colony's clergy. Visitors from surrounding churches who attended her meetings brought her perspective back to their own communities. Prophesying sessions allowed believers in Boston and other churches the opportunity to challenge the teachings of their clergy, prompting bitter divisions over how saving grace was received by God's chosen. This "Free Grace controversy" threatened both the civil and religious stability of the colony. The threat to the civil order led to a trial, with the General Court banishing Hutchinson and some of her leading supporters. During that trial Hutchinson claimed support for her views from the immediate revelation of the Spirit. A synod held in 1637 defined doctrinal errors believed to be circulating, which was followed by a church trial resulting in Hutchinson's banishment.[18]

Like Anne Hutchinson, Samuel Gorton believed in immediate revelation, but he evidently went beyond her in rejecting the value of education and a trained ministry, though it was not until some years later that his more extreme views became evident.[19] Gorton also believed in the equality of all men, denying that any individual owed deference to another—not ruled to ruler, servant to master, or wife to husband. He also rejected predestination and infant baptism.[20]

Observing the proceedings against Hutchinson, John Wheelwright, and others who were associated with her, Gorton undoubtedly realized his own ideas would be controversial. He may have discussed his decision to move to Plymouth with Ralph Smith. The Plymouth pastor was in Boston consulting with the Bay clergy, having been invited to represent Plymouth in the 1637 synod that was meeting to condemn the errors circulating in the colony.[21] Smith was likely one of the few representatives who eventually rejected the findings of that synod.[22] At the time he was also in the process of giving up his position as pastor in Plymouth, though he and his wife would remain there for some years. Faced with financial problems, Smith was happy to rent half of his house to Gorton. When Gorton first arrived in Plymouth, he "gave some hopes that he would have proved an useful instrument."[23] He allowed his neighbors to join his family at their morning and evening religious exercises. Such conferences were accepted by most puritans, and even viewed as important means of furthering one's faith, but at this time in New England some may have drawn worrisome comparisons with those that had recently been held by Anne Hutchinson in her home. According to Gorton's later statement, Smith's wife, members of the Smith household, a maid in the household of the new minister (John Reyner), and others frequently attended. "Mistress Smith," he wrote, expressed herself "how glad she was that she could come into a family where her spirit was refreshed in the ordinances of God as in former days."[24]

This certainly would have been seen as a slight to Reyner, Smith's successor. Faced with this situation, Smith evidently sought to break Gorton's lease. At around the same time, Gorton acknowledged that he had helped Ellen Alderedge, his own wife's servant, when she got in trouble with the authorities. Alderedge had publicly criticized the doctrines and ordinances of the Plymouth congregation. In November 1638 the colony's General Court summoned Gorton to answer for his support of the maid. During his appearance he verbally attacked the magistrates and ministers. On December 4 the court fined and banished him for this abuse, giving him fourteen days to leave the colony.[25] The church elders, Brewster and Reyner, also accused Gorton of heresy, though in the absence of detailed early church records it is unclear whether he was excommunicated. There is a record, however, of the congregation excommunicating John Weekes and his wife, who, according to Nathaniel Morton, "became very Atheists" due to Gorton's influence, "and were cast out of the church for their abominable opinions, by which said damnable opinions several young folks belonging to the church had like to be carried aside into the paths of darkness."[26] While these individuals were not readmitted to the church, it should be noted that excommunication was regarded as a last effort to recover an individual to the community of faith. It was for those, as Bradford expressed it, who were "incurable and incorrigible, when after much patience used no other means would serve."[27] But the hope was that this would shock the offender into repentance, which in many cases reported in New England it did, with the offender readmitted to the church.[28]

Banishment was a separate judgment. When the time came to depart there was, Gorton recalled, "as mighty a storm of snow as I have seen in the country."[29] Together with some of his followers, he moved to Aquidneck (present-day Newport, Rhode Island), where he joined Anne Hutchinson, William Coddington, and others who had settled there following the Free Grace controversy. He supported Hutchinson in a quarrel with Coddington, and then moved on to Providence. In 1641 Roger Williams wrote to John Winthrop that "Master Gorton having foully abused high and low at Aquidneck, is now bewitching and bemaddening poor Providence, both with his unclean and foul censures of all the ministers of this country . . . and also denying all visible and external ordinances in depth of Familism," a heresy that was perceived as leading to sexual excess.[30] Williams eventually succeeded in ridding Providence of Gorton, who was eventually arrested and tried in Massachusetts, and returned to England. As with the case of Anne Hutchinson, Gorton's career may have raised some doubts about the extent to which the laity should be empowered to express their views.

While the story of Gorton was unfolding, Plymouth had been changing in significant ways. A series of agreements discharged the colonists from their obligation to English investors and led to allocation of land to individual colonists.[31] Early in the colony's history the population was small and lacked domestic livestock. There were some pigs and goats but no cattle until March 1624, when Edward Winslow returned from a journey to England with "three heifers and a bull, the first beginning of any cattle of that kind in the land."[32] Over the following years the number of cattle would grow, and the new settlements in Massachusetts provided a market for livestock that became an important prop of the economy. The increase in pigs and cattle would contribute to deteriorating relations with the Natives. The animals, generally allowed to forage outside town boundaries, rooted out and ate the seedlings planted by Native women, trampled fields, uprooted corn stored in the ground, and scavenged in the woods for nuts and berries.[33] Over the long run the physical expansion of English settlement and the threat that their practices posed to Native lifestyles would be significant causes in upending the long peace with the Wampanoags, precipitating King Philip's War.[34]

Despite setbacks caused by a "great hurricane" in 1635 and a major earthquake in 1638, the colony continued to grow in the 1630s and beyond.[35] As the settler population and the need for livestock pasturage grew, families began to move away from the original town of Plymouth to tend the herds they grazed on outlying lands. As a result, Bradford wrote, "they were scattered all over the [Cape Cod] Bay quickly and the town in which they lived compactly till now was left very thin and in a short time almost desolate."[36]

The earliest new settlement occurred in the late 1620s in the area across a small bay to the north of Plymouth town. William Brewster purchased lands there in 1631 and built a home.[37] The community became known as Duxbury. By 1632, John Alden, Myles Standish, Jonathan Brewster, and Thomas Prence also lived there much of the year but returned to their Plymouth homes in the winter. Despite a pledge that they would live in the town of Plymouth in the winter to better be able to attend worship, that alone posed serious implications for the church. Bradford noted that "those that lived on the other side of the Bay, called Duxbury, . . . could not long bring their wives and children to the public worship and church meetings here, but with such burden as, growing to some competent number, they sued to be dismissed and become a [congregational] body, of themselves." The Plymouth church agreed to this, "though very unwillingly," around 1632.[38] In 1637 Duxbury became a separate township.[39]

In 1633 the colony General Court had supervised the cutting of a canal that would connect Green Harbor with Cape Cod Bay. By the mid-1630s, land had been granted there to Edward Winslow, William Bradford, and others in what became Marshfield. The population became large enough in 1637 for the settlers to organize militia drills, a regular feature of every New England town's efforts to defend itself.[40] This early expansion north along the Bay brought the new towns of Duxbury and Medford closer to the Massachusetts Bay Colony. Later in the decade, settlements were established to the south (Sandwich) and east (Yarmouth and Barnstable) of Plymouth town and one to the west (Taunton).

North of Marshfield, not far from the Massachusetts town of Hingham, lay Scituate. English settlers lived there by 1633 and a congregation was organized by 1635, when John Lothrop, an important figure in the puritan movement, arrived. In 1624 Lothrop had joined the semiseparatist London congregation formed earlier by Henry Jacob in Southwark. With Jacob having emigrated to Virginia, the congregation chose Lothrop as their pastor. In 1630 Lothrop's congregation split over whether to reject all connections with the Church of England. Lothrop, reflecting a position similar to that previously adopted by Robinson and Brewster, opposed such a move, "not knowing what in time God might further manifest to them."[41] Those who disagreed with his position seceded from the church.

In 1632 Lothrop and forty-one members of his congregation were arrested in London while worshipping in the home of one of its members, a brewer's clerk named Humphrey Barnet. While they languished in prison they engaged in a discussion with John Davenport, then rector of St. Stephens Coleman Street. Having received notes of a sermon that Davenport had preached against separatism, Lothrop responded to Davenport's position. Davenport found their arguments persuasive, prompting him to cease participating in aspects of the liturgy they criticized, adopting a nonconformist stance, and emigrating to the Netherlands, and later to New England.[42] Following their release from prison, the Lothrop congregation further divided on the question of infant baptism, with some members leaving to form a Baptist church.[43]

Lothrop was freed on bond in June 1634 on the stipulation that he appear before the church High Commission at its next term and in the meantime cease attending what they viewed as conventicles. When he failed to appear, he was cited for contempt twice and finally, in February 1635, the Commission ordered his arrest.[44] By that time he had already emigrated to New England with the intention of settling in the Plymouth colony.[45] Lothrop arrived in Boston in September 1634. During a brief stay there, he asked to be allowed to observe the administration of the Lord's Supper in the Boston church but declined to participate since he had been dismissed by his previous congregation and was not a member of a recognized church.[46]

By the end of September, Lothrop and some of those who had journeyed with him settled in Scituate.[47] Within months, members of the Plymouth town congregation then living in Scituate were "dismissed from their membership in case they joined in a body at Scituate." Those individuals, along with people who had come with Lothrop, formed a church and subscribed to a covenant following a day of humiliation on January 8, 1635.[48] James Cudworth, the stepson of the English puritan divine John Stoughton, had been a member of the Southwark congregation and settled in Scituate. Writing to his stepfather in December 1634, he referred to Lothrop as "a holy, reverent, and heavenly minded man" whom "the Lord hath brought to us in safety."[49] The congregation elected Lothrop as their pastor at a meeting in his house on January 19.[50] Nathaniel Morton referred to him as one who "was endowed with a competent measure of gifts and eminently endowed with a great measure of brokenness of heart and humility of spirit."[51] Starting with the formation of the congregation by its lay members and their selection of Lothrop, the early history of that church reinforces what is known about Plymouth Congregationalism. Over the following years there were days of humiliation to seek God's help in settling church differences and days of thanksgiving on which they praised God for the blessings he had bestowed on them.[52]

Lothrop recorded a day of thanksgiving on December 26, 1636, that describes the form such services took in Scituate and likely in the rest of the colony's churches. On that very cold day the congregation assembled around 8:30 in the morning. They joined in a short prayer, then sang a psalm, offered a longer prayer, sang another psalm, and then listened to the preaching of the Word. Following the sermon there was another prayer and the singing of another psalm. The congregation then dispersed around noon "for making merry . . . , the poorer sort being invited of the richer."[53] A day of thanksgiving on October 12, 1637, underscores the congregation's concern and engagement with issues that concerned the larger New England religious community. Two reasons were cited for this observance—"for the victory over the Pequots" and "reconciliation between Mr. Cotton and the other ministers," referring to the divisions caused by the Free Grace controversy. The Boston clergyman had been subjected to sharp questions by his clerical colleagues, but had eventually reconciled with the other ministers.[54]

The controversy that divided members of Lothrop's church in London followed him to Scituate. Agitation of this issue, along with an interest in acquiring richer land, convinced Lothrop and most members of the church to uproot and settle Barnstable, also in the Plymouth colony, in 1639. He presented the decision as a means of advancing "God's own glory, our Sion's better peace and prosperity, and the sweet and happy regiment of the prince of our salvation more jointly embraced, and more fully exalted."[55] Lothrop remained in Barnstable until his death in 1653. The rump of the congregation, which included William Vassall (one of the original assistants in Massachusetts), was forced to rely on lay preaching.[56]

The expansion of the Plymouth colony from one town to many required changes in its political structure. Each town was granted representatives in the colony government. Freemen were expected to be males over the age of twenty-one with an estate of at least £20 in taxable value. They were expected to be of good character and to have taken an oath of loyalty, but they were not required to belong to a church. In 1636 a committee that included Brewster was appointed to prepare a code of laws.

Bradford feared this expansion would be "the ruin of New England, at least of the churches of God there, and will provoke the Lord's displeasure."[57] A major challenge for the colonists was finding adequate religious leadership. Brewster remained the elder of what might be called the "Mother Church" in the town of Plymouth itself, but he sought to provide what spiritual assistance he could to Duxbury, where he owned land, until that township found a minister of its own in 1637. While Brewster may have been able to preach and lead prayer in both Plymouth town and Duxbury for a time, providing spiritual counsel to an ever larger and more diffuse group of believers would have been challenging.[58]

Brewster's role in the colony's religious life was gradually reduced as the colony began to attract English puritan ministers. The first of these had been Ralph Smith, who was elected pastor of the Plymouth congregation after he moved there from Nantasket in 1629. In 1633 he had married the widow of Richard Masterson, who had two young children. In subsequent years, Smith corresponded with Hugh Goodyear in Leiden, an old friend, in an effort to arrange for the sale of a house in Leiden that Richard Masterson had bequeathed to his children. Smith gave up his ministry in Plymouth around 1636. In a letter to Goodyear in 1638, he indicated he had been worn down by "long sickness in London and many-fold sorrows in Europe and America here in New England." He was "weakened and unable to labor as formerly." He also referred to having gained "freedom 20 months since"—which would have been about when he left Plymouth—"of mine intolerable charge pressing me nigh 7 years." Most likely he was referring to the burden of responsibilities he had labored under as the congregation's pastor since his arrival in New England.[59] But his tenure may have been more contentious than we know, since Nathaniel Morton wrote that when Smith laid down his charge it was "partly by his own willingness as thinking it too heavy a burden, and partly at the desire and by the persuasion of others."[60]

Edward Winslow was in England in 1634 to defend the colony against various charges, during which he commented on the lack of ministers in the colony. While he was successful in explaining the colony's positions, in one of his appearances before the Commissioners for Plantations, Archbishop William Laud questioned him for his lay preaching in Plymouth, which was prohibited in the Church of England. Winslow responded by acknowledging that this was the practice in Plymouth and explained the reasons for it, stating that "some time ([the church] wanting a minister) he did exercise his gift to help the edification of his brethren when they wanted better means, which was not often." At Laud's request, the commissioners sent Winslow to the Fleet Prison, where he remained for seventeen weeks until the intercession of friends led to his release.[61]

During his stay in England, Winslow, knowing Smith's inclination to leave, sought a clergyman who would be able to assist or possibly replace Smith. He found a "Mr. Glover," but "when he was prepared for the voyage, he fell sick of a fever and died."[62] Winslow then persuaded John Norton to accept the position. Norton agreed to take the post on the understanding that he would reimburse the congregation for the costs of transporting him if he decided to leave. Norton, who was a Peterhouse, Cambridge, graduate, had adopted strong puritan views after his graduation and was unwilling to conform to practices required to hold a church living. Arriving in Plymouth in October 1635, he preached there during that winter. Norton "was well liked of them [the congregation] and much desired by them," but he left in less than a year to accept an offer from Ipswich, Massachusetts.[63]

At around the same time that Norton left, John Reyner arrived in Plymouth. Nothing is known about his career between his attendance at Magdalene College, Cambridge, and his arrival in Plymouth. Bradford referred to him as "an able and godly man," of "a meek and humble spirit, sound in the truth and in every way unreprovable in his life and conversation." After a trial period in which they had a chance to listen to his preaching, the congregation elected Reyner as their teacher and they enjoyed "the fruits of [his] labor" for "many years with much comfort, in peace and good agreement."[64]

The religious histories of the towns that hived off from Plymouth provide further insight into congregational practices as they existed in the colony. One of the more significant figures was Ralph Partridge, who arrived in Boston on a ship from England in 1636.[65] A graduate of Trinity College, Cambridge, Partridge had been licensed in 1605 and appointed a curate in Sutton-by-Dover, Kent in that same year.[66] He was evidently a puritan nonconformist. Cotton Mather colorfully described him as "one who bore the name as well as the state of a hunted partridge, who, distressed by ecclesiastical setters, had no defense neither of beak nor claw, but a flight over the ocean." Mather also wrote of him as "having the innocency of the dove, conspicuous in his blameless and pious life, but also the loftiness of an eagle, in the great soar of his intellectual abilities."[67] Nathaniel Morton, who knew Partridge, likewise attested to his personal character and his "sound and solid judgment in the main truths of Jesus Christ, and very able in his disputation to defend them."[68] When he died, in 1658, his inventory totaled more than 418 volumes, a library even larger than Brewster's.[69] It is striking that, despite his attainments, he was content to remain in Duxbury and minister to that small church for the rest of his life. When representatives from churches throughout New England were called to Cambridge, Massachusetts, in 1646 to prepare a statement of the principles of the New England Way, Partridge represented Plymouth colony. He prepared one of the three drafts considered by the assembly as it crafted the Cambridge Platform, regarded as the definitive statement of the New England Way in the mid-seventeenth century.[70]

Charles Chauncy would serve the church in Plymouth town but then moved to Scituate. He had arrived in Plymouth in 1638. A graduate and fellow of Trinity College, Cambridge, as well as lecturer there in Hebrew and Greek, Chauncy had been appointed vicar of Ware in Hertfordshire in 1627. On more than one occasion he was called before the High Commission to answer for his views and he was deprived of his living for refusing to read the *Book of Sports*—a royal proclamation authorizing Sabbath practices puritans found objectionable—to his parishioners. In Plymouth he preached while on trial for three years. The length of the trial was likely due to some of Chauncy's unusual views, including a belief that the Lord's Supper was to be administered every Sabbath in the evening, and that baptism had to be by immersion. The congregation did not agree that immersion was the only scripturally approved way to baptize and they brought in Duxbury's Ralph Partridge and others to publicly dispute him on this point.[71] In the end, after sharing views in prophesying, the congregation accepted the legitimacy of immersion, but "in this cold country not so convenient."[72]

Not willing to decide definitively on either method, the congregation sought a compromise whereby Chauncy, if he was called to the pastorate, would baptize by immersion, while those who wished the alternative of sprinkling for their children would go to John Reyner for the sacrament. Chauncy was not willing to accept this compromise, so the congregation sent letters to other churches in the region, including Boston, Hartford, and New Haven, to solicit their views. Despite the letters from ministers that "all concluded against him," Chauncy persisted in his view. Given the impasse, he left Plymouth town and accepted a call to the church in Scituate.[73] There, according to John Winthrop, Chauncy "persevered in his opinion of dipping in baptism, and practiced accordingly, first upon two of his own, which being in very cold weather, one of them swooned away. Another, having a child about three years old, feared it would be frightened (as others had been, and one caught hold of Mr. Chauncy and had near pulled him into the water)."[74] The remainder of Lothrop's congregation in Scituate did not accept Chauncy, leading to a lengthy dispute between two "congregations," each claiming to be the true church. Efforts to reconcile the two groups by church leaders in Plymouth and Massachusetts failed, and the division was only healed after Chauncy moved on, accepting an invitation to become president of Harvard College.[75]

Within a few years of their settlement, the outlying towns of Plymouth were able to find ministers—Partridge in Duxbury, Lothrop and then Chauncy in Scituate, William Leveridge in Sandwich, Joseph Mayo in Barnstable and then Eastham, and Joseph Hull and Matthew Marmaduke in Yarmouth.[76] The ability of the Plymouth towns to obtain clergymen had improved when greater pressure was placed on English puritan clergy to conform following the accession of Charles I in 1625. The Plymouth colony's new clergymen had not been separatists in England, but rather nonconforming members of the Church of England who had run afoul of the increasing demands of the bishops for conformity. By the time they arrived in New England, the distinction between separatist and no-separatist had little meaning in the region, save for a few such as Roger Williams. Of course, Plymouth itself reflected the irenic views of Robinson and Brewster and was deemed insufficiently separatist by Williams. While there were a few outliers, virtually all of the churches followed the pattern that had been set in Salem in 1629, largely due to the influence of Plymouth.

During the 1630s the unity of Plymouth with the churches of the Bay was evident in the consultations that occurred between the churches of the colonies. Francis Higginson had corresponded with Brewster about baptismal practices in 1629. There are references to other such exchanges where, as in this case, the actual letters do not survive. But correspondence does survive as evidence of such consultation.

Both the Plymouth and Massachusetts colonies had to deal with the problems of population growth and expansion. As men moved to outlying farms they found it more difficult to attend worship. In 1639 Plymouth's William Brewster and John Reyner wrote to Boston's John Wilson and John Cotton about these issues. Brewster and Reyner, noting that the Lord had called "you with us in the fellowship of the Gospel to mutual helpfulness," asked the Boston ministers' views on the extent to which those laboring on the farms—owners and servants—should be obliged to attend worship. Expressing a desire for "what light you have received," the two Plymouth leaders asked help in "guiding our feet in the ways of truth & peace." While the response of the Boston divines does not survive, Cotton's view on the issue in general was expressed in his *Pouring Out of the Seven Vials* (1642), in which he wrote that believers should "sit down nowhere without good ministers," and "never make a beginning, but where you may come and partake of waters of God's house every Lord's day."[77]

A few months later, Reyner and Cotton again exchanged letters, though on a different subject. Reyner asked Cotton's views on what should be required of admitting someone to a congregation, but he moved on to a more personal concern. The Plymouth minister was contemplating marrying Frances Clarke, a maid in the household of John Wilson, and he wanted to know if she had yet been admitted to the Boston church. In his response Cotton indicated that she had not been admitted, but solely because of a backlog of applicants. Church records show that she was subsequently admitted, married Reyner, and was released in good standing to the Plymouth church. But the correspondence also speaks to ongoing interaction between the Plymouth and Boston churches. Reyner refers to having been together with Cotton on more than one occasion. In his response Cotton asks that his love be given to Brewster, Bradford, and Charles Chauncy.[78]

A more momentous exchange of views occurred in 1642, when Massachusetts governor Richard Bellingham wrote to William Bradford to solicit the advice of the colony's ministers on the appropriate punishment for "heinous offences in point of uncleanness."[79] Bellingham's account of the offense in question was at some point excised from Bradford's manuscript history, but the details were presented by John Winthrop in his journal. Three servants of John Humfrey, an early leader of the Massachusetts Bay Colony, were accused of having sexually abused two of Humfrey's daughters, Dorcas and Sarah, who were as young as seven years old. When they were charged, Daniel Fairfield, Jenkin Davis, and John Hudson confessed to "all but entrance to her body." There was no law that dealt specifically with what they were willing to admit to, and there was uncertainty as to whether they could be charged with rape, sodomy, or some other offense, and if so what the penalty should be. The Bay authorities solicited the views of the elders in Plymouth, Connecticut, and New Haven.[80] Because the accused denied penetration, Bellingham evidently inquired about whether torture might be acceptable to obtain that confession.[81]

John Reyner, Ralph Partridge, and Charles Chauncy all wrote out their opinions, which Bradford sent on to the Massachusetts authorities. Others, perhaps including Brewster, had not responded, he said. In sending the opinions, the governor reflected John Robinson's cautions against judicial excess, indicating that if there was doubt about the details of a crime it should not be punished with death. All three clergymen drew on the scriptures, particularly the book of Leviticus, in developing their views. John Reyner explored various circumstances that might surround a sexual crime and indicated that the death penalty "might" be appropriate so long as there were two witnesses, but he did not pass judgment on the particular case. He was, however, emphatic in rejecting the use of torture to extract a confession and likewise rejected the use of a self-incriminating ex officio oath.[82]

Partridge had less to say about evaluating the crime but was similarly emphatic about the need for two witnesses and also rejected the use of torture to extract a confession. A magistrate was to draw a confession from force of argument, but not "by an oath imposed" or "any punishment inflicted or threatened to be inflicted." Chauncy was far more convinced that the servants deserved capital punishment even if their actions had not resulted in penetration, and he listed among crimes worthy of such punishment adultery, incest, rape, bestiality, and sodomy. He also believed that "if a man witness against himself, his own testimony is sufficient," without a second witness. As for extracting a confession, he too rejected the use of an ex officio oath and rejected torture in most capital cases, though "in matters of highest consequence, such as do concern the safety or ruin of states or countries, magistrates may proceed so far to bodily torments, as racks, hot irons, etc. to extract a confession."[83] Because the Massachusetts authorities could not reach consensus on whether the offense was a capital crime, the men who had abused the Humphrey children were merely punished with a whipping and a fine.

The request for advice on how to deal with those accused came at a time when Plymouth was facing a similar "heinous crime." The son of a couple who lived in Scituate, Thomas Granger, was employed as a servant on the Duxbury farm of Love Brewster. Granger was seen engaging in sex with an animal and when questioned admitted to "the same, with a mare, a cow, two goats, five sheep, two calves, and a turkey." He was found guilty by a jury and executed in September 1642. This was likely particularly troubling for the Brewsters, as it implied a failure to properly supervise their Duxbury household.[84]

Bradford viewed these incidents, as well as similar offenses in New Haven and elsewhere in New England, as an eruption of behaviors that threatened the godly commonwealths of the region. In the opening of his account of 1642, he wrote of "wickedness [that] did grow and break forth here, in a land where the same was so much witnessed against and so narrowly looked unto, and severely punished when it was known, as in no place more, or so much, that I have known or heard of." He mentioned drunkenness, fornication, adultery, and, "which is worse, even sodomy and buggery." He wondered if this might not be because "the Devil might carry a greater spite against the churches of Christ and the gospel here, by how much the more they endeavor to preserve holiness and purity amongst them and stain upon them in the eyes of [the] world." Reflecting his suspicions of Native life, he also wondered if Satan might have more power in New England because it was a "heathen land." Yet in the end he decided that there were no more sins in Plymouth than elsewhere, but that the faith and zeal of the population led to more of them being discovered.[85]

The 1630s saw a rapid growth of New England, including the founding of the new colonies of Connecticut (1636) and New Haven (1638), as well as the de facto establishment of what would officially become Rhode Island when the towns of Providence, Newport, and Portsmouth were settled by various puritan dissenters. During this period and into the following decades new religious ideas were brought to the region, as well as a growing number of immigrants who sought economic rather than religious success. The overthrow of the English bishops, which Bradford applauded, gave new life to transatlantic debates over church structure and practices. While Plymouth's influence continued to be felt, it was Massachusetts that would increasingly lead in defining the evolving New England Way and finding ways to maintain religious unity.

Conclusion

Defending Plymouth Congregationalism

William Brewster remained at the center of the religious life of the Plymouth colony until his death in April 1644.[1] Although the precise date of his birth is unknown, he was likely seventy-seven or seventy-eight when he died. Over his last years he had witnessed the deaths of his wife Mary (1627), his daughter Frances (1633), his daughter Patience (1634), and his son Wrestling (1635). He had been defrauded by his son-in-law Isaac Allerton and embarrassed by the discovery of Thomas Granger's crimes on his son Love's farm. Through all of this he maintained his faith and continued his labors as elder of the church.

In writing of his "dear and loving friend" and mentor, William Bradford noted that Brewster had played a key role with "this poor persecuted church above 36 years in England, Holland, and this wilderness, and done the Lord and them faithful service in his place and calling."[2] From walking the corridors of power in the employ of William Davison he had taken on the mantle of a shepherd to a humble flock of religious dissidents. As his life took him from Scrooby to Leiden to Plymouth he had accepted steadily diminishing material circumstances. Bradford's nephew Nathaniel Morton detailed this in his own history of the colony. Of Brewster, he wrote that he had laid aside the comforts of England and accepted "a new course of living . . . unto which he was no way unwilling to take his part and to bear his burden with the rest, living many times without bread or corn many months together, having many times nothing but fish and often wanting that also, and drank nothing but water for many years together, yea until within five or six years of his death." He "would labor with his hands in the fields as long as he was able," alongside performing his duties as a church leader.[3]

By 1639, his advanced age was evident from what one scholar has referred to as his "quavering handwriting."[4] Yet he remained active up to the end. Even when he sickened he did not take to his bed until the day he died, though ill health may have led to the cancellation of a meeting of the colony church elders at Ralph Partridge's house intended to reconcile a religious dispute that was dividing Scituate.[5] His speech did not fail him until the end. Around nine or ten at night "he died in peace, amongst the midst of his friends, who mourned and wept over him and ministered what help and comfort they could unto him," while he in turn sought to comfort them. "A few hours before, he drew his breath short, and some few minutes before his last, he drew his breath long as a man fallen into a short sleep without any pangs or gaspings, and so sweetly departed this life unto a better."[6]

By the time of Brewster's death, aspects of the Congregationalism that Plymouth represented were under attack in New England and, indeed, back in England, where Presbyterian puritanism was for a time in the ascendant. At the heart of Plymouth's religious life was lay empowerment, a characteristic strengthened by the lack of a strong clerical

Fig. C.1 A scene in Plimoth Plantation, a living history museum representing the community in the 1620s. Photo by Francis J. Bremer.

presence in the colony during its first decade and expressed through the practice of prophesying. The essence of Congregationalism was the authority of the believers in a congregation to control their affairs and the autonomous freedom of each such congregation from influence by external clerical conferences, assemblies, synods, or civil government. As New England grew more populous some religious and civil leaders became worried about how the unity of the region could be sustained.

During the early 1630s, clergy in Massachusetts gathered informally to discuss problems they all experienced in organizing and leading their churches, with each taking turns in hosting the meeting once a fortnight. These ministers produced a "Model of Church and Civil Power" that justified such gatherings as a means of providing one another "help in regard of daily emergent troubles, doubt, and controversies"; to share in fellowship; to organize to promote the welfare of the region's churches as well as those abroad; and to demonstrate the "communion of love [by which] others shall know they are disciples of Christ."[7] Notably, Salem's Samuel Skelton and Roger Williams refused to engage in such meetings, "fearing it might grow in time to a Presbytery or superintendency to the prejudice of the churches' liberties," a charge those engaged in such gatherings rejected.[8] There is no evidence that Plymouth clergy participated in such meetings during the early history of the colony, although such gatherings may have occurred.

Congregationalists accepted the value of clergymen gathering in assemblies or synods if, and only if, the results of their deliberations were purely advisory. Representatives of the Plymouth churches did participate in regional clerical assemblies called to deal with specific issues. One such gathering was held in Cambridge, Massachusetts, in 1637, attended by Ralph Smith.[9] This was the meeting that arose from the Free Grace controversy.[10] Though there were congregations that were uneasy about the convening of a synod, that body produced and condemned a list of eighty-two errors.[11]

Few if any Plymouth residents had sympathy for most of the ideas condemned by that synod, but there would likely have been disquiet about the classification as an error the belief that "the weakest minister may edify the strongest Christian which had more experience than himself," implying as it did the superior insight of clergy over

Spirit-inspired laity.[12] Equally troubling would have been the synod's resolutions to restore order in the churches. These included a statement that the type of conference hosted by Anne Hutchinson—"where sixty or more did meet every week, and one woman (in a prophetical way . . .) took upon her the whole exercise . . . was agreed to be disorderly and without rule." The synod statement conceded that it was appropriate for lay members of a congregation to ask questions in church for information, but "utterly condemned" questions whereby "the doctrines delivered were reproved, and the elders reproached."[13] Charles Chauncy, an eighteenth-century Boston minister (not the seventeenth-century Plymouth clergyman), had a manuscript copy of the synod's proceedings and wrote that that representatives at the synod who dissented from the conclusions included "diverse of Boston, one or two of Charlestown, one at Salem, one at Plymouth, one at Duxbury, one at Watertown."[14] Most likely Smith was there as a representative from Plymouth and Partridge was Duxbury's representative. The possibility of Brewster being there cannot be discounted. Interestingly, the Massachusetts churches whose representatives dissented were those in the towns where Fuller had been most engaged in explaining the Plymouth way in 1629 and 1630.

Suddenly, in 1639, a series of events began that suggested that the long-sought reform of the Church of England might be possible. The attempt by Charles I to impose new, English-style worship on Scotland had prompted a rebellion in 1637. Failing in his initial attempts to suppress the insurgents, in 1640 the king called a parliament to raise the funds needed to fight the Scots. When that body (which became known as the Short Parliament) refused to enact revenue measures unless the king undertook a range of reforms, he dissolved the assembly. But the success of Scottish armies forced Charles to call a new parliament (the Long Parliament) that pressured the king into measures to guarantee future Parliaments and reform the church. Pushed too far, in 1642 the king raised his standard and declared Parliament in rebellion. During the resulting English Civil Wars, the Parliament took steps to reform the Church, starting in 1643 with the calling of the Westminster Assembly of Divines, charged with recommending the forms and doctrines of a new national church.[15]

On the battlefield the parliamentary forces and their Scottish allies recovered from early reverses to win significant battles at Marston Moor and Naseby. In 1646 Charles surrendered to the Scots, who turned him over to the English Parliament in January 1647, ushering in a puritan Commonwealth. The fighting was resumed, with royalists in England and Scotland rallying to support Charles II, but this Second Civil War came to a swift conclusion with victories at Dunbar and Worcester by the Parliament's New Model Army commanded by Oliver Cromwell. In 1653 the parliament was dissolved and a new government, the Protectorate, formed with Cromwell as Lord Protector.[16]

In 1646 William Bradford, who had begun to write his history "Of Plimmoth Plantation" around 1630, picked up his pen and made a lengthy entry on the reverse side of one of the early pages of his manuscript. "Full little did I think that the downfall of the Bishops, with their courts, canons and ceremonies, etc. had been so near when I first began these scribbled writings. . . . But it is the Lord's doing, and ought to be marvelous in our eyes." He rhetorically asked his fellow colonists, "Do you now see the fruits of your labors, O all ye servants of the Lord?" After reeling off a series of scriptural references, Bradford summarized the implications of the recent news—"The tyrannous Bishops are ejected, their courts dissolved, their canons forceless, their services cashiered, their ceremonies useless and despised, their plots for popery prevented, and all their superstitions discarded and returned to Rome from whence they came, and the monuments of idolatry rooted out of the land."[17]

Bradford's joy typified that of most New Englanders, who sympathized with Parliament from the start. Taunton's William Hooke asserted that it was the duty of the colonists to "lie in wait in the wilderness, to call down upon the backs of God's enemies with deadly Fasting and Prayer, murderers that will kill point blank from one end of the world to the other."[18] Prayer was a weapon available to all the colonists. Days of humiliation brought members of particular congregations together to pray for favors, and many such occasions were called throughout New England to solicit God's aid for the parliamentary cause.[19] The records kept by John Lothrop in Scituate document what was typical of Plymouth congregations. Between September 23, 1642, and May 1653, Lothrop recorded twelve such days observed "for old

England." Good news brought the congregation together for a day of thanksgiving. On September 2, 1641, the Scituate believers joined to thank God for "good tidings from old England, of a most happy beginning of a gracious Reformation." In October 1647 thanks were offered for the "admirable success . . . by the hand of Sir Thomas Fairfax and his [parliamentary] army." In January 1650 it was the "good success of the army . . . under Colonel Cromwell" that was a cause for thanking God.[20]

In addition to sending up prayers to God, clergy dispatched numerous tracts setting out and defending the New England Way as a blueprint for English reform, since "great pity were it," as stated by John Cotton, "that they should want any light which might possibly be afforded them."[21] Some colonists went further and returned to England to personally aid the cause in pulpits and on the battlefield. Ten former New Englanders would rise to the rank of major general or higher in the parliamentary armies. Plymouth's Edward Winslow would serve the new puritan regime established in England and led by Oliver Cromwell.[22]

During the debates over the reform of the English church a variety of positions evolved that helped shape New England's religious history. This was the period when English puritanism began to assume denominational identities, with proponents of various forms of church governance and practice hardening into Presbyterians, Congregationalists, and Baptists. Initially the momentum was with those who favored a Presbyterian settlement. English clergy favoring this choice and Scottish observers represented the majority in the Westminster Assembly of Divines. But a minority, largely ministers who had experience in guiding congregations in the Netherlands, advocated a congregational polity that was soon identified as the New England Way. When these Dissenting Brethren were unable to stop Parliament from taking steps to establish Presbyterianism, they formed a coalition with various sectarian groups (such as the Baptists) to prevent effective implementation of that decision. These Congregationalists, or Independents, as they came to be known, were supported by many members of Parliament and the army, particularly Oliver Cromwell. The religious establishment during the Protectorate loosely reflected what the Independents had advocated.[23]

Presbyterians saw their church order as more conducive to social order at a time when too many of their fellow Englishmen were
seeking to turn the world upside down.[24] The army, whose exploits
Bradford commended, was a place where godly men gathered around
campfires much as in a conventicle to debate religious issues and how
these related to political reform. In a more formal setting delegates
of ordinary soldiers as well as officers discussed the civil and religious settlement of the realm in debates at Putney and Whitehall.[25]
One of the strategies of the Presbyterians in England was to discredit
Congregationalism by claiming that in New England it had led to radical ideas and practices. To support this claim, Presbyterians sought to
connect the churches of Massachusetts with separatism by drawing a
direct path linking Plymouth to radical separatism and arguing that
the New England churches of Salem, Boston, and elsewhere were modeled on the Plymouth example. This was especially true in the works of
the Scottish Presbyterian Robert Baillie, such as his *A Dissuasive from
the Errours of the Time* (1645), who according to Bradford claimed that
"in a few years most who settled in the land [New England] did agree
to model themselves after Mr. Robinson's pattern."[26]

The second strategy of the Presbyterians was to attribute the radicalism of Anne Hutchinson, Roger Williams, and others to the practice
of prophesying. This was particularly effective at a time when the end
of effective censorship allowed men and women of all backgrounds to
espouse a variety of religiously and socially radical views in print and
from street pulpits. John Milton connected lay preaching with freedom
of the press, arguing that truth in the scripture was a "streaming foun-
tain" but that "if her waters flow not in a perpetual progression, they
sicken in a muddy pool of conformity and tradition."[27] One of the
leading Presbyterian writers, Thomas Edwards, set out to provide a
compendium of all the errors of the day in *Gangraena, or, A Catalogue
and Discovery of many of the Errors, Heresies, Blasphemies and
Pernicious Practices of the Sectaries of this Time* (1646). He inveighed
against the "laymen, weavers, tinkers, and cobblers" and other ordinary sorts who were "suffered to turn preachers, and to go up and down
seducing people."[28] Edwards wrote of a particular instance during a
service he was conducting when "up stands one Colonel Washington
of Hartfordshire . . . and spake openly against what I had preached,

that I had not rightly given the sense of that parable of the tares, and that I was a false prophet, or, beware of false prophets."[29] Some of these street preachers were women, including a former New Englander, Sarah Dudley Keayne.[30] William Rathband specifically pointed to New England as the source of such behavior because of the socially disruptive aspects of allowing "mere private persons . . . to exercise their gifts." Even worse, he cited a sermon—the 1621 Plymouth sermon of Robert Cushman—as preached by a "comber of wool," arguing that Cushman's emphasis on the common good encouraged community of property and led to Familism, a heresy identified with licentiousness.[31]

On the other side of the spectrum from the Presbyterians were some of the more radical groups that had joined the English Congregationalists seeking independence of all the churches. But as the Presbyterian threat diminished, members of that coalition on the extreme fringes of doctrinal orthodoxy saw English Congregationalists, moderate Presbyterians, and Baptists working together with Protector Cromwell to establish a religious consensus that would have excluded them. These radicals then expressed suspicions of the embrace of the New England Way by their Congregationalist allies, pointing to the persecution of dissenters in the colonies.

The principal colonial contributions to these English debates were written by clergymen such as Massachusetts's John Cotton and Richard Mather, New Haven's John Davenport, and Connecticut's Thomas Hooker. But Brewster and other Plymouth leaders also sought to defend their practices and beliefs against critics from the right and the left, and particularly to assert their true role in having shaped New England. This task was primarily undertaken by Edward Winslow, who contributed a number of works to the English debates of the 1640s, and by William Bradford, who wrote a series of dialogues seeking to explain the Plymouth heritage to the young men born in the colony after 1620.

As Bradford explained it, Plymouth and its church leaders had in fact played a key part in shaping the New England Way. Their ability to exercise such a role was made easier by the fact that Brewster and John Robinson had abandoned the rigid separatism that condemned any contact with those who retained an identification with the Church of England. This, of course, is what Roger Williams had found wanting in both Plymouth and Massachusetts. Responding to the criticisms of Robert Baillie and others, Bradford explicitly denied the effort of critics to associate the Plymouth congregation, or even other separatists, as followers of Robert Browne, writing that "rigid Brownists . . . lie under much aspersion and their names [were] much blemished and beclouded not only by enemies but even by godly and reverend men."[32] He further argued that "it is very injurious to call those after his name [Browne] whose person they never knew and whose writings (few if any of them) ever saw and whose backslidings they have constantly borne witness against."[33]

Bradford's task was made more difficult by the fact that some defenders of the New England Way, including John Cotton, had initially tried to free themselves from any taint of separatism by minimizing the influence that Plymouth had exerted on their churches. It suited their polemic purposes of such New England writers to argue that their Congregationalism was different from that of Plymouth; that it was instead a middle way between separatism and Presbyterianism. In composing his dialogue Bradford generally praised Cotton for kind words the Boston clergyman had offered regarding Plymouth, but criticized Cotton's early efforts to distance himself from early separatism, something he believed was contrary to the evidence.[34]

Bradford explained to the "young men" of Plymouth that within a few years of the settlement of New England "the most whole [churches] settled in the land did agree to model themselves after Mr. Robinson's pattern." He further asserted that the "famous men and churches in New England" not only agreed with Plymouth in their practice, but so did the "godly party" in England, which stood "for the same way under the new name of Independents put upon them."[35] In another conference with the "young men" he clarified the meaning of the term "Independent," noting that the name "is not a name of choice made by any of themselves, but a title imposed by others which are their opposite." He further explained that it was "no fit name for our churches, in that it holdeth us forth as independent from all others," whereas in fact they professed "dependency upon magistrates for civil government and protection, dependency upon Christ and his word for the sovereign government and rule of our administrations," and recognized the value of the advice of "other churches and synods when our own variance or ignorance may stand in need of such help from them."[36]

Following the lead of John Robinson, the Plymouth puritans had always been open to the possibility that the positions they reached might be in error. Discussion within the church through prophesying was intended to minimize mistakes. But consultation with other clergy and churches was always part of their practice. In Leiden, Robinson and Brewster learned from discussions with Ames and Jacob. In New England, Fuller offered advice to the puritans who arrived in 1629 and 1630; consultation between Brewster and Higginson helped both sides refine their positions on infant baptism; and the contributions of Winthrop and Wilson to the October 1632 prophesying in the Plymouth church helped shape a consensus on using the English practice of calling individuals "goodman," without implying their moral worth. Agreement was not always possible, of course. Roger Williams could not persuade Brewster and the Plymouth church to accept some of his more extreme views and was dismissed with Christian charity to return to Salem. Granting dismissal was a recognition that the person who wished to move and join another congregation was in good standing with the church he or she was leaving.

What distinguished Plymouth, the other New England churches, and England's Congregationalists from the Presbyterians was that they viewed consultation as advisory only. Bradford accepted that "the officers of one or many churches may meet together or discuss and consider of matters for the good of the church or churches . . . so they infringe no order of Christ or liberty of the brethren." He referenced New Haven's John Davenport in support of his position.[37] In his "third dialogue" Bradford further denied the validity of any "combination of churches as whereby the true liberty of every particular church is taken away," citing this as one of the key differences between the Congregationalists and the Presbyterians.[38] On this and other matters he cited the works of the Dissenting Brethren.[39]

Related to this were other criticisms of the Presbyterians, whom Bradford believed in some things rather "follow the example of the worst, than the best Reformed Churches." He rejected their position that ordination was a permanent empowerment that gave the clergyman the right to enter the ministry of a new church "without a new call and ordination." He disputed the authority of such ministers when it interfered with the liberty of the covenanted believers. And he rejected their practice of baptizing all children, not just those of covenanted members.[40]

Many of the sharpest English attacks on New England practices focused on the practice of lay prophesying, and in their dialogue the "young men" of Plymouth asked the "Ancient men" to respond to those criticisms. It likely did not help New England's reputation abroad that some of those who most strongly approved of and used the practice were perceived as religious radicals. But it had been common in early New England. Laymen had often preached in the first settlements of Massachusetts when there were no ministers.[41] John Clarke, a Rhode Island Baptist, wrote in his *Ill Newes from New England* (1652): "Quench not the spirit," and "despise not prophesyings."[42] Roger Williams wrote that many "of what rank soever" had the gifts of "prophets and witnesses" and could expound the "heavenly mysteries." To prove his point Williams, who had spent time in England, pointed to Samuel How, "an eminent Christian witness and prophet of Christ," who despite no formal education could far excel trained ministers in his teaching.[43]

By the 1640s, some New Englanders, especially in Massachusetts, were defensive and downplayed the extent of the practice, which appeared to be encouraged less after the Free Grace controversy.[44] In 1672 William Coddington, one of the first Massachusetts puritans, complained to William Hathorne and other old friends who had emigrated with him that in the early days of the colony they had spoken out against any attempt to limit "the spirit of prophesy," but had since degenerated "from Christianity to hardness and cruelty."[45] But Bradford had no doubt that prophesying, having been the foundation of Plymouth's religious life, was scriptural. He claimed, "it had been an ancient practice of the people of God" and was justified by the scriptures. It was "not an unheard novelty that God should enlarge private men with public gifts and to dispense them to edification."[46]

Many of these issues were debated at a new gathering of spokesmen for the region's churches that became known as the Cambridge Assembly. The Massachusetts General Court issued a call in 1646 for representatives of the region's churches to gather, explaining that "divers of Christian countrymen and friends in England, both of the ministry and others . . . have sundry times, out of their brotherly faithfulness and love, and care of our well-doing, earnestly by letters from thence solicited and called upon us that we would not neglect the opportunity which God has put in our hands" for explaining the New England Way.[47] The magistrates also expressed a desire for the assembly to address the controversial issues of infant baptism and church membership.

The court's invitation was originally phrased as a call or demand for the churches to send delegates. The first session opened on September 1, but four Massachusetts churches had failed to send representatives— Hingham, whose Presbyterian impulses set it apart; Concord, which was having difficulty finding a suitable person; Salem; and Boston. These last two were suspicious of anything that might be seen to impinge on the autonomy of an individual congregation.[48] While John Winthrop attributed this suspicion to the influence of some members newly arrived from England, where they had been influenced by Independency, it is notable that these were the two congregations most influenced by the Plymouth Way.[49] After John Norton was brought to Boston to deliver a sermon making the case for the assembly, a majority of the congregation voted to send messengers. Salem likely fell into agreement, but the delays led to an adjournment of the assembly until the following spring.[50]

When the assembly reconvened in June 1647, all of the Massachusetts churches but Hingham were represented. Churches from Connecticut, New Haven, and Plymouth had also sent representatives. There is no list enumerating the actual representatives, but Ralph Partridge of Duxbury certainly attended, as did William Bradford. At one of the first sessions Ezekiel Rogers, the pastor of the Rowley, Massachusetts, congregation preached to the group. In addition to criticisms about various moral failings, he "reproved . . . the practice of private members making speeches in the church assemblies to the disturbance and hindrance of their ordinances." John Winthrop indicated that "divers were offended at his zeal in some of these passages" and, interestingly, immediately after this comment recorded that "Mr. Bradford, the Governor of Plymouth, was there as a messenger of the church of Plymouth."[51] Presumably Bradford was offended and had spoken out against Rogers's attack on prophesying, which in the end the assembly did not condemn.

There is no further evidence of Bradford's involvement in the assembly. More is known about Ralph Partridge's participation. The Duxbury clergyman was one of three ministers, along with John Cotton and Richard Mather, invited to draft a "model of church government."[52] The selection of Partridge is striking because there were more prestigious clergymen in the colonies, and it attests to the influence Plymouth still had on New England polity. In the end it was Richard Mather's draft that became the core of the Cambridge Platform, as the assembly adopted a modification of his draft. The court requested that it be read to every Massachusetts congregation. But there is no evidence of official action on the Platform in Connecticut, New Haven, or Plymouth.[53]

Ralph Partridge's draft provides an idea of how closely Plymouth was aligned with the churches of Massachusetts in the late 1640s, though it reflected unity rather than uniformity in views.[54] In discussing the ruling elders of a congregation (the ministers and lay elders), Partridge perhaps took a more conservative stance than Robinson and Brewster may have set out in that he explicitly stated that "we do not hold that the government of the church is democratical, or merely popular." But he affirmed that "neither do we believe that it is by the Lord's appointment merely aristocratical, wherein the church government should be so in the hands of the elders as that the rest of the body should be wholly excluded from intermeddling by way of power therein."[55] The text of the Platform recognized the importance of the congregation, particularly in admitting new members, but went further in the direction of "aristocratical" rule than Partridge was willing to go in stating that "Church-government, or Rule, is placed by Christ in the officers of the church, who are therefore called rulers. . . . Yet in case of maladministration they are subject to the power of the church."[56]

As for the use of church councils, such as the one in which he was participating, Partridge emphasized that they could only offer advice. He believed, as had Robinson and Brewster, that the counsel of other churches was to be sought when a church needed further "light or peace." When a question was "more difficult and intricate than others," and some churches of less spiritual ability than other, the Lord not dispensing his gifts alike to all churches, nor alike to any at all times, . . . one church ought to be helpful to another, as one member to another."[57] Here, too, the Platform goes further than Partridge would, giving the "magistrate power to call a synod," and asserting that "the synod's directions and determinations, so far as consonant with the word of God, are to be received with reverence & submission."[58] The Plymouth clergyman did not accept the submission of churches to synod findings. In regard to governance within the congregation and governance over congregations, Partridge's draft and that published as the *Cambridge Platform* could both be interpreted as upholding Congregationalism, but the official version strongly reflected a growing drift in New England toward a more authoritarian system. This may well explain the concerns of John Lothrop's congregation in Barnstable, which observed a day of humiliation on April 22, 1647, "partly for the state of this country, to prevent any evil that might come by their synod."[59]

Partridge addressed in his draft practices that were omitted from the approved Platform but represented an important element of Plymouth's religious practice. He wrote that "we do further conceive that the celebration of marriage and burial of the dead be no ecclesiastical actions proper to the ministry but are civil acts." These were matters that not only affected church members but also were important "to all the people, whether Christians or Pagans." Furthermore, Partridge was worried that making these activities church concerns would "confirm the popish error in the one, that marriage is a sacrament, and in the other that prayer is to be used for the dead, or over the dead."[60] While this accords with early practice throughout New England, the assembly majority did not deem such a statement necessary to be included in the Cambridge Platform, perhaps suggesting that the majority of clergymen at the assembly had considered expanding their roles into these activities.

Of more significance is the fact that Partridge was not willing to grant as much authority to the civil magistrates as the majority of the assembly voted for. The Platform required civil authorities to enforce the first as well as the second table of the Ten Commandments, and specifically to take notice of, restrain, and punish "idolatry, blasphemy, heresy, and venting corrupt and pernicious opinions."[61] Partridge drew a sharp distinction between the two realms—"the power of the magistrate over the church being temporal and not spiritual, and all the power of the Church over magistrates being spiritual and not temporal."[62] This reflected the view that Robinson and Brewster had expressed in the "Seven Articles" they had sent to the Privy Council in 1617, acknowledging the king had authority over the church, but only in temporal but not doctrinal aspects of the church.[63]

The willingness of the Cambridge Assembly to entrust the civil magistrate with greater power over doctrine was likely due to the sense that orthodoxy in New England was being challenged by the influx of radical religious ideas. Massachusetts was at the time dealing with Samuel Gorton's challenges to puritan orthodoxy and ministerial authority. The Bay authorities also felt threatened by the influx of Baptist ideas and the support that those ideas received among some colonists. Within a few years Quakers would arrive in New England. The approach favored by Massachusetts and most of its leaders was to legislate against and punish these ideas.[64]

Because Baptists and Quakers were associated with lay preaching—Quaker worship in particular featured lay sharing of the promptings of the "Inner Light" in the soul of each believer—the opponents of these groups sought to suppress the practice of lay prophesying.[65] When the growth of Boston necessitated it, a Second Church (later known as North Church) was organized in 1650. That new congregation had difficulty finding a university-trained minister to assume the pastorate and so relied on the layman Michael Powell, who preached by way of prophesying. The congregation found Powell's "services so satisfactory that the church would have proceeded to ordain him," but because he was not university trained the civil magistrates forbade it. Then, in 1652, the Massachusetts General Court passed a law designed to regulate if not forbid lay preaching. The court recognized that some new towns were "destitute of persons fitly qualified to undertake the work of ministry" but feared the calling of "persons of bolder spirits and erroneous principles," which led to "the infection of their hearers and the disturbance of the peace of the country." Consequently they ordered that no one "shall undertake any constant course of public preaching or prophesying within this jurisdiction without the approbation of the elders of the four neighboring churches or the county court to which the place belongs."[66] Not only did the magistrates seek to limit lay preaching, but in their treatment of Michael Powell and the passage of this law they were also asserting the authority of external bodies to oversee the affairs of an individual congregation.[67]

All of this posed particular challenges for Plymouth in the decades following the death of Brewster. The potential for prophesying leading to radicalism was evident in the earliest years of the colony. Samuel Hicks, who had questioned the legitimacy of the Plymouth congregation, had gone on to become a Quaker, while John Cooke, at one time a deacon of the church, became a Baptist.[68] But as prophesying came under new criticism elsewhere in New England, it became more important for the towns of the Plymouth colony. The success of the puritan cause in England, from which Bradford took satisfaction, led many established clergy in the colonies to return home and aid in the cause of reformation. Noted clergy such as Hugh Peter and Thomas Welde went to England, never to return. In Plymouth, Taunton's William Hooke, who had urged on New Englanders the need to launch their prayers as arrows across the Atlantic, himself returned to England. It was not only established clergymen who crossed the ocean. Harvard graduates in large numbers sought ministerial posts in England. One of them, Nathaniel Mather, wrote to his friends who were still in Massachusetts, "'Tis a notion of mighty great and high respect to have been a New England man, 'tis enough to gain a man very much respect, yea almost any preferment."[69] With this return migration the Plymouth churches, which had always struggled financially, found it increasingly difficult to find qualified ministers. Following the death of John Reyner, the Plymouth church on a number of occasions wrote to the churches of Massachusetts "craving their best help for a supply, but could not obtain any help notwithstanding their said endeavors, which also were accompanied by fasting and prayer."[70] In his appreciation of Ralph Partridge, Cotton Mather praised him for the fact that the Duxbury clergyman stayed at his post at "a time when most of the ministers in the colony of Plymouth left the colony, upon the discouragement [from] . . . the want of a competent maintenance."[71] Those churches were left to rely on lay prophesying as in the past. Shortly after Brewster's death Thomas Cushman, Robert Cushman's son, was chosen as the new elder, assisting John Reyner.[72] Cushman, along with another layman, Thomas Southworth (who "had a good ability to preach publicly"), were largely responsible for the services until John Cotton Jr. was chosen as the congregation's pastor in 1659.[73]

The puritans who settled Plymouth had embraced the idea of searching for further light. The 1632 prophesying showed an openness to considering opposing views. Roger Williams was given an opportunity to share his ideas, and although they were considered troublesome by Brewster and others, Williams was not expelled. Recognizing that he had not won over the local congregation, he moved on to Salem. But the congregation dismissed him as being in good standing. So too did the church consider and seek to accommodate Charles Chauncy's somewhat eccentric views on full immersion baptism. When he settled elsewhere in Plymouth's jurisdiction, his call by the Scituate church was not questioned—a sharp difference from when the Massachusetts authorities intervened to pressure Salem into not calling Williams to the ministry after he arrived there from Plymouth.

One of the concerns that Brewster had expressed regarding Williams was that the young man was proceeding along the path that John Smyth had traveled in the Netherlands. Baptist ideas caused unease because they were associated with the capture of the German city of Munster by radical Anabaptists in 1534, an event that other Protestants believed had led to social disruption, moral anarchy, and ultimately the loss of lives in a siege and capture of the city. But while fearful of the extremes of Baptist views, the Plymouth puritans were open to discussing the issues surrounding baptism. Brewster had exchanged views with Higginson in the early 1630s. Chauncy's views were entertained. When Harvard's president Henry Dunster became persuaded that infant baptism was not justified, efforts were made to convince him otherwise. When he was unwilling to reach an accommodation, he left Massachusetts Bay and was welcomed as pastor of the Plymouth colony church in Scituate.

The advocacy of a toleration for their own ideas by England's Dissenting Brethren was well known in New England, and in the mid-1640s there were a number of efforts to ensure tolerance toward diverse views in the colonies. In 1645 William Vassall, who had been one of the lay leaders of the Scituate church following the departure of John Lothrop, petitioned the Plymouth General Court "to allow and maintain full and free tolerance of religion to all men that would pre-serve the civil peace." Its genesis may very well have been in the disputes that were roiling Scituate. Charles Chauncy, who had moved from the town of Plymouth to become that town's minister, had sought to ex-communicate those members of the congregation who did not accept his views on communion and baptism. Vassall and his supporters, who had considered themselves the remnants of the Scituate church estab-lished by John Lathrop, having failed to be recognized as the town's legitimate church, had sought and been thwarted in their efforts to get their congregation separately recognized. There was a political context to this division as well, with Chauncy maintaining that freemanship should be limited to members of recognized congregations and Vassall with his supporters denying that there should be such a test.

Information about the Vassall petition for toleration is known from a letter Edward Winslow sent to John Winthrop. Winslow complained that the proposal made no "limitation or exception against the Turk, Jew, Papist, Arian, Socinian, Nicholaytan Familist or any other, etc." These last were clearly beyond the pale of acceptable discourse, but the deputies apparently supported the petition while the colony leaders opposed it. Winslow complained about the supporters, noting how "sweet this carrion relished to the palates of most of the deputies!" The procedures of the Plymouth General Court required that such a petition be put to a vote, but Bradford "would not suffer it to come to a vote as being that indeed would eat out the power of godliness, etc." Presumably the governor ensured that no mention of it would appear in the official records.[74] But the episode reveals that there was considerable sentiment for toleration in the colony, a sentiment that likely explains the relatively modest actions taken in Plymouth against dissenters.

Over the next decade Plymouth did begin to crack down on Baptists and on the newly arrived Quakers, though the punishments meted out were not as severe as those in the Bay colony. Massachusetts had begun to exert a stronger cultural influence, drawing Plymouth to-ward its example. The English monarchy had been restored in 1660, and in 1685 the English courts revoked the Massachusetts Bay charter, demanded the surrender of the other New England colonial charters, and merged the region into a single Dominion of New England under a governor-general appointed by the king. That regime was toppled by a revolt of Bostonians in 1689, and the old order was partially restored. A new charter granted to Massachusetts in 1691 saw the absorption of Plymouth into Massachusetts, making official what had become a cultural reality.

Toward the close of Bradford's final dialogue with the colony's young men, he expressed the hope that the next generation would not "lose what your fathers have obtained with so much hardships" such as those detailed in his history of the colony. He told them, "you have been called unto liberty," and urged them to "use not liberty for an occasion to the flesh, but by love serve one another."[75] That was the legacy of Brewster, Bradford, and the group of believers who had first gathered in the Scrooby manor house. Tested by their voyage and their "starving time," they had learned to trust one another and to care for one another. In America, they had sacrificed to create a colony in which ordinary men and women governed themselves. The colony was never effectively controlled by the king, nor by a proprietor, nor by a corporation of investors. From the signing of the Mayflower Compact to the suppression of their colony's identity over a half-century later, the people of Plymouth had governed themselves. Their churches were created not by the action of bishops or presbyteries but were by and for lay believers. The participatory character of this rule sometimes led to policies and actions that failed to live up to the highest ideals of the founders, and in others facilitated the expression of prejudices that later generations would condemn. But as they would have readily admitted, they were fallible sinners who hoped that they could move beyond their present imperfections to receive further light.

Acknowledgments

This book is the product of my half-century of seeking to engage with the world and ideas of the men and women who settled New England. I first became engaged in the subject as a student at Fordham College, where I was introduced to Perry Miller's "Errand into the Wilderness" essay in a historiography course taught by Raymond Cunningham. I was able to explore the interrelationship between New England puritans and England in a Columbia University dissertation under the supervision of Alden T. Vaughan, who became and remains a friend and sounding board. Chilton Williamson Jr., a fellow student at Columbia, became an editor at St. Martin's Press and encouraged me to organize the notes on puritans that I had compiled for my doctoral orals study group into a book. That became *The Puritan Experiment: New England Society from Bradford to Edwards.* Shortly after that I was awarded a summer fellowship to participate in a seminar on anthropological approaches to early America directed by Timothy H. Breen at Northwestern University. While there I met Stephen Foster, and both have been fonts of information and advice over the succeeding years.

Over those years I have been able to draw on the knowledge and support of numerous scholars who participated in programs I organized and to spend time at some of the principal universities of England and Ireland. Christopher Hill came from Oxford to Thomas More College in Kentucky, where I was teaching, to keynote a conference titled "Puritanism in Old and New England," and subsequently became a good friend. While at Cambridge University on a Fulbright Fellowship I met Patrick Collinson and John Morrill, who were supportive and introduced me to many young scholars of Tudor-Stuart England, some of whom are acknowledged in what follows. John Morrill became a close friend and collaborator on a variety of projects. All of these contacts reinforced a focus on puritanism as a transatlantic movement, which became characteristic of my work. Another friend, Diarmaid MacCulloch, secured a fellowship for me at St. Cross College, Oxford, which gave me an opportunity to pursue research there. And Crawford Gribben suggested I apply for a Long Room Fellowship at Trinity College, Dublin, where the two of us had many fruitful exchanges of ideas. It was there that I began to devote increasing interest to the role of the laity in the shaping of puritanism.

Martin Wood was an avid local historian in Groton, Suffolk, England, who, along with his wife, Jane, provided hospitality and local expertise when I explored the world of John Winthrop and puritanism in general through East Anglia.

As for this current book, I owe much to Rebecca Fraser, David Lupher, Donald Yacovone, and Rose Doherty. Rebecca, fresh from the research for her own study of *The Mayflower: The Families, the Voyage, and the Founding of America* (2017), read drafts of this entire work and offered suggestions and encouragement. David Lupher, who had similarly immersed himself in the sources for early Plymouth for his impressive study of *Greeks, Romans, and Pilgrims: Classical Receptions in Early New England* (2017), took extraordinary pains to save me from errors of fact and infelicitous expression of my ideas, as well as discussing some critical issues regarding the congregation. Robert Charles (Bob) Anderson shared his vast knowledge of the men and women who settled in Plymouth. Donald Yacovone and Rose Doherty both read the entire manuscript and provided essential insights.

I first met Jeremy Bangs when I was researching John Davenport's years in the Netherlands. He went out of his way to guide me through the archives, show me the American Pilgrim Museum in Leiden, and discuss the puritan presence in the Netherlands in the early seventeenth century. As the four hundredth anniversary of the settlement of Plymouth approached, I came to rely more and more on his work and have joined with him on a number of projects. He is more knowledgeable than anyone else on the history of the group that originated in Scrooby and ended up in New England.

In the course of research and writing I reached out to many for information on various points. Among those who have helped are Adrian Chastain Weimer, Anthony Milton, Michael Braddick, John Morrill, Jan Van de Kamp, Sue Allan, Andrew Fitzmaurice, Diarmaid MacCulloch, Ken Minkema, Chad Van Dixhoorn, Tom Freeman, and Paula Peters.

I am grateful to John Demos, who read the proposal for this book for Oxford University Press and encouraged the press to publish it. At Oxford I am very fortunate to have worked with Susan Ferber. She was the editor for *John Winthrop: America's Forgotten Founding Father* (2003) and largely responsible for its success. Once again she has been a supportive and meticulous editor who has saved me from errors of fact and style, and constantly reminded me of the importance of being understood by the audience I have been writing for.

As always, my wife, Bobbi, our children, and our grandchildren provide the foundations of my life that make all my scholarship possible.

Notes

The most important source for the history of the Plymouth colony is William Bradford's *Of Plimoth Plantation*. A new edition of that work will be published in two forms in 2020 through a project supported by the Colonial Society of Massachusetts and the New England Historic and Genealogical Society under the aegis of New England Beginnings. The editorial team consists of Kenneth P. Minkema, Francis J. Bremer, and Jeremy Bangs, with a special introduction by Paula Peters of the Wampanoag nation and Bradford's Hebrew lists edited and introduced by Eric D. Reymond. First, there will be a born-digital online resource that features a verbatim transcription, within the constraints of typography, that includes notes on textual and historical material. The result will be viewable at the websites of the Massachusetts State Library (mass.gov/orgs/state-library-of-massachusetts), the Colonial Society of Massachusetts (colonialsociety.org), and the New England Historic Genealogical Society (americanancestors.org). Second, there will be a print edition, with slight modernization of the text and extensive annotation on the content. This will be published as Kenneth Minkema, Francis J. Bremer, and Jeremy Bangs, editors, *"Of Plimoth Plantation" by William Bradford* (Boston: The Colonial Society of Massachusetts and the New England Historic and Genealogical Society, 2020). In both these versions as well as most earlier editions, the manuscript pages are indicated in brackets. In the following notes the work is abbreviated as OPP and page references are to the actual manuscript pages.

Prologue: Disease and Death in Early Plymouth

1. Scurvy had not been anticipated by the colonists, but they learned enough so that in a 1621 letter Plymouth's Edward Winslow recommended lemon juice be taken by those who journeyed to America. Jeremy Dupertuis Bangs, *Pilgrim Edward Winslow: New England's First International Diplomat* (Boston: New England Historic and Genealogical Society, 2004), 47.

2. OPP, 55.

3. *A Journal of the Pilgrims at Plymouth: Mourt's Relation*, ed. Dwight B. Heath (New York: Corinth Books, 1963), 45.

4. *Mourt's Relation*, 47.

5. Godfrey Hodgson, *A Great and Godly Adventure: The Pilgrims and the Myth of the First Thanksgiving* (New York: Public Affairs, 2006), 89–90.

6. OPP, 55.

7. Seventy-eight percent of the women who sailed on the *Mayflower* died in the first winter, leaving only five alive—Eleanor Billington, Elizabeth Hopkins, Mary Brewster, Susanna (White) Winslow, and Katherine Carver.

8. OPP, 55. At this distance of time we cannot fully appreciate some of the physical aspects and sensory experiences involved in tending the sick and other aspects of everyday life, a point made by Martha L. Finch in *Dissenting Bodies: Corporalities in Early New England* (New York: Columbia University Press, 2010), 20–21.

9. Edward Arber, ed., *The Story of the Pilgrim Fathers . . . as Told by Themselves, Their Friends, and Their Enemies* (Boston: Houghton Mifflin, 1897), 359–360.

10. *Mourt's Relation*, 42.

11. Bangs, *Winslow*, 96.

12. *Mourt's Relation*, 44.

13. Francis Higginson, quoted in Francis J. Bremer, *First Founders: American Puritans and Puritanism in an Atlantic World* (Hanover, NH: University Press of New England, 2012), 33. It might be noted that Higginson himself died within a year of arriving in New England.

14. George Percy, *A Trewe Ralacion*, quoted in *Captain John Smith: Writings with Other Narratives of Roanoke, Jamestown, and the First English Settlement of America* (New York: Library of America, 2007), 1100. Percy's account had not yet been published, but his story was known to those who followed the progress of England's efforts at colonization.

15. Robert C. Anderson, *The Great Migration Begins: Immigrants to New England 1620–1633*, Volume 1: *A–F* (Boston: New England Historic and Genealogical Society, 1995), 274.

16. *Mourt's Relation*, 35–37.

17. *Mourt's Relation*, 42, 43.

18. James Horn, *Adapting to a New World: English Society in the Seventeenth-Century Chesapeake* (Chapel Hill: University of North Carolina Press, 1994), 55–56.

19. OPP, 24.

Introduction

1. Among the histories are John Demos, *A Little Commonwealth: Family Life in Plymouth Colony* (New York: Oxford University Press, 1970); Darrett B. Rutman, *Husbandmen of Plymouth: Farms and Villages in the Old Colony, 1620–1692* (Boston: Beacon Press, 1967); Eugene A. Stratton, *Plymouth Colony: Its History and People, 1620–1691* (Salt Lake City: Ancestry Publications, 1986); Jeremy Dupertuis Bangs, *Strangers and Pilgrims, Travelers and Sojourners: Leiden and the Foundations of Plymouth Plantation* (Plymouth, MA: General Society of Mayflower Descendants, 2009); Nathaniel Philbrick, *Mayflower: A Story of Courage, Community, and War* (New York: Viking, 2006); Nick Bunker, *Making Haste from Babylon: The Mayflower Pilgrims and Their World* (New York: Knopf, 2010); James Deetz and Patricia Scott Deetz, *The Times of Their Lives: Life, Love, and Death in Plymouth Colony* (New York: W. H. Freeman, 2000); Rebecca Fraser, *The Mayflower: The Families, the Voyage, and the Founding of America* (New York: St. Martin's, 2017); David A. Lupher, *Greeks, Romans, and Pilgrims: Classical Receptions in Early America* (Leiden: Brill, 2017); Douglas Anderson, *William Bradford's Books: Of Plimmoth Plantation and the Printed Word* (Baltimore: Johns Hopkins University Press, 2003); and George D. Langdon Jr., *Pilgrim Colony: A History of New Plymouth, 1620–1691* (New Haven: Yale University Press, 1966). The poetic treatment is Longfellow's "Courtship of Miles Standish." Novels include Ernest Gebler's *The Plymouth Adventure* (Garden City, NY: Doubleday, 1950), and Sue Allan's *The Mayflower Maid* (Burgess Hill, Sussex: Domtom Publishing, 2006). The 1952 Hollywood production of Gebler's novel centered on a fictional love triangle between the *Mayflower's* Captain Christopher Jones (Spencer Tracy), Dorothy Bradford (Gene Tierney), and Dorothy's husband, William Bradford (Leo Glenn). More recently, documentaries include the History Channel's *Desperate Crossing, American Experience: The Pilgrims*, and National Geographic's *Saints and Strangers*. Books touching on the early puritan history of New England and Plymouth in particular that are scheduled to appear around the time of the four hundredth anniversary of the Mayflower's journey and the establishment of the colony include works by Michael Winship, Andrew Lipman, Abram van Engen, David Silverman, Michael Oberg, Linford Fisher, John Turner, and others.

2. Exceptions to this are Jeremy Bang's *Strangers and Pilgrims*, which provides unparalleled treatment of the organization of the congregation in Scrooby, England, and their stay in the Netherlands, and also Michael

P. Winship's *Godly Republicanism: Puritans, Pilgrims, and a City on a Hill* (Cambridge, MA: Harvard University Press, 2012).

3. They were using it in the same general sense that another seventeenth-century puritan, John Bunyan, would apply it in his story of the *Pilgrim's Progress* (1678).

4. While some scholars question the use of the term "puritan," the scholarly consensus, particularly among English historians, is that it does help to identify a broad range of individuals in the sixteenth and seventeenth century who sought to "purify" the Church of England from Roman Catholic remnants and to advance ideas and practices generally derived from the Reformed Protestant tradition. My use of a lowercase "p" in talking about these individuals—puritans rather than Puritans—follows a practice that seeks to avoid defining the movement and beliefs too precisely, and suggests the breadth of the spectrum on which these individuals found themselves. For further discussion of these issues, see Francis J. Bremer, *Puritanism: A Very Short Introduction* (New York: Oxford University Press, 2009).

5. Typical of these works was Charles Francis Adams, *Three Episodes of Massachusetts History* (Boston: Houghton Mifflin, 1892).

6. See Fred C. Hobson, *Mencken: A Life* (New York: Random House, 1994), 190.

7. See, for example, Samuel Eliot Morison, *The Puritan Pronaos: Studies in the Intellectual Life of Colonial New England* (New York: New York University Press, 1936), and *Builders of the Bay Colony* (Boston: Houghton Mifflin, 1930); Perry Miller, *Orthodoxy in Massachusetts* (Boston: Beacon Press, 1959), *The New England Mind: The Seventeenth Century* (Cambridge, MA: Harvard University Press, 1939), and *The New England Mind: From Colony to Province* (Cambridge, MA: Harvard University Press, 1953); Edmund S. Morgan, *The Puritan Family* (Boston: Trustees of the Public Library, 1944), and *Visible Saints: The History of a Puritan Idea* (New York: New York University Press, 1963); and Stephen Foster, *The Long Argument: English Puritanism and the Shaping of New England Culture* (Chapel Hill: University of North Carolina Press, 1991).

8. Examples of works that take religion seriously are David D. Hall, *A Reforming People: Puritanism and the Transformation of Public Life in New England* (New York: Knopf, 2011); and Michael P. Winship, *Godly Republicanism: Puritans, Pilgrims and a City on a Hill* (Cambridge, MA: Harvard University Press, 2012) and *Hot Protestants: A History of Puritanism in England and America* (New Haven: Yale University Press, 2019).

9. Examples include Lyle Koehler, *Search for Power: The "Weaker Sex" in Seventeenth-Century New England* (Urbana: University of Illinois Press, 1980), and Darren Staloff, *Making of an American Thinking Class: Intellectuals and Intelligentsia in Puritan Massachusetts* (New York: Oxford University Press, 1997).

10. The first claim that Cromwell said this was in Horace Walpole's *Anecdotes of Painting in England* (1754). It is surprising that no one previously would have recorded such an instruction in the almost hundred years since Cromwell's death. But it is likely that the Lord Protector gave some such instruction to Lely, since the portrait's realism is different from how the artist painted other prominent individuals, and because Cromwell was known to disdain all forms of personal vanity. I thank John Morrill (email November 22, 2018) for his views on the subject.

11. My thinking on this point has been influenced by James L. Kugel's *The Great Shift: Encountering God in Biblical Times* (New York: Houghton Mifflin Harcourt, 2017).

12. I have discussed this general theme in *Lay Empowerment and the Development of Puritanism* (London: Palgrave Macmillan, 2016) and elsewhere.

13. OPP, 181.

Chapter 1

1. Christopher Marsh, *Popular Religion in Sixteenth-Century England* (Basingstoke: Macmillan, 1998), 169.

2. One of the Lollards, quoted in Claire Cross, *Church and People, 1450–1660: The Triumph of the Laity in the English Church* (Hassocks: Harvester Press, 1976), 9–10.

3. My thinking on this point has been influenced by James L. Kugel's *The Great Shift: Encountering God in Biblical Times* (New York: Houghton Mifflin Harcourt, 2017).

4. John Robinson, *A Justification of Separation from the Church of England* (1610), 32.

5. William Tyndale, *The Whole Works of W. Tyndal, John Frith, and Doc. Barnes* (1573), 285–286. See David Daniell, *William Tyndale: A Biography* (New Haven: Yale University Press, 1994).

6. For an overview of this background, see Michael P. Winship, *Hot Protestants: A History of Puritanism in England and America* (New Haven: Yale University Press, 2019).

7. Robert Cushman, *The Cry of a Stone: A Treatise Showing What Is Right Matter, Form and Government of the Visible Church of Christ*, reprinted from edition of 1642; edited by Michael R. Paulick; transcription and annotation by James Baker (Plymouth, MA: General Society of Mayflower Descendants, 2016), 141.

8. Browne himself, whose name became synonymous with separatism, eventually reconciled with the Church of England, though retaining many of his general puritan positions. See Robert Charles Anderson, *Puritan Pedigrees: The Deep Roots of the Puritan Migration to New England* (Boston: New England Historic and Genealogical Society, 2019), ch. 7.

9. The date is generally given as 1566. Sue Allan argues for 1564 or 1565. Sue Allan, *William Brewster, The Making of a Pilgrim* (Burgfess Hill Sussex: Domton Publishing, 2016), 20.

10. Godfrey Hodgson, *A Great and Godly Adventure: The Pilgrims and the Myth of the First Thanksgiving* (New York: Public Affairs, 2006), 23; H. Kirk-Smith, *William Brewster, "The Father of New England": His Life and Times, 1567–1644* (Boston, UK: Richard Kay, 1992), 15.

11. Mary B. Sherwood, *Pilgrim: A Biography of William Brewster* (Falls Church, VA: Great Oaks Press, 1982), 14–18.

12. Kirk-Smith, *Brewster*, 17.

13. OPP, 254.

14. Allan, *Brewster*, 69.

15. Francis J. Bremer, *Congregational Communion: Clerical Friendships in the Anglo-American Puritan Community, 1610–1692* (Boston: Northeastern University Press, 1994), 27.

16. For the puritan influence at Oxford at this time, see Francis J. Bremer, *Building a New Jerusalem: John Davenport, a Puritan in Three Worlds* (New Haven: Yale University Press, 2012), 26–34. For the puritan presence at Cambridge, see Bremer, *Congregational Communion*, ch. 1.

17. William Patterson, *William Perkins and the Making of Protestant England* (New York: Oxford University Press, 2014), has argued that Perkins was not a puritan, but this is not entirely convincing. Perkins's Calvinist credentials are unquestioned, and Patterson's judgment is dependent on how one defined "puritans," a matter that is more difficult than often presented, as I will discuss in the next chapter.

18. Kirk-Smith, *Brewster*, 28; Sherwood, *Pilgrims*, 19; Hodgson, *Godly Adventure*, 28; David A. Lupher, *Greeks, Romans, and Pilgrims: Classical Republicanism in Early New England* (Leiden: Brill, 2017), 187–188.

19. In examining what he was likely reading at this time and in later periods of his life, I have broken Brewster's career into key periods and make

the assumption that he acquired and read most of the books when they were published or soon thereafter. While it is of course possible that he acquired some books long after they were published, by grouping his reading in this fashion we may get an idea of his intellectual development. With some exceptions, grouping books to a particular time in his life does seem to illuminate shifts in his thought and interests. An examination of these particular titles makes it likely that they were part of his college education. What is, of course, impossible to determine is whether the books altered his views or were acquired because of changes in his beliefs.

20. Lupher, *Greeks, Romans, and Pilgrims*, 211–212.

21. Analysis based on the inventory as presented in Jeremy Duperius Bangs, *Plymouth Colony's Private Libraries* (Leiden: Leiden American Pilgrim Museum, 2016).

22. Henry Martyn Dexter and Morton Dexter, *The England and Holland of the Pilgrims* (Boston: Houghton Mifflin, 1905), 282–283.

23. OPP, 254.

24. Dorothy Brewster, *William Brewster of the Mayflower: Portrait of a Pilgrim* (New York: New York University Press, 1970), 27.

25. Pearson, *Cartwright*, 189–190; one of those letters is published as Appendix XIII.

26. A. F. Scott Pearson, *Thomas Cartwright and Elizabethan Puritanism, 1535–1603* (Cambridge, UK: Cambridge University Press, 1925), 170–176.

27. Stubbs to William Davison, April 30, 1578, in Lloyd E. Berry, *John Stubbs' Gaping Gulf, with Letters and Other Relevant Documents* (Charlottesville: University of Virginia Press, 1968), 106–107.

28. Jeremy Dupertuis Bangs, *Strangers and Pilgrims, Travelers and Sojourners: Leiden and the Foundations of Plymouth Plantation* (Plymouth, MA: General Society of Mayflower Descendants, 2009), 130–136.

29. OPP, 254.

30. OPP, 254; Douglas Anderson, *William Bradford's Books: Of Plimmoth Plantation and the Printed Word* (Baltimore: Johns Hopkins University Press, 2003), 212.

31. Pearson, *Cartwright*, 210–211.

32. Sandys had replaced Grindal as archbishop in 1577. Scrooby manor was one of the holdings of the archbishopric.

33. Kirk-Smith, *Brewster*, 255–256.

34. OPP, 254.

35. There is ample documentary evidence of Brewster as postmaster. While there is no surviving evidence that demonstrates that he followed his

father in the position of the archbishop's bailiff and receiver, it is generally assumed that this was the case.

36. Kirk-Smith, *Brewster*, 47–50.

37. Bangs, *Strangers and Pilgrims*, 29–31; Hodgson, *Godly Adventure*, 31.

38. I thank Sue Allan, Jeremy Bangs, and Bob Anderson for discussion of this.

39. Willem J. op 't Hof, "The Eventful Sojourn of Willem Teellinck (1579–1629) at Banbury in 1605," *Journal for the History of Reformed Pietism*, 1 (2015), 15–16. For more on Teellinck, see Ariwe de Reuver, *Sweet Communion: Trajectories of Spirituality from the Middle Ages through the Further Reformation*, translated by James A. De Jong (Grand Rapids: Reformation Heritage Books, 2007), 105–162.

40. Bangs, *Strangers and Pilgrims*, 31–32.

41. OPP, 254.

42. Bangs, *Strangers and Pilgrims*, 27; Kirk-Smith, *Brewster*, 75–76.

43. OPP, 254.

Chapter 2

1. For the challenges to Calvinism in Cambridge, see Francis J. Bremer, *Congregational Communion: Clerical Friendship in the Anglo-American Puritan Community, 1610–1692* (Boston: Northeastern University Press, 1994), 35ff.

2. For Arminianism see Anthony Milton, *Catholic and Reformed: The Roman and Protestant Churches in English Protestant Thought, 1600–1640* (Cambridge, UK: Cambridge University Press, 1995).

3. Eamon Duffy, *The Stripping of the Altars* (New Haven: Yale University Press, 2005).

4. For a full discussion of this, see John Craig, "The Growth of English Puritanism," in John Coffey and Paul C. H. Lim, eds., *The Cambridge Companion to Puritanism* (Cambridge, UK: Cambridge University Press, 2008), 34–47; and Tom Webster, "Early Stuart Puritanism," in Coffey and Lim, *Companion*, 48–66.

5. For much of this, see Patrick Collinson, *The Elizabethan Puritan Movement* (London: Cape, 1967).

6. Peter Lake, *The Boxmaker's Revenge: "Orthodoxy," "Heterodoxy," and the Politics of the Parish in Early Stuart London* (Stanford: Stanford University Press, 2001), writes about "a world . . . of godly seeking, where conversations with and rumours about a variety of more or less sectarian experiments and claims were commonplace," 183.

7. See Michael P. Winship, *Godly Republicanism: Puritans, Pilgrims, and a City on a Hill* (Cambridge, MA: Harvard University Press, 2012), 41–44; and Karl Gunther, *Reformation Unbound: Protestant Visions of Reform in England, 1525–1590* (Cambridge, UK: Cambridge University Press, 2014), 119.

8. Matthew Reynolds, *Godly Reformers and Their Opponents in Early Modern England: Religion in Norwich, c.1560–1643* (Woodbridge: Boydell, 2005), 88–89.

9. Reynolds, *Godly Reformers*, 89.

10. M. Moody, "Browne, Robert (1550?–1633), religious separatist," in *Oxford Dictionary of National Biography*, September 23, 2004, retrieved April 16, 2019, from http://www.oxforddnb.com/view/10.1093/ref:odnb/ 9780198614128.001.0001/odnb-9780198614128-e-3695.

11. Ibid. For more on Browne's later career, see Robert Charles Anderson, *Puritan Pedigrees: The Deep Roots of the Great Migration* (Boston: New England Historic and Genealogical Society, 2018), ch. 7.

12. R. Bayne, "Harrison, Robert (d. c. 1585), Brownist and writer," in *Oxford Dictionary of National Biography*, September 23, 2004, retrieved April 16, 2019, from http://www.oxforddnb.com/view/10.1093/ref:odnb/ 9780198614128.001.0001/odnb-9780198614128-e-12442.

13. M. Moody, "Johnson, Francis (bap. 1562, d. 1617), separatist minister and religious controversialist," in *Oxford Dictionary of National Biography*, September 23, 2004, retrieved April 16, 2019, from http:// www.oxforddnb.com/view/10.1093/ref:odnb/9780198614128.001.0001/ odnb-9780198614128-e-14877.

14. M. Moody, "Greenwood, John (c. 1560–1593), religious controversialist," in *Oxford Dictionary of National Biography*, May 24, 2007, retrieved April 16, 2019, from http://www.oxforddnb.com/view/10.1093/ref:odnb/ 9780198614128.001.0001/odnb-9780198614128-e-11436.

15. Freke quoted in Reynolds, *Godly Reformers*, 91.

16. P. Collinson, "Barrow, Henry (c. 1550–1593), religious separatist," in *Oxford Dictionary of National Biography*, September 23, 2004, retrieved April 16, 2019, from http://www.oxforddnb.com/view/10.1093/ref:odnb/ 9780198614128.001.0001/odnb-9780198614128-e-1540.

17. Francis Fulwood, *The Church-History of Britain . . . endeavored by Thomas Fuller* (1655), 472.

18. Fulwood, *Church-History*, 470–471.

19. Edward Winslow, *Hypocrisie Unmasked* (1646), 97–98.

20. In a talk that was part of a program at Suffolk University in Boston on New England Puritans and Native Americans, October 25, 2018, David D. Hall

asserted that Robinson was a hard-core Calvinist. While that description fits with his stance on some issues it does not extend to all aspects of his thought.

21. Godfrey Hodgson, *A Great and Godly Adventure: The Pilgrims and the Myth of the First Thanksgiving* (New York: Public Affairs, 2006), 31.

22. OPP, 6. When he was "about twelve years old," which is how Cotton Mather described Bradford's attendance on Clfyton's preaching would have meant that he was traveling to Babworth, which was about nine miles from Austerfield. However, in 1605, when Bradford would have been fifteen, Clifton was deprived of his living in Babworth and began preaching without license in Bawtry, which was less than a mile from Austerfield and less than two miles from Scrooby, which makes it more likely that he first heard Clifton at Bawtry.

23. Jeremy Dupertuis Bangs, *Strangers and Pilgrims, Travellers and Sojourners: Leiden and the Foundations of Plymouth Plantation* (Plymouth, MA: Society of Mayflower Descendants, 2009), 29.

24. Nick Bunker, *Making Haste from Babylon: The Mayflower Pilgrims and Their Worlds* (New York: Knopf, 2010), 151–152.

25. Bangs, *Strangers and Pilgrims*, 1.

26. Ronald A. Marchant, *The Puritans and the Church Courts in the Diocese of York, 1560–1642* (London: Longmans, 1960), 141–143. The preacher who was rotating between Scrooby and Bawtry was John Deacon. Deacon was a "godly preacher," likely suggested to James Brewster by William. At the time Deacon was engaged in the debate centered on an outbreak of witchcraft in Lancashire. John Darrell was a Cambridge graduate who had earned a reputation as a spiritual healer, having on more than one occasion cast out demons from individuals possessed as a result of witchcraft. The exorcisms attracted popular audiences that were viewed with suspicion by the authorities. Archbishop John Whitgift ordered an investigation that resulted in the prosecution of Darrell for fraud when some of the possessed admitted that they had feigned their symptoms. Darrell was deprived of holy orders and imprisoned, though released in 1599. Deacon coauthored two tracts on the controversy in which he was critical of Darrell, possession in postbiblical times, and exorcism. But he defended his fellow puritan against the charges of fraud and sought to prevent the controversy being used to discredit the godly. See Thomas Freeman, "Demons, Deviance and Defiance: John Darrell and the Politics of Exorcism in Late Elizabethan England," in Peter Lake and Michael Questier, eds., *Conformity and Orthodoxy in the English Church, c.1650–1660* (Woodbridge, Suffolk: Boydell, 2000), 51–55. Marion

Gibson notes that in one of his treatises Deacon mentions Bawtry in his text as "Eirtwb." She also believes that Darrell certainly knew John Smyth and John Robinson as well as Deacon. Gibson, *Possession, Puritanism and Print: Darrell, Harsnett, Shakespeare and the Elizabethan Exorcism Controversy* (London: Routledge, 2006), 145–150.

27. Quoted in Marchant, *Diocese of York*, 141–143.

28. See Jeremy Bangs, "William Brewster's Preaching in St. Wilfrid Church, Scrooby, 1598," *Mayflower Quarterly*, 72 (2006), 239–241.

29. John Robinson, *A Justification of Separation from the Church of England against Mr. Richard Beernard* (1610), 236.

30. For a further discussion of this aside from the remainder of this book, see Francis J. Bremer, *Lay Empowerment and the Development of Puritanism* (London: Palgrave Macmillan, 2015). This practice bore a striking resemblance to the future Quaker meetings, reinforcing the roots of the Religious Society of Friends in the broad puritan movement. See also Peter Iver Kaufman, *Thinking of the Laity in Late Tudor England* (South Bend: University of Notre Dame Press, 1994).

31. For a fuller discussion of this topic and women who assumed such roles, see Bremer, *Lay Empowerment,* especially 39–42.

32. The texts are 1 Corinthians 14:34 and 1 Timothy 2:12–13.

33. Robinson, *Justification of Separation*, 237; John Robinson, *The Peoples Plea for the Exercise of Prophesy Against Mr. Yates* (1618), 66–67.

34. Joel Halcomb, "Godly Order and the Trumpet of Defiance: The Politics of Congregational Church Life during the English Revolution," in Michael Davies, Anne Dunnan-Page, and Joel Halcomb, eds., *Church Life: Pastors, Congregations, and the Experience of Dissent in Seventeenth-Century England* (Oxford: Oxford University Press, 2019), 32.

35. Keith Sprunger, *Dutch Puritanism* (Leiden: Brill, 1973), 333–334.

36. Stephen Goffe in the Hague, April 26, 1633, to William Laud, SP 16/286/202.

37. Keith Sprunger points out that the practice of women voting for officers was evidently discontinued after Peter's departure, but that women "did have a special role in the Rotterdam church through their own weekday prayer, praise, and communion service." Sprunger, *Dutch Puritanism*, 331.

38. It has been suggested that this was also the case in the selection of John Bunyan to minister to the Bedford church. See Davies, Dunnan-Page, and Halcomb, "Introduction," *Church Life*, 5.

39. For this campaign, see Patrick Collinson, *Bancroft and Elizabethan Antipuritanism* (Cambridge, UK: Cambridge University Press, 2013).

40. S. J. Brachlow, "John Robinson," in Richard L. Greaves and Robert Zalleer, eds., *Biographical Dictionary of British Radicals in the Seventeenth Century*, 3 vols. (Brighton, UK: Harvester Press, 1984), 3:103.

41. Bangs, *Strangers and Pilgrims*, 22–26.

42. Brachlow, "Robinson."

43. John Robinson, *A Manumission to a Manuduction, or Answer to a Letter Inferring Public Communion in the parish Assemblies* (1615), 20.

44. Timothy George, *John Robinson and the English Separatist Tradition* (Macon, GA: Mercer University Press, 1982), 82–83.

45. The idea that such naming was common among puritans is a myth. But it was adopted by some zealous believers, which makes the practice of the Brewsters suggestive.

46. Nathaniel Morton, *New-Englands Memorial* (1669), 20–21.

47. H. Kirk-Smith, *William Brewster, "The Father of New England": His Life and Times, 1567–1644* (Boston, Lincolnshire: Richard Kay, 1992), 81.

48. OPP, 255.

49. Quoted in George, *Robinson*, 84–85.

50. OPP, 6.

51. A discussion of this first covenant of the Scrooby-Leiden-Plymouth congregation is provided by Douglas Horton in "The Scrooby Covenant," *Unitarian Historical Society Proceedings*, 11 (1957), 1–13.

52. Fuller quoted in Horton, "Scrooby Covenant," 2–3.

53. Jacob, quoted in Stephen Brachlow, *The Communion of the Saints: Radical Puritans and Separatist Ecclesiology, 1570–1625* (New York: Oxford University Press, 1988), 37.

54. Polly Ha, "The Freedom of Association and Ecclesiastical Independence," in Davies, Dunnan-Page, and Halcomb, *Church Life*, 113–114.

55. Walter Craddock, quoted in Geoffrey F. Nuttall, *The Holy Spirit in Puritan Faith and Experience*, with a new introduction by Peter Lake (Chicago: University of Chicago Press, 1992), 142.

56. Robinson, *Justification of Separation*, 126.

57. Hodgson, *Godly Adventure*, 31.

58. "A Dialogue or the Summe of Conference between some young men born in New England and sundry Ancient Men that came out of Holland and Old England," in *Publications of the Colonial Society of Massachusetts*, Volume 22: *Plymouth Church Records, 1620–1859, Part One*, 140.

59. Dorothy Brewster, *William Brewster of the Mayflower: Portrait of a Pilgrim* (New York: New York University Press, 1970), 59.

60. Kirk-Smith, *Brewster*, 72.

61. Bangs, *Strangers and Pilgrims*, 26.

62. Quoted in Henry Martyn Dexter and Morton Dexter, *The England and Holland of the Pilgrims* (Boston: Houghton Mifflin, 1905), 400.

63. Bunker, *Making Haste*, 176.

64. Kirk-Smith, *Brewster* (73), suggests that for a time at least the members of these two churches continued to attend some services and receive the sacraments at their parish churches, pointing out that no residents of Scrooby, Worksop, Sutton-cum-Lound, and Austerfield were presented by the church authorities for being absent from the sacraments, and only two in Babworth. This is not conclusive but does suggest a group of believers searching for further light on these matters. Eventually, the Scrooby congregation would reject all contact with parish churches and their ceremonies, but then reverse themselves so far as to allow attendance to join in prayer and listen to sermons, while forbidding joining in the administration of sacraments.

65. William Bradford, *A Dialogue or Third Conference between some young men born in New England, and some Ancient Men which came out of Holland and Old England*, ed. Charles Deane (Boston: J. Wilson & Son, 1870), 2, 10, 13–14.

66. Bradford, *Third Conference*, 30.

67. Bradford, *Third Conference*, 22, 24.

68. Bradford, *Third Conference*, 31, 26, 25.

69. Printer's letter to John Robinson, *A Treatise of Hearing of the Ministers in the Church of England* (1634).

70. John Robinson, *New Essays or Observations Divine and Moral* (1628), 2–3.

71. This discussion of puritan beliefs is drawn from my larger treatment of the issue in Francis J. Bremer, *Puritanism: A Very Short Introduction* (New York: Oxford University Press, 2009), especially chapters 3 and 4.

72. Robinson, *New Essays*, 152–154.

73. Bangs, *Strangers and Pilgrims*, 45–46.

74. OPP, 6.

75. Walter H. Burgess, *Pastor of the Pilgrim Fathers: A Study of His Life and Times* (New York: Harcourt, Brace, 1920), 79–80.

76. OPP, 7.

Chapter 3

1. OPP, 8.

2. Since the early 1540s licenses to pass overseas had been required by the English government, in part to prevent Catholics from enrolling in Continental

seminaries. Expanding on this, in 1606 a royal proclamation had required anyone leaving the country to pledge an oath of allegiance, and requiring a license for any women or children under the age of twenty-one desiring to emigrate. These additional requirements were intended to control the flight of Catholics as part of a crackdown following the discovery of the Gunpowder Plot. The following July another royal proclamation, citing precedents from the reigns of Edward I and Edward III, forbade anyone except lords of the realm, "notable merchants," and mariners to leave the country without a special license from the king or four members of the Privy Council. This was modified by the Privy Council in December 1608. The Council required all traveling abroad to be examined and registered and restricted passage to certain ports. William Bradford, *History of Plymouth Plantation 1620–1647*, edited by Worthington Chauncey Ford (Boston: Massachusetts Historical Society, 1912), I, 30, n3. Nick Bunker alludes to this—*Making Haste from Babylon: The Mayflower Pilgrims and Their Worlds* (New York: Knopf, 2010), 187—but students of the Pilgrims have generally passed over the issue of why the group would have been liable to arrest for seeking to leave England, content to repeat Bradford's narrative without seeking the reasons for their arrest. I would like to thank John Morrill for helping me to understand this.

3. OPP, 8.

4. OPP, 8.

5. OPP, 255.

6. Though we don't know how he did so, William Brewster was able to find ways to hide much of his wealth from the authorities, since he was able to draw on his resources to assist others to migrate, to establish himself in the Netherlands, and to contribute to the costs of the move to New England.

7. Mary B. Sherwood, *Pilgrim: A Biography of William Brewster* (Falls Church, VA: Great Oaks Press, 1982), 105.

8. OPP, 8–9.

9. OPP, 9–10.

10. Bradford wrote in some detail of the two attempts to leave England mentioned in my text, presumably because he was a witness to both. But he refers to these as two examples, implying that there were other efforts.

11. Henry Martyn Dexter and Morton Dexter, *The England and Holland of the Pilgrims* (Boston: Houghton Mifflin, 1905), 406.

12. A good contemporary description of Amsterdam is to be found in Sir William Brereton, *Travels in Holland, the United Provinces, England, Scotland and Ireland*, Remains Historical and Literary Published by the Cambden Society (1844).

13. For an overview of them all, see Keith Sprunger, *Dutch Puritanism* (Leiden: Brill, 1973).

14. The "Ancient Church" was not really ancient. The name was given to the congregation of English separatists that formed a church in 1596 in the city of Amsterdam. It was distinct from the churches of the Dutch Reformed Church, and also different from the English Reformed Church, which had been authorized by the Dutch authorities to serve the needs of the English community in the city, and which the authorities provided a place to worship.

15. Sprunger, *Dutch Puritanism*, 48–50.

16. M. Moody, "Ainsworth, Henry (1569–1622), separatist minister and religious controversialist," *Oxford Dictionary of National Biography*, September 23, 2004, retrieved April 19, 2019, from http://www.oxforddnb.com/view/10.1093/ref:odnb/9780198614128.001.0001/odnb-9780198614128-e-240.

17. "A Dialogue or the Summe of Conference between some young men born in New England and sundry Ancient Men that came out of Holland and Old England," in *Publications of the Colonial Society of Massachusetts*, Volume 22: *Plymouth Church Records, 1620–1859, Part One*, 136–137 (hereafter "First Dialogue").

18. For some of the disputes in the Ancient Church, see Michael P. Winship, *Godly Republicans: Puritans, Pilgrims, and a City on a Hill* (Cambridge, MA: Harvard University Press, 2012), 68–87.

19. "First Dialogue," 137.

20. OPP, 12.

21. Quoted in Jeremy Dupertuis Bangs, *Strangers and Pilgrims, Travellers and Sojourners: Leiden and the Foundations of Plymouth Plantation* (Plymouth, MA: Society of Mayflower Descendants, 2009), 85.

22. See Bangs, *Strangers and Pilgrims*, passim.

23. Bangs, *Strangers and Pilgrims*, 138.

24. "First Dialogue," 139.

25. Bangs, *Strangers and Pilgrims*, 303–306. A typical small house that some of the English might have acquired would be sixteen feet deep and twelve feet wide, with a front door and window. The interior was dominated by a fireplace and a bed. The fireplace provided warmth, light, and a place to cook. If one was fortunate enough to find employment as a weaver he had to fit a loom into the house.

26. OPP, 255.

27. Bangs, *Strangers and Pilgrims*, 343–347.

28. H. Kirk-Smith, *William Brewster, "The Father of New England": His Life and Times 1567–1644* (Boston, Lincolnshire: Richard Kay, 1992), 111.

29. Godfrey Hodgson, *A Great and Godly Adventure: The Pilgrims and the Myth of the First Thanksgiving* (New York: Public Affairs, 2006), 39–40.

30. Hodgson, *Godly Adventure*, 39.

31. OPP, 255. The following discussion of what this entails is from David Lupher, in an email communication, August 22, 2019: "Brewster's facility in spoken Latin, acquired in grammar school and honed during his brief time at Cambridge, would have enabled him to teach English to an international assortment of students by using the standard tongue of university instruction. Also, in the Europe and Britain of his day the grammatical rules of Latin were regarded (not always helpfully) as paradigmatic for other European languages as well. Thus, an Englishman who was sufficiently learned in Latin could be confidently hired to teach his own native language to foreigners not only because he could offer explanations in that shared pedagogical language, but also because he could be assumed to understand how all European languages are (supposedly) structured and could thus effectively teach English to students who had mastered the paradigmatic Latin tongue. English grammars were rare in Brewster's day, but he could have made use of Paul Greaves's *Grammatica Anglicana* (Cambridge, 1594), whose Latin text and Latin-English glossary his students would have found useful. But Greaves's handbook proclaimed that it followed the "single method" of Peter Ramus and thus challenged the standard Latin model for understanding English. It seems more likely that Brewster drew up his own rules to share with his students, rules modeled on the Latin grammatical instruction of his youth. Not only does this fit Bradford's wording ("he drew rules"), but it also reflects common pedagogical practice in his time. John Gallagher (University of Leeds), a prominent specialist in early modern language learning, writes, "It seems to me, from looking at vernacular language-learners and teachers, that it was not uncommon for people to draw up their own grammatical materials in manuscript, likely building on language-learning experiences at grammar schools" (personal communication, August 17, 2019). Brewster's own grammar school experience of learning Latin was surely based on the Latin grammar attributed to William Lily, which appeared in various forms and under various titles. For over a century after it first appeared in 1527, it was the only Latin grammar royally authorized for use in English grammar schools, and it would have provided Brewster with the template of his "rules . . . after the Latine maner."

32. OPP, 255. Jeremy Dupertuis Bangs, *Pilgrim Edward Winslow: New England's First International Diplomat. A Documentary History* (Boston: New England Historic and Genealogical Society, 2004), 8, suggesting that this instruction took place in his home.

33. "First Dialogue," 131.

34. John Robinson, *A Justification of Separation from the Church of England against Mr. Richard Bernard his invective, entitled the Separatists Schism* (1610), 73.

35. Robinson, *Justification*, 92.

36. Robinson, *Justification*, 93.

37. Robinson, *Justification*, 141.

38. Robinson, *Justification*, 454, 236.

39. Thomas Prince, *A Chronological History of New England* (1826), 176.

40. Winnifred Cockshott, *The Pilgrim Fathers: Their Church and Colony* (London: Methuen, 1909), 140.

41. "First Dialogue," 140.

42. Norman Gevitz, "Samuel Fuller of Plymouth Plantation: A 'Skilful Physician' or 'Quacksalver'?," *Journal of the History of Medicine and Allied Sciences*, 47 (1992), 32–33.

43. Kirk-Smith, *Brewster*, 138–139.

44. Thanks to Jeremy Bangs for clarifying some of this in an email, May 30, 2018.

45. Inventories of early settlers indicated ownership of psalm books. William Brewster had a copy of Ainsworth's *The Book of Psalms: Englished both in prose and metre*. He also had a book described as "Davids Musick," which was likely *A Paraphrase upon the Divine Poems, A Paraphrase upon the Psalms of David* (1636), which was written by George Sandys, a son of Edwin Sandys, Archbishop of York, for whom Brewster's father managed Scrooby Manor. Jeremy Duperius Bangs, *Plymouth Colony's Private Libraries* (Leiden: Leiden American Pilgrim Museum, 2016), 133.

46. Kirk-Smith, *Brewster*, 114; K-S, 114–115; Bangs, *Stranger and Pilgrims*, 269.

47. Sprunger, *Dutch Puritanism*. 324. A group of members of the English Reformed Church in Amsterdam who had been thwarted in their efforts to elect first Thomas Hooker and then John Davenport to be ministers in that church by the pastor, John Paget, evidently petitioned Paget in the 1630s to make changes in the governance of that church. Women signed the petition and among the points debated in the church consistory was allowing women a role in ministerial elections. Sprunger, *Dutch Puritanism*, 333–334.

48. John Robinson, *Justification of Separation from the Church of England* (1610), quoted in Martha L. Finch in *Dissenting Bodies: Corporalities in Early New England* (New York: Columbia University Press, 2010), 120.

49. Robinson quoted in Keith Thomas, "Women and the Civil War Sect," *Past and Present*, 13 (1958), 44, 46.

50. On this, see Finch, *Dissenting Bodies*, 121.

51. Hooker and Craddock quoted in Geoffrey F. Nuttall, *The Holy Spirit in Puritan Faith and Experience*, with a new introduction by Peter Lake (Chicago: University of Chicago Press, 1992), 142. For further discussion see Bremer, *Lay Empowerment*, 71–72.

52. Edward Winslow, *Hypocrisie Unmasked* (1646), 98–99.

53. The details of the dispute were set out by Ainsworth in his *An Animadversion to Mr. Richard Clifton's Advertisement* (1613). The letter from Brewster and Robinson is printed on pp. 132–134.

54. The quote is from the account by Christopher Lawne, *The Prophane Schisme of the Brownists or separatists* (1612), 232–238. For a fuller discussion of the dispute, see Bangs, *Strangers and Pilgrims*, 248–253.

55. Robinson, *Justification*, 32.

56. Keith L. Sprunger, "The Meeting of Dutch Anabaptists and English Brownists, Reported by P. J. Twisck," in *The Contentious Triangle, Church, State, and University, A Festschrift in Honor of Professor George Huntston Williams*, ed. Rodney L. Petersen and Calvin Augustine Pater, Sixteenth-Century Essays and Studies, 51 (Kirksville: Thomas Jefferson University Press, 1999), 221–231.

57. D. Plooij, *The Pilgrim Fathers from a Dutch Point of View* (New York: New York University Press, 1932), 93–94.

58. John Robinson, *Of Religious Communion Private & Publique with the Silencing of the Clamours Raised by Mr. Thomas Helwys against Our retaining the Baptism Received in England & Administering our Baptism unto Infants* (1614).

59. Bangs, *Strangers and Pilgrims*, 142–144; Plooij, *Pilgrim Fathers*, 47–48.

60. See Francis J. Bremer, *Congregational Communion: Clerical Friendship in the Anglo-American Puritan Community, 1610–1692* (Boston: Northeastern University Press, 1994), 93–94.

61. Plooij, *Pilgrim Fathers*, 86, 100; Sargent Bush, ed., *The Correspondence of John Cotton* (Chapel Hill: University of North Carolina Press, 2001), 139–141.

62. "First Dialogue," 131.

63. Polly Ha, ed. and introduction, *The Puritans on Independence: The First Examination, Defence, and the Second Examination* (New York: Oxford University Press, 2018), 2–7.

64. Ha's *Puritans on Independence* introduces, presents, and comments on this manuscript.

65. Ha, *Puritans on Independence*, 13–15.

66. Champlin Burrage, *The Early English Dissenters in the Light of Recent Research (1550–1641)* (Cambridge, UK: Cambridge University Press, 1912), 1:313–314. The rejection of the Jacob congregation is discussed by John Robinson in *A Treatise of the Lawfulness of Hearing of the Ministers in the Church of England* (1634) and A. T., *A Christian Reproof against Conention, Wherein is declared and manifested a just defense of the Church against such slanders and reproaches which Sabine Staresmore hath laid upon us in his two books* (1631).

67. Jacob quoted in Winship, *Godly Republicanism*, 99–100.

68. Burgess, *John Robinson*, 123–124. Their views were expressed in Robinson, *Manumission*, and *A Second Manduction for Mr. Robinson, or a Confutation of the former, in answer to his Manumission* (1615).

69. A. T., *Christian Reproof*, 20.

70. K. Sprunger, "Parker, Robert (c. 1564–1614), religious controversialist," *Oxford Dictionary of National Biography*, January 3, 2008, retrieved April 20, 2019, from http://www.oxforddnb.com/view/10.1093/ref:odnb/9780198614128.001.0001/odnb-9780198614128-e-21334.

71. Winship, *Godly Republicanism*, 97.

72. Both Samuel Fuller and William Brewster owned copies of editions of Whately's *God's Husbandry* in the libraries inventoried at their death. See Bangs, *Private Libraries*, 28, 136.

73. Willem J. op 't Hof has recently published an important article, "The Eventful Sojourn of Willem Teellinck (1579–1629 at Banbury in 1605," *Journal for the History of Reformed Pietism*, 1 (2015), 5–34, on which much of this paragraph is based. See also Philip Benedict, *Christ's Churches Purely Reformed: A Social History of Calvinism* (New Haven: Yale University Press, 2002), 360–361.

74. Kirk-Smith, *Brewster*, 207–208.

75. Winslow, *Hypocrisie Unmasked*, 94–96.

76. Lawne, *Prophane Schisme*, 11.

77. Lawne, *Prophane Schisme*, 76–77. The same letter was quoted (probably from Lawne's book) by Ephraiem Pagitt, *Heresiography* (1645), 54.

78. See Gevitz, "Fuller," 29–48, which is skeptical about Fuller having acquired any medical knowledge in Leiden, but I thank Jeremy Bangs for having pointed out the ways in which he could have done so.

79. Robert C. Cushman and Michael R. Paulick, "Robert Cushman, Mayflower Pilgrim in Canterbury, 1586–1607," *Mayflower Quarterly*, 79 (2013), 226–235.

80. Michael R. Paulick and Robert C. Cushman, "Pilgrim Robert Cushman, A Chronology, 1577–1625," *Mayflower Journal*, 3 (2018), 65.

81. Bangs, *Strangers and Pilgrims*, 157 n1.

82. William Bradford, "Of Plimoth Plantation," OPP, 13.

83. Douglas Anderson, *William Bradford's Books: Of Plimmoth Plantation and the Printed Word* (Baltimore: Johns Hopkins University Press, 2003), 18.

84. Winslow, *Hypocrisie Unmasked*, 95.

85. "First Dialogue," 139–140.

86. Anderson, *Bradford's Books*, 18

87. Jeremy D. Bangs, ed., *Pilgrims in the Netherlands: Recent Research* (Leiden: The Center, 1998), 34.

88. William Brewster's own search for further light can be followed in his readings. The inventory of his estate when he died included over a hundred and twenty works published between his departure from England and the migration to New England. There were likely other works that did not end up in his New England library, but those that did were largely of a religious nature. These included a small number of specifically anti-Catholic polemics and a number of aids to scriptural analysis such as concordances and lexicons. He read works by theologians across the Protestant spectrum including Lutherans, German Reformed, and Dutch Reformed. His library included treatises by leading separatists such as Henry Jacob, John Smyth, Henry Ainsworth, Francis Johnson, and Henry Barrow as well as individuals who had repented of their separatism such as Peter Fairlambe. Church of England theologians and preachers found a place on his shelves. Most of the books, however, were by English puritans. These included five titles by William Perkins and three by John Dod. Taken as a whole, the collection represents the reading of a man who was still engaged in godly seeking.

89. Anderson, *Bradford's Books*, 17; see Keith Sprunger, *Trumpets from the Tower: English Puritan Printing in the Netherlands, 1600–1640* (Leiden: Brill, 1994).

90. Bangs, *Winslow*, 5.

91. Sprunger, *Dutch Puritanism*, 141–142.

92. Sprunger, *Dutch Puritanism*, 141–142.

93. Bangs, *Strangers and Pilgrims*, 555–568.

Chapter 4

1. Edward Winslow, *Hypocrisie Unmasked* (1646), 88–90; and see Michael P. Winship, *Godly Republicanism: Puritans, Pilgrims and a City on a Hill* (Cambridge, MA: Harvard University Press, 2012), 112ff. The subject of this chapter can be followed as well in Rebecca Fraser, *The Mayflower: The Families, the Voyage, and the Foundation of America* (New York: St. Martin's Press, 2017), 26–30.

2. OPP, 256.

3. OPP, 16.

4. Jeremy Dupertuis Bangs, *Strangers and Pilgrims, Travellers and Sojourners: Leiden and the Foundations of Plymouth Plantation* (Plymouth, MA: Society of Mayflower Descendants, 2009), 569–573.

5. OPP, 14.

6. Jeremy Dupertuis Bangs, *Plymouth Colony's Private Libraries* (Leiden: Leiden American Pilgrim Museum, 2016), 38ff.

7. OPP, 16.

8. Quoted by Jeremy Bangs, citing a copy of the document in an article published by J. H. Trap, "Een Reis die niet Doorging," *Jaarboekje voor Geschiedenis en Oudheidkunde van Leiden en Omstreken*, 91 (1998), 54–57.

9. I owe this information to Rebecca Fraser, who also pointed out that John Pory, who expressed a friendship with Brewster in a letter from Plymouth, had previously been an assistant to Hakluyt.

10. John Smith, *The True Travels, Adventures and Observations* (1630) and *Advertisements for the Unexperienced Planters of New England* (1631), in *Captain John Smith: Writings with Other Narratives of Roanoke, Jamestown, and the First English Settlements of America* (New York: Library of America, 2007), 750, 798.

11. Jeremy Bangs makes a strong case for Standish's connections with the Leiden congregation in *Strangers and Pilgrims*, 177ff.

12. David S. Lovejoy, *Religious Enthusiasm in the New World: Heresy to Revolution* (Cambridge, MA: Harvard University Press, 1985), 44.

13. See Scott Culpepper, *Francis Johnson and the Separatist Influence* (Macon, GA: Mercer University Press, 2011), 95–102; David B. Quinn, "The First Pilgrims," *William and Mary Quarterly*, 3rd series, 23 (1966), 360–390.

14. Walter Ralegh had explored the region in the 1590s and published a book, *Discoverie of the Large, rich, and beautiful Empire of Guiana, with a relation of the great and Golden Citie of Manoa (which the Spaniards call El Dorado)* (1596), which included a map showing the city. An attempt to establish an English colony there in 1609 had failed.

15. OPP, 18. This referred to a French Protestant settlement established along what is now the St. John's River in Florida. Furious at this infringement on their territory, the Spanish attacked the settlement in 1565 and killed 111 of the Frenchmen when they refused to abandon their faith and revert to Catholicism. See Scott Weidensaul, *The First Frontier: The Forgotten History of Struggle, Savagery, and Endurance in Early America* (Boston: Houghton Mifflin Harcourt, 2012).

16. Wesley Frank Craven, *The Dissolution of the Virginia Company: The Failure of a Colonial Experiment* (New York: Oxford University Press, 1932), 37–38, 62–63.

17. *A sermon preached in London before the right honorable the Lord Lavvarre, Lord Gouernour and Captaine Generall of Virginea, and others of his Maiesties Counsell for that kingdome, and the rest of the aduenturers in that plantation At the said Lord Generall his leaue taking of England his natiue countrey, and departure for Virginea, 21. 1609* (1609).

18. See David A. Lupher, *Greeks, Romans, and Pilgrims: Classical Receptions in Early New England* (Leiden: Brill, 2017).

19. Bangs, *Strangers and Pilgrims*, 587.

20. Craven, *Dissolution*, 63.

21. Andrew Fitzmaurice, "The Civic Solution to the Crisis of English Colonization, 1609–1625," *The Historical Journal*, 42, no. 1 (March 1999), 45. Sandys's statement about "a free popular state" is quoted in Fitzmaurice, "The Company Commonwealth," an essay forthcoming in a collection edited by Jim Horn and Paul Musselwhite. I thank Professor Fitzmaurice for allowing me to read that essay and for his further suggestions. See also Andrew Fitzmaurice, *Humanism and America: An Intellectual History of English Colonization, 1500–1625* (New York: Cambridge University Press, 2003), and Margo Todd, *Christian Humanism and the Puritan Social Order* (New York: Cambridge University Press, 1987).

22. Theodore K. Robb, *Jacobean Gentleman: Sir Edwin Sandys, 1561–1629* (Princeton: Princeton University Press, 1998), 330–331. Sandys was attacked by his enemies for his purported support of the separatists. In 1621 he was interrogated about the discovery of letters with the Leiden group (particularly Thomas Brewer) in his correspondence; Rabb, *Jacobean Gentleman*, 204).

23. OPP, 22.

24. Winship, *Godly Republicans*, 113.

25. Bangs, *Strangers and Pilgrims*, 580–581.

26. OPP, 22.

27. Craven, *Dissolution*, 59.

28. James Horn, *Adapting to a New World: English Society in the Seventeenth-Century Chesapeake* (Chapel Hill: University of North Carolina Press, 1994), 55–56.

29. John Bennett Boddie, *Seventeenth-Century Isle of Wight County, Virginia* (Chicago: Chicago Law Printing Company, 1938), 20–22.

30. Cushman in Edward Archer, ed., *The Story of the Pilgrim Fathers* (Boston: Houghton Mifflin, 1897), 290–291.

31. I thank Andrew Fitzmaurice for this suggestion.

32. Francis J. Bremer, *John Winthrop: America's Forgotten Founding Father* (New York: Oxford University Press, 2002), 140–143.

33. Rabb, *Jacobean Gentleman*, 204.

34. Winslow, *Hypocrisie Unmasked*, 90, 210.

35. Fitzmaurice, "The Company-Commonwealth," 16.

36. OPP, 17; Bangs, *Strangers and Pilgrims*, 583–584.

37. Bangs, *Strangers and Pilgrims*, 265–266.

38. OPP, 23.

39. H. Kirk-Smith, *William Brewster, "The Father of New England": His Life and Times, 1567–1644* (Boston, Lincolnshire: Richard Kay, 1992), 141.

40. Letter of Robert Cushman to the leaders of the Leiden church, May 8, 1619, in OPP, 24. We know from this same letter that Brewster was in contact about the negotiations with Robinson and the church, but his letters have not survived.

41. OPP, 24.

42. OPP, 26.

43. Minutes of the Virginia Company of London. Wincop was likely one of three clerical brothers (Thomas and Samuel were the others) who all studied at Cambridge. In Easter week 1632 they would take turns preaching on the Monday, Tuesday, and Wednesday at St. Mary's Spital in London (*The Survey of London . . . begun by . . . John Stowe . . . and now completely finished . . .* [1633], 781–782).

44. This is suggested by Fraser, *Mayflower*, 28.

45. Susan Kingsbury, ed., *Records of the Virginia Company of London*, 129–130.

46. OPP, 24.

47. Quoted in *Virginia Company of London*, 129.

48. For this possibility, see Bangs, *Strangers and Pilgrims*, 564–565.

49. Bangs, *Strangers and Pilgrims*, 590ff.

50. Morton, *New-Englands Memorial* (1669), 5.

51. Winslow, *Hypocrisie Unmasked*, 97–98.

52. Winslow, *Hypocrisie Unmasked*, 90–91.

53. OPP, 36.

54. The distinction was made a major theme by George F. Willison in his 1945 book *Saints and Strangers*. But Willison exaggerated the number of passengers on the *Mayflower* who were not members of the Leiden congregation. Furthermore, it has been demonstrated that some of the passengers who were not members of the congregation were puritans who were in sympathy with the religious outlook of the Leiden group. Also, Bradford was describing the self-awareness of those departing from Delftshaven—which was before the non-Pilgrims had joined the expedition.

55. The full passage, in the Geneva translation of 1560, which was favored by the puritans, was: "All these died in the faith, and received not the promises, but saw them a far off, and believed them, and received them thankfully, and confessed that they were strangers and pilgrims on the earth. For they that said such things, declare plainly that they seek a country. And if they had been mindful of that country, from whence they came out, they had leisure to have returned. But now they desire a better, that is an heavenly, wherefore God is not ashamed of them to be called their God, for he hath prepared for them a city."

56. OPP, 37.

57. OPP, 41.

58. Quoted in Stephen R. Berry, *A Path in the Mighty Waters: Shipboard Life and Atlantic Crossings to the New World* (New Haven: Yale University Press, 2015), 206.

59. A good description of the voyage can be found in the opening chapter of Nathaniel Philbrick, *Mayflower* (New York: Viking, 2006).

60. OPP, 256.

61. OPP, 45; Berry, *Waters*, 210–221. See Jeremy Bangs, *Strangers and Pilgrims*, 607–608, and Bangs, *Winslow*, 9–10, who discounts the idea that the screw was part of a printing press.

62. OPP, 46.

Chapter 5

1. Frank Shuffleton, "Devils and Pilgrim Fathers: Squanto, Hobomok, and the English Conception of Indian Religion," *New England Quarterly*, 49 (1976), 109.

2. As Lisa Brooks has pointed out, English guests too often misinterpreted Native hospitality, so that when they were told they were "welcome," that

"did not mean they were 'welcome' to possess it." Lisa Brooks, *Our Beloved Kin: A New History of King Philip's War* (New Haven: Yale University Press, 2018), 20.

3. For excellent examples of such new scholarship by Native scholars, see Brooks, *Beloved Kin*, and Jean O'Brien, *Firsting and Lasting: Writing Indians out of Existence in New England* (Minneapolis: University of Minnesota Press, 2010).

4. For an overview of the Natives of the region, see Kathleen Bragdon, *Native People of Southern New England, 1500–1650* (Norman: University of Oklahoma Press, 1999).

5. Harald E. L. Prins and Bunny McBride, *Asticou's Island Domain: Wabanaki Peoples of Mount Desert Island 1500–2000; Acadia National Park Ethnographic Overview and Assessment* (Boston: National Park Service, 2007), 2, 48.

6. Not until the late seventeenth century do we find this tribe designated as the Wampanoag. Before that time the term "Pokanoket" was used to designate them. However, because it is the term widely accepted today, most importantly by their descendants, I have used "Wampanoag," meaning "eastern people," throughout this book. See Christina B. Johannsen, "European Trade Goods and Wampanoag Culture in the Seventeenth Century," in Susan G. Gibson, ed., *Burr's Hill: A 17th-Century Wampanoag Burial Ground in Warren, Rhode Island* (Providence: Brown University Press, 1980), 25.

7. Neal Salisbury, *Manitou and Providence: Indians, Europeans, and the Making of New England, 1500–1643* (New York: Oxford University Press, 1982), 32–33.

8. Bragdon, *Native People*, 37.

9. Bragdon, *Native People*, 113–117.

10. Bragdon, *Native People*, 128.

11. Lisa Brooks discusses the authority of the female sachem Weetamoo (Namumpum) in the course of *Our Beloved Kin*.

12. Ronald G. Handsman, "Landscapes of Memory in Wampanoag Country—and the Monuments upon Them," in Patricia E. Robertone, ed., *Archaeologies of Placemaking: Monuments, Memories, and Engagement in Native North America* (Walnut Creek, CA: Left Coast Press, 2008), 165; Lisa Blee and Jean M. O'Brien, *Monumental Mobility: The Memory Work of Massasoit* (Chapel Hill: University of North Carolina Press, 2019), 11.

13. Ramona L. Peters, "Consulting with the Bone-Keepers," in Jordan E. Kerber, *Cross-Cultural Collaboration: Native Peoples and Archaeology in the Northeastern United States* (Lincoln: University of Nebraska Press, 2006), 43.

14. Blee and O'Brien, *Monumental Mobility*, 70.
15. Johannsen, "Wampanoag Culture," 32.
16. Quoted in Bragdon, *Native People*, 127.
17. Shuffleton, "Indian Devils," 109. For discussion of the challenges facing Englishmen seeking to understand Native life, see Alden T. Vaughan, "From White Man to Redskin: Changing Anglo-American Perceptions of the American Indian," in Vaughan, *Roots of American Racism: Essays on the Colonial Experience* (New York: Oxford University Press, 1995), 3–33; and Karen Ordahl Kupperman, *Indians and English: Facing Off in America* (Ithaca, NY: Cornell University Press, 2000).
18. Quoted in Bragdon, *Native People*, 184.
19. The major efforts to convert Natives took place after the time period covered in this book and remain a contentious subject. There is no denying that those converted to Christianity abandoned traditional cultures and in so doing undermined Native societies. But there were many who embraced Christian ideas. A sensitive portrait of a number of such individuals, including Caleb Cheeshateaumuck, is to be found in Brooks, *Our Beloved Kin*.
20. Bristol records quoted in Alden T. Vaughan, *Transatlantic Encounters: American Indians in Britain, 1500–1776* (New York: Cambridge University Press, 2006), 11.
21. Vaughan, *Encounters*, 11. See also Neil Chesire, Tony Waldron, Alison Quinn, and David Quinn, "Frobisher's Eskimos in England," *Archivaria*, 10 (1980), 23–50. Thanks to David Lupher for pointing me to this.
22. Quoted in Vaughan, *Encounters*, 21.
23. Ralegh's interpreters are fully covered in Vaughan, *Encounters*, ch. 2.
24. "The Voyage of Martin Pring, 1603," Wisconsin Historical Society Digital Library and Archives, Document No. AJ-040.
25. See Mary Beth Norton and Emerson W. Baker, "'The Names of the Rivers': A New Look at an Old Document," *The New England Quarterly*, 80, 3 (September 2007), 459–487.
26. All quoted are from James Rosier, *A True Relation of the most prosperous voyage made this present year 1605, by Captain George Weymouth* (1605), which is not paginated. Quotes are from the eleventh to eighteenth pages in the text.
27. Vaughan, *Encounters*, 64–65.
28. Quoted in Vaughan, *Encounters*, 66.
29. Quoted in Vaughan, *Encounters*, 79.
30. D. E. M. Rose, "Did Squanto Meet Pocahontas, and What May They Have Discussed?," guest post in *The Junto* online blog, November 22, 2017.

31. See Neal Salisbury, "Squanto, Last of the Patuxets," in David Sweet and Gary Nash, eds., *Struggle and Survival in Colonial America* (Berkeley: University of California Press, 1982), 242–243. Other information on Tisquantum is derived from this essay.

32. Kathleen Donegan, *Seasons of Misery: Catastrophe and Colonial Settlement in Early America* (Philadelphia: University of Pennsylvania Press, 2014), 127–128.

33. Timothy Bratton, "The Identity of the New England Indian Epidemic of 1616–19," *Bulletin of the History of Medicine*, 62 (1988), 351–383; John S. Marr and John T. Cathey, "New Hypothesis for Cause of an Epidemic among Native Americans, New England, 1616–1619," *Emerging Infectious Diseases*, 16, no. 2 (2010), 281–286.

34. David J. Silverman, *Red Brethren: The Brotherhood and Stockbridge Indians and the Problem of Race in Early America* (Ithaca, NY: Cornell University Press, 2010), 14.

35. Quoted in Donegan, *Seasons of Misery*, 127–128.

36. Salisbury, *Manitou and Providence*, 101–106.

37. Silverman, *Red Brethren*, 14.

38. Donegan, *Seasons of Misery*, 127–129.

39. OPP, 63.

40. Andrew Lipman, *The Saltwater Frontier: Indians and the Contest for the American Coast* (New Haven: Yale University Press, 2015), 100–101.

41. Prins, *Island Domain*, xvi.

42. Quoted in Prins, *Island Domain*, 116–117.

Chapter 6

1. OPP, 46.

2. OPP, 47; see David A. Lupher, *Greeks, Romans, and Pilgrims: Classical Republicanism in Early New England* (Leiden: Brill, 2017), 177–178.

3. Nathaniel Morton, *New-Englands Memorial* (1669), 13.

4. *A Journal of the Pilgrims at Plymouth: Mourt's Relation*, ed. Dwight B. Heath (New York: Corinth Books, 1963), 17.

5. OPP, 53.

6. The passage alluded to was Hebrews 11:13–16: "13. All these all died in faith, and received not the promises, but saw them a far off, and believed them, and received them thankfully, and confessed that they were strangers and pilgrims on the earth. 14. For they that say such things declare plainly that they seek a country. 15. And if they had been mindful

of that *country* from whence they came out, they had leisure to have returned. 16. But now they desire a better, that is, an heavenly: wherefore God is not ashamed of them to be called their God: for he hath prepared for them a city." For an important discussion of this, see Jeremy Dupertuis Bangs, *Strangers and Pilgrims, Travellers and Sojourners: Leiden and the Foundations of Plymouth Plantation* (Plymouth, MA: Society of Mayflower Descendants, 2009), 614–615.

7. Bangs, *Strangers and Pilgrims*, 614.

8. Robert C. Anderson, *The Great Migration Begins: Immigrants to New England, 1620–1633*, Volume 1: *A–F* (Boston: New England Historic and Genealogical Society, 1995), 315.

9. OPP, 43.

10. Babette Levy, "Early Puritanism in the Southern and Island Colonies," *Proceedings of the American Antiquarian Society*, 70, no. 1 (April 1960), 163–165; see also Bangs, *Strangers and Pilgrims*, 616–617; and Alexander Mazzaferro, "'Such a Murmur': Innovation, Rebellion, and Sovereignty in William Strachey's 'True Reportory,'" *Early American Literature*, 53 (2018), 3–32. Thanks to David Lupher for directing me to this source.

11. *Mourt's Relation*, 12.

12. OPP, 54.

13. For Carver's possible membership in the Walloon church, see Bangs, *Strangers and Pilgrims*, 157.

14. OPP, 54. See also Rebecca Fraser, *The Mayflower: The Families, the Voyage, and the Founding of America* (New York: St. Martin's Press, 2017), 56.

15. H. Kirk-Smith, *William Brewster, "The Father of New England": His Life and Times, 1567–1644* (Boston, Lincolnshire: Richard Kay, 1992), 71–72.

16. Following the voyages of Columbus, writers drew on a tradition that was already centuries old that denied rights of self-rule to peoples whose cultures were different from that of Christian Europe. To buttress its own right to lands it had "discovered" in South America, Portugal appealed to the pope, who in 1493 issued a papal bull titled *Inter Caestera*, which divided the world of countries and islands recently and yet to be discovered between Spain and Portugal, presumably as a step to Christianize those lands. Though this was disputed by the Spaniards Francisco de Vitoria and Bartholome de Las Casas, both of whom rejected the notion that the pope could bestow the property of Native peoples on whom he wished, both countries drew on the papal pronouncement to assert full sovereignty over the lands they colonized. This bull was, of course, rejected by nations that rejected papal authority after the Reformation.

17. For the definitive treatment of Plymouth colony treaties with the Natives of the region, see Jeremy Bangs, *Indian Deeds: Land Transactions in Plymouth Colony, 1620–1691* (Boston: New England Historic Genealogical Society, 2002).

18. *Mourt's Relation*, 19.

19. *Mourt's Relation*, 20–21.

20. OPP, 16. It should be noted that whereas Edward Winslow's accounts of the Natives showed an interest in them and their way of life, Bradford's comments in his history and other writings displayed all the negative stereotypes about the Natives.

21. OPP, 17.

22. Ronald G. Handsman, "Landscapes of Memory in Wampanoag Country—and the Monuments on Them," in Patricia E. Robertone, ed., *Archaeologies of Placemaking: Monuments, Memories, and Engagement in Native North America* (Walnut Creek, CA: Left Coast Press, 2008), 167–168.

23. *Mourt's Relation*, 21–22.

24. Winslow's accounts of Native life were written close to the events, at a time when the colonists had established favorable relations with the Native tribes. William Bradford, who also described these events, lacked his fellow colonist's sensitivity, but was writing after regional relations had been fractured in the Pequot War.

25. *Mourt's Relation*, 22.

26. *Mourt's Relation*, 26, 28–29. These expeditions are discussed in Jeremy Dupertuis Bangs, *Pilgrim Edward Winslow: New England's First International Diplomat; A Documentary History* (Boston: New England Historic and Genealogical Society, 2004), 15–20, and Fraser, *Mayflower*, 58–59.

27. *Mourt's Relation*, 35–37.

28. The idea that Dorothy Bradford committed suicide was first suggested by Jane Goodwin Austin in an 1869 story in *Harper's Weekly*. But it became popular with a 1950 novel and subsequent film that seemingly influenced Samuel Eliot Morison in his edition of Bradford's OPP and was then repeated by various historians, all with no clear evidence. For a discussion of the historiography of this, see David A. Lupher, *Greeks, Romans, and Pilgrims: Classical Republicanism in Early New England* (Brill, Leiden: 2017), 281–284.

29. *Mourt's Relation*, 39–41.

30. *Mourt's Relation*, 42–43.

31. *Mourt's Relation*, 45.
32. *Mourt's Relation*, 47.
33. Kathleen Donegan has argued that the dead were buried on a hill below the fort and that the dead were buried at night and corn planted over their graves to hide the losses from the Natives. She also accepts the claim of Phineas Pratt, who arrived in the colony in 1622 (after the events he claimed to know about) and didn't testify to this for forty years, that sick men were propped up outside with their muskets; Donegan, *Seasons of Misery*, 136. But David Lupher effectively discounts this; Lupher, *Greeks, Romans, and Pilgrims*, 289, n44.
34. OPP, 46.
35. *Mourt's Relation*, 48–50.
36. *Mourt's Relation*, 50–51.
37. Information on Samoset is primarily drawn from Harald E. L. Prins and Bunny McBride, *Asticou's Island Domain: Wabanaki Peoples at Mount Desert Island, 1500–2000. Acadia National Park Ethnographic Overview and Assessment* (Boston: National Park Service, 2007). I thank Dr. Prins for his assistance.
38. *Mourt's Relation*, 53–55.
39. This character of the contact between the two groups is pointed out by Brooks, *Beloved Kin*, 159.
40. Robert Cushman, *A Sermon Preached at Plimoth in New-England December 9, 1621. In an Assembly of his Majesty's faithful Subjects there inhabiting. Wherein is Showed the Danger of Self-Love, and the Sweetness of True Friendship. Together with a Preface Showing the State of the Country, and Condition of the Savages. Rom. 12. 10. "Be affectioned to love one another with brotherly love." Written in the year 1621.* (London, 1622), epistle dedicatory.
41. David J. Silverman, *Red Brethren: The Brotherhood and Stockbridge Indians and the Problem of Race in Early America* (Ithaca: Cornell University Press, 2010), 105 and 292, n18.
42. *Mourt's Relation*, 55–57. Winslow's account refers to a "Mr. Williamson." Brewster, whose father was also named William, appears to have used the patronymic "Williamson"—"William's son"—to avoid attention of the English authorities when he was being pursued for his role in the Pilgrim Press.
43. *Mourt's Relation*, 56–57. Bradford's summary of the treaty omitted the provision that Englishmen visiting Wampanoag villages should leave their weapons outside the encampment.

44. Mary B. Sherwood, *Pilgrim: A Biography of William Brewster* (Falls Church, VA: Great Oaks Press, 1982), 188.

45. See Jenny Hale Pulsipher, *Subjects unto the Same King: Indians, English, and the Contest for Authority in Colonial New England* (Philadelphia: University of Pennsylvania Press, 2005), 9–11, 18–19.

46. See Bangs, *Winslow*, 28–34.

47. Fraser, *Mayflower*, 81–82; OPP, 63.

48. For these events, see OPP, 65; and Alden T. Vaughan, *New England Frontier: Puritans and Indians, 1620–1675*, 3rd ed. (Norman: University of Oklahoma Press, 1995), 75–77.

49. Morton, *New England's Memorial*, 29. It is important but difficult to parse the language of these agreements and to understand how each side understood the words. It is possible that the wording of the submission reflected Bradford's more suspicious attitude toward the Natives.

50. Letters are to be found in OPP, 109, 108.

51. There are numerous suggestions as to where this was, including Braintree and Quincy, but I have found Nick Bunker's identification of North Weymouth the most persuasive; Nick Bunker, *Making Haste from Babylon: The Mayflower Pilgrims and Their Worlds* (New York: Knopf, 2010), 319.

52. Vaughan, *New England Frontier*, 82–83.

53. For extended discussion of this, see Winslow's account, printed in Bangs, *Winslow*, 69–75.

54. Vaughan, *New England Frontier*, 85.

55. Winslow in Bangs, *Winslow*, 79.

56. OPP, 113.

57. Just as we need to avoid simplifying the religious views of the men and women of Plymouth, we need to avoid assuming that all of the colonists thought alike on matters of America's Native people. The most obvious distinction is between William Bradford and Edward Winslow, though even here care is necessary. Bradford showed little sympathy for the Natives in his account of the colony's history or in his poetry, though he was writing these at a time when relations with the tribes of the region had taken a downward turn. Winslow, on the other hand, writing in the 1620s, showed an interest in native lives and beliefs and showed considerable sympathy with figures such as Ousamequin, even if his understanding of their culture was in some respects flawed. It is perhaps notable, however, that the original treaty negotiated by Brewster and Carver with the Wampanoags was an alliance of "friends," whereas the submission of 1621

forced on Native leaders by Bradford identified them as "subjects" of King James. As to the attack on the Massachusetts, it is Winslow who gives us the details of the expedition and its outcome while Bradford passes over the details but does copy Robinson's letter into his text.

58. See Brooks, *Beloved Kin*, and Christine DeLucia, *Memory Lands: King Philip's War and the Place of Violence in the Northeast* (New Haven: Yale University Press, 2019).

Chapter 7

1. Mark Peterson, "The Plymouth Church and the Evolution of Puritan Religious Culture," *The New England Quarterly*, 66 (1993), 573–574.

2. Jeremy Dupertuis Bangs, *Pilgrim Edward Winslow: New England's First International Diplomat; A Documentary History* (Boston: New England Historic and Genealogical Society, 2004), 149–152.

3. Nathaniel Morton, *New-Englands Memorial* (1669), 37.

4. Email from Jeremy Bangs, July 1, 2018.

5. One of the most common misconceptions of the Plymouth colony is the assumption that the education of the ordinary colonists there was inferior to that of those who settled in Massachusetts, a judgment extended to the church leaders. One scholar has written, "the church in the village of New Plymouth had more sporadic and generally less well-educated and theologically rigorous ministerial leadership than did other New England churches" (Martha L. Finch in *Dissenting Bodies: Corporalities in Early New England* [New York: Columbia University Press, 2010], 25). I have often felt that one of the few flaws in the presentation of early Plymouth in Plimoth Plantation, the generally excellent living history reconstruction of Plymouth in 1627, is the failure to re-create the libraries that Brewster, Bradford, Standish, and others brought to the New World in 1620 and that they continued to add to.

6. Isaac de Rasieres to Samuel Blommaert, c. 1628, in Sydney V. James Jr., ed., *Three Visitors to Early Plymouth* (Plymouth, MA: Plimoth Plantation, 1963), 76–77.

7. See Arnold Hunt, *The Art of Hearing* (New York: Cambridge University Press, 2011), 41, who points to Sabine Staresmore's pamphlet uncompromisingly titled *The Unlawfulness of Reading in Prayer* (1619). Staresmore was a separatist well known to Brewster and his fellow congregants.

8. OPP, 256. For a general discussion of the puritan preaching style, see Francis J. Bremer and Ellen Rydell, "Puritans in the Pulpit: Center Stage in the Theater of God's Judgment," *History Today*, September 1995.

9. Finch, *Dissenting Bodies*, 144–145.

10. *The Journal of John Winthrop 1630–1649*, ed. Richard Dunn, James Savage, and Laetitia Yeandle (Cambridge, MA: Harvard University Press, 1996), 82. This is a significant point for a number of reasons. It indicates that the Plymouth church was celebrating the Lord's Supper since they had properly ordained Ralph Smith and had a pastor to administer the sacrament. But it also signifies that the Plymouth church recognized the Boston church as properly formed on congregational principles so that its members could be accorded the right to join in communion.

11. *Winthrop's Journal*, 82.

12. When Samuel Gorton was in Plymouth he and his wife hosted such conferences in their home. See Samuel Gorton to Nathaniel Morton, Peter Force, ed. *American Archives* 9 vol (1837–1853), Volume Four, item 7.

13. See David S. Lovejoy, *Religious Enthusiasm in the New World: Heresy to Revolution* (Cambridge, MA: Harvard University Press, 1985), 50ff.

14. See Francis J. Bremer, *Lay Empowerment and the Development of Puritanism* (London: Palgrave Macmillan, 2015), especially 40–41.

15. Among the women with such books listed in the inventories published by Jeremy Bangs in *Plymouth Colony's Private Libraries as Recorded in Wills and Inventories, 1633–1692* (Leiden: Leiden American Pilgrim Museum, 2018) are Ann Atwood, Elizabeth Bacon, Elisha Besby, Alice Bradford, Margaret Carpenter, Elizabeth Howe, Sarah Howes, Margaret Howland, Sarah Jenney, Hannah Kempton, Joanna Martin, Martha Nelson, Judith Parker, Mary Ring, Judith Smith, widow Sutton, and Joan Swift. While in some cases these may reflect books inherited from a deceased husband, there are undoubtedly other women whose books did not show up in inventories. Thus, we know that the wife of Samuel Fuller conducted a school in Plymouth, but there is no inventory for her.

16. R. G. Marsden, ed., "A Letter of William Bradford and Isaac Allerton, 1623," *American Historical Review*, 8 (1903), 299.

17. See Phyllis Mack, *Visionary Women: Ecstatic Prophecy in Seventeenth-Century England* (Berkeley: University of California Press, 1993); and also Bremer, *Lay Empowerment*.

18. Lovejoy, *Religious Enthusiasm*, 55–56, Morton quoted on 55.

19. OPP, 255.

20. David Pulsipher, ed., *Records of the Colony of New Plymouth in New England* (Boston, 1861), 57–58; see J. M. Bumsted, *The Pilgrim's Progress: The Ecclesiastical History of the Old Colony, 1620–1775* (New York: Garland, 1989), 8.

21. OPP, 161.

22. OPP, 255.

23. Winslow acknowledged this in a statement to the Privy Council, published in Bangs, *Pilgrim Edward Winslow*, 149–152.

24. There are some indications that a manuscript of Brewster's sermons, possibly referred to in the inventory of his estate, did survive and is in the hands of a private individual who queried Jeremy Bangs about it in a phone call when Dr. Bangs was working at Pilgrim Hall. The individual would not provide details and has not come forward to this date with the volume. Email from Jeremy Bangs, March 19, 2014.

25. Robert Cushman, *A Sermon Preached at Plimoth in New-England December 9, 1621. In an Assembly of his Majesty's faithful Subjects there inhabiting. Wherein is Showed the Danger of Self-Love, and the Sweetness of True Friendship. Together with a Preface Showing the State of the Country, and Condition of the Savages. Rom. 12. 10. "Be affectioned to love one another with brotherly love." Written in the year 1621.* (London, 1622).

26. This was also a practice adopted in Massachusetts. Lori Rodgers-Stokes's recent transcription of the deacon's book of the Cambridge Church from 1638 to 1646 offers a fascinating insight into early Congregationalism, but particularly the collection and distribution of funds for "the needy people of Cambridge." Included are donations of clothes and food, but also loans to assist individuals who had fallen on hard times. The transcript and introduction to it are on the "Hidden Histories" website of the Congregational Library and Archives.

27. OPP, 255.

28. Jeremy Dupertuis Bangs, *Strangers and Pilgrims, Travellers and Sojourners: Leiden and the Foundations of Plymouth Plantation* (Plymouth, MA: Society of Mayflower Descendants, 2009), 379–380.

29. Emmanuel Altham to Sir Edward Altham, September 1623, in Sydney V. James Jr., ed., *Three Visitors to Early Plymouth* (Plymouth, MA: Plimoth Plantation, 1963), 29.

30. OPP, 65.

31. *A Journal of the Pilgrims at Plymouth: Mourt's Relation*, ed. Dwight B. Heath (New York: Corinth Books, 1963), 82.

32. Christine O'Neill Grace and Margaret M. Bruchac, *1621: A New Look at Thanksgiving* (Washington DC: National Geographic Society, 2011), 33, 37.

33. There is a claim that the Spanish explorer Coronado observed a thanksgiving in 1541 outside of Canyon, Texas. There is a record of Spanish conquistadors under Pedro Menéndez de Avilés in September 1565 landing at what would be named St. Augustine, Florida, embracing a

cross, joining in the celebration of a mass, and then indulging in a feast. Another "Texas" thanksgiving was held by Spanish explorers in El Paso in 1598. In the English settlements there was a harvest celebration in the Popham Colony in what is now Maine. The following year the colony was abandoned. The Jamestown settlers offered prayers of thanksgiving when the arrival of supply ships in the spring of 1610 brought an end to the "starving time." And, also in Virginia, in 1619 the investors behind the Berkeley Hundred instructed the settlers there to commemorate the date of their arrival with prayers of thanksgiving.

34. As Theodore D. Bozeman has pointed out, puritans were committed to the effort to "live ancient lives," looking to biblical times to find models for their behavior. Theodore D. Bozeman, *To Live Ancient Lives: The Primitivist Dimension in Puritanism* (Chapel Hill: University of North Carolina Press, 1988).

35. Horton Davies, *Worship and Theology in England from Andrewes to Baxter and Fox, 1603–1690* (Princeton: Princeton University Press, 1975), 224.

36. *The Book of Common Prayer* (1559), in William Keatinge Clay, ed., *Liturgies and Occasional Forms of Prayer Set Forth in the Reign of Queen Elizabeth* (1847), 260–261. The specified proclamations are in Clay, *Liturgies*, 508, 583, 587, 595, 604, 619; and for others 538, 548, 654, 668, 679.

37. Bangs, *Strangers and Pilgrims*, 643–646.

38. Francis J. Bremer, *Congregational Communion: Clerical Friendship in the Anglo-American Puritan Community, 1610–1692* (Boston: Northeastern University Press, 1994), 28.

39. Bangs, *Strangers and Pilgrims*, 644–645.

40. OPP, 103.

41. *Plymouth Colony Records*, 11:18.

42. *Mourt's Relation*, 82.

43. Emmanuel Altham to Sir Edward Altham, September 1623, in James, *Three Visitors*, 29.

44. George D. Langdon Jr., *Pilgrim Colony: A History of New Plymouth, 1620–1691* (New Haven: Yale University Press, 1966), 16–17.

45. OPP, 65.

46. John Winthrop, for instance, took notes on a Christmas sermon preached in Groton in 1618. See Winthrop, *Religious Writings*, forthcoming from Massachusetts Historical Society.

47. These quotes and those in the following paragraph are from OPP, 70.

48. Bradford's objection was not to the sports, but to when they were being played, which is further indication that such activities may well have been part of the earlier Thanksgiving celebrations.

Chapter 8

1. OPP, 141.

2. John Robinson to William Brewster, December 20, 1623, in OPP, 115.

3. H. Kirk-Smith, *William Brewster, "The Father of New England": His Life and Times, 1567–1644* (Boston, Lincolnshire: Richard Kay, 1992), 272.

4. Samuel Deane, *History of Scituate, Massachusetts from Its Settlement to 1831* (1831), 77.

5. For the inventories, see Jeremy Dupertuis Bangs, *Plymouth Colony's Private Libraries*, rev. ed. (Leiden: Leiden American Pilgrim Museum, 2018). See also David A. Lupher, *Greeks, Romans, and Pilgrims: Classical Republicanism in Early New England* (Leiden: Brill, 2017).

6. Robinson to Brewster, December 20, 1623, in OPP, 113–115.

7. Stephen Brachlow, *The Communion of Saints: Radical Puritan and Separatist Ecclesiology 1570–1625* (New York: Oxford University Press, 1989), 195. See Lupher, *Greeks, Romans, and Pilgrims*, 304, n8.

8. OPP, 129. The fact that the Plymouth group had not reconstituted themselves as a separate congregation may have been a factor that led Brewster to resist such pressure.

9. OPP, 111.

10. I thank Bob Anderson for directing me to the possible college career of Lyford, as identified by Nick Bunker (Nick Bunker, *Making Haste from Babylon: The Mayflower Pilgrims and Their Worlds* [New York: Knopf, 2010], 345), and the listings in the Clergy of the Church of England Database.

11. Thomas Morton, *New English Canaan, or New Canaan* (1632), 118–119. Michael Winship has suggested that separate from his ordination Lyford may have received a calling from lay members of the church he had ministered to in England or Ireland and that he would have been reluctant to renounce this. Michael P. Winship, *Godly Republicanism: Puritans, Pilgrims, and a City on a Hill* (Cambridge, MA: Harvard University Press, 2012), 126. We do know that some English clergy insisted on a call from their parishioners in addition to their appointment by church authorities; John Wilson requested and received such a call from his Sudbury parish (see Francis J. Bremer, *First Founders: American Puritans and Puritanism in an Atlantic World* [Hanover, NH: University Press of New England, 2011], 47). But there is no evidence to suggest that Lyford ever had such a calling. Winship also writes of Lyford having a good reputation in Ireland (286, n28), but there is no evidence of this.

12. Quoted in Robert Charles Anderson, *The Great Migration Begins, 1620–1633* (Boston: New England Historic and Genealogical Society, 1995–), 2:954.

13. William Hubbard, *A General History of New England* (Cambridge, MA; 1815), 93.

14. This may have been the John Pemberton who was a clergyman who was sent to Virginia at this time. But in Sydney V. James Jr., ed., *Three Visitors to Early Plymouth* (Plymouth, MA: Plimoth Plantation, 1963), 53, n1, James suggests that Pemberton was a merchant and leader of an antipuritan faction among the adventurers.

15. OPP, 123.

16. OPP, 126.

17. OPP, 129.

18. I thank Bob Anderson for the information on Hooker, sent in an email, January 17, 2018.

19. The preceding discussion has been influenced by Winship, *Godly Republicanism*, 120–121.

20. The church cited these "as they have published the same in the Harmony of Confessions [*An Harmony of the Confessions of Faith of the Christian and Reformed Churches* (1586)]."

21. OPP, 134–135.

22. Letter to "the Church of Christ in London" in John Robinson, *A Treatise of the Lawfulness of Hearing of the Ministers in the Church of England . . . Together with a letter written by the same author and approved by his church* (1634), 65. The preface to this work (published after Robinson's death) alluded to a schism in the Leiden church over this issue once death had removed Robinson's healing presence. The position of the Ancient Church had been set out in A. T. [member of Ancient Church], *A Christian Reproof against contention Wherein is declared and manifested a just defense of the Church against such slanders and reproaches which Sabine Staresmore hath laid upon us in his two books* (1631).

23. I thank Jeremy Bangs for this information and insight. Dr. Bangs has also suggested that it is possible that Goodyear presided over the Lord's Supper for the congregation on occasion.

24. Hubbard, *History*, 65.

25. OPP, 162.

26. George D. Langdon, *Pilgrim Colony: A History of New Plymouth, 1620–1691* (New Haven: Yale University Press, 1966), 22.

27. Hubbard, *History*, 65.

28. For a full list, see Bang's *Plymouth Libraries*.

29. Quoted in Kirk-Smith, *William Brewster*,, 221–222

30. *Mourt's Relation*, 54.

31. Jenny Hale Pulsipher, *Subjects unto the Same King: Indians, English, and the Contest for Authority in Colonial New England* (Philadelphia: University of Pennsylvania Press, 2005), 6.

32. OPP, 68. Bradford acknowledged that there was much discussion of various issues, but was denying that this was so extensive as to prevent the colonists from fulfilling their economic tasks.

33. *The Journal of John Winthrop 1630–1649*, ed. Richard S. Dunn, James Savage, and Laetitia Yeandle (Cambridge, MA: Harvard University Press, 1996), 71.

34. Kirk-Smith, *Brewster*, 255–256. The particular copy that was used in Plymouth had originally belonged to William Cecil, Lord Burghley. Cecil was a close friend of William Davison, and it has been suggested that he gifted the copy to Brewster, Davison's aide.

35. Quoted in Douglas Anderson, *William Bradford's Books: Of Plimmoth Plantation and the Printed Word* (Baltimore: Johns Hopkins University Press, 2003), 295.

36. Anderson, *Bradford's Books*, 196, quoting Martyr; and 169, n39.

37. OPP, 180; *Winthrop's Journal*, 40.

38. One of the precipitating factors had been the murder of John Oldham by Natives on Block Island in 1636. The Pequots tribe had been wrongly accused of this and in seeking to punish that tribe for this and other offenses, John Endecott and a force from Massachusetts attacked the Pequots, triggering their assaults on English settlements along the Connecticut River. As the war erupted Massachusetts decided to launch a major assault on the Pequots. Plymouth reluctantly agreed to join with the Bay colony but before the colony's General Court could vote to provide a land force of thirty men, the war was over. Meanwhile Massachusetts and Connecticut forces attacked and destroyed the main Pequot fort on the Mystic River. Somewhere between 400 and 700 Natives were killed, with one of the English commanders noting that "many were burnt in the fort, both men, women, and children" while others were killed as they fled the flames. See Rebecca Fraser, *The Mayflower: The Families, the Voyage, and the Founding of America* (New York: St. Martin's Press, 2017), 148–156; Alden T. Vaughan, *New England Frontier: Puritans and Indians, 1620–1675*, 3rd ed. (Norman: University of Oklahoma Press, 1995), 140, on Plymouth's involvement.

39. OPP, 227; Anderson, *Bradford's Books*, 179–183.

40. OPP, 227–228.

Chapter 9

1. Rebecca Fraser, *The Mayflower: The Families, the Voyage, and the Founding of America* (New York: St. Martin's Press, 2017), 116; David A. Lupher, *Greeks, Romans, and Pilgrims: Classical Republicanism in Early New England* (Leiden: Brill, 2017), ch. 2.

2. OPP, 160.

3. Thomas Morton, *New English Canaan, or New Canaan* (1637), 132.

4. Morton, *New English Canaan*, 134. My reading of the poem is one advanced by Joanne van der Woude, "Indians and Antiquity: Subversive Classicism in Early New England Poetry," *New England Quarterly*, 93 (2017), 418–441; Edith Murphy, "'A Rich Widow Not to Take Up or Lay Down': Solving the Riddle of Thomas Morton's 'Rise, Oedipus,'" *William and Mary Quarterly*, third series, 53 (1996), 755–768; and Jack Dempsey, "Reading the Revels: The Riddle of May Day in New England Canaan," *Early American Literature*, 34 (1999), 283–312. But David Lupher cautioned that the identification of the woman as the land and the husband the Natives is not self-evident in a reading of the poem. See his thoughtful exegesis in Lupher, *Greeks, Romans, and Pilgrims*, ch. 2.

5. OPP, 159.

6. Morton, *New English Canaan*, 138.

7. OPP, 161; details and the list of contributing communities is given in *Governor William Bradford's Letter Book*, reprinted from *The Mayflower Descendant* (Bedford, MA, 2001), 40–43.

8. This evaluation of Conant's early years in New England is based on Robert Charles Anderson, ed., *The Pilgrim Migration: Immigrants to Plymouth Colony, 1620–1633* (Boston: New England Historic and Genealogical Society, 2004), 134–143.

9. John Gorham Palfrey, *History of New England* (1858), 1:220–221.

10. For White and his efforts in Dorchester, see David Underdown, *Fire from Heaven: Life in an English Town in the Seventeenth Century* (New Haven: Yale University Press, 1992).

11. Michael P. Winship, *Godly Republicanism: Puritans, Pilgrims, and a City on a Hill* (Cambridge, MA: Harvard University Press, 2012), 132–133.

12. Samuel Eliot Morison mentions that no clergyman had been found for the Cape Ann settlement "until 1625, when a weak vessel expelled from Plymouth was thus employed." Samuel Eliot Morison, *Builders of the Bay Colony* (1964 edition), 29.

13. Winship, *Godly Republicanism*, 132–133.

14. Samuel Fuller has often been referred to as a physician. While his role as a deacon of the church in Leiden likely included visiting and comforting the sick, there is no evidence that Fuller studied medicine in any way or was referred to as a doctor before his arrival in Plymouth. However, Jeremy Bangs has pointed out that anatomical lessons (dissections) in the university's anatomy theater were open to the public; and that the university's botanical garden was provided with explanatory labels referring to the medicinal value of the different plants. That *Dodoens' Herball* (1578) was among the Pilgrims' books indicates familiarity with the university's garden, where Dodoens had been the hortulanus. The fact that as the congregation's deacon his responsibilities would have included visits to the sick may have encouraged him to seek such information. His medical training was likely furthered during his journey to America. At the time it was customary for ships to have a surgeon serve as a member of the crew. On the *Mayflower* that person was Giles Heale, who had served a surgical apprenticeship in London and been admitted to the Guild of Surgeons in 1619. A qualified surgeon, Heale attended the sick on the *Mayflower*'s journey to America and until the ship returned to England. Fuller likely assisted and learned from him during this time. Supplementing what he learned from Heale, Fuller would have had access to medical books that William Brewster brought with him to the colony— in particular Timothy Bright's *A Treatise wherein is declared the sufficiency of English medicines for cure of all diseases* (1615). Over time Fuller acquired medical books and tools of his own, as indicated in the inventory of his estate, which included "physic books" and a "surgeon's chest with the things belonging to it," and refers to a medical volume he had lent to Roger Williams. Plymouth's governor William Bradford memorialized Fuller as the colony's "surgeon and physician . . . [who] had been a great help and comfort to" the colonists. Fuller's skills and usefulness were attested to when Bradford dispatched him in 1629 to Salem in response to a request from John Endecott requesting medical aid for that community. The colonists were evidently suffering from scurvy, and though Fuller and others recognized the efficacy of citrus (thus, in a 1621 letter Plymouth's Edward Winslow recommended lemon juice be taken by those who journeyed to America) there was none available in the region. Shortly thereafter he again visited Massachusetts to lend his medical skills. We don't know how successful Fuller's efforts were on either occasion. Fuller died in Plymouth while treating his fellow colonists during what was likely a smallpox epidemic in 1633. For an excellent discussion of Fuller, including his medical knowledge, see Norman Gevitz, "Samuel Fuller of

Plymouth Plantation: A 'Skilful Physician' or 'Quacksalver'?," *Journal of the History of Medicine and Allied Sciences*, 47, no. 1 (1992), 29–48.

15. William Hubbard, *A General History of New England* (1815), 115.

16. OPP, 165.

17. John Endecott to William Bradford, May 11, 1629, in *Governor William Bradford's Letterbook*, 46–47.

18. Endicott to Bradford, in *Letterbook*, 46–47.

19. Charles Gott to William Bradford, July 30, 1629, in *Governor William Bradford's Letterbook*, 47–48.

20. Hubbard, *History*, 116–117.

21. *Records of the Governor and Company of the Massachusetts Bay, New England*, Volume I: *1628–1641*, edited by Nathaniel B. Shurtleff (Boston: 1853), 390.

22. "Higginson's Journal of the Voyage to New England," reprinted in Alexander Young, *Chronicles of the First Planters of the Colony of Massachusetts Bay* (Boston: Little and Brown, 1846), 224.

23. Francis J. Bremer, *Building a New Jerusalem: John Davenport, a Puritan in Three Worlds* (New Haven: Yale University Press, 2012), 82, 95.

24. Clergy of the Church of England database.

25. There is a lengthy historiography dealing with the formation of the Salem church, beginning with minister historians such as William Hubbard and Cotton Mather who asserted the clerical role in the founding. That position was adopted by later historians, including Perry Miller. But over a hundred years ago Williston Walker, in his *The Creeds and Platforms of Congregationalism* (Boston: Pilgrim Press, 1893), made clear that there was a church with members *before* the July 20 meeting for election of officers, and certainly before the August 6 meeting that formalized the formation.

26. Hubbard, *History*, 181–182, describing the general practice of the earliest churches formed in Massachusetts.

27. Gott to Bradford, in *Letterbook*, 47–48. Nathaniel Morton's account differs slightly from this, minimizing somewhat the lay role, which might be indicative of how the early history of the region was being rewritten to emphasize clerical influence when Morton wrote. See Morton, *New-Englands Memorial* (1669), 74–76. Hubbard's account is similar to Gott's.

28. OPP, 172.

29. Edward L. Smith, *Rev. Ralph Smith, First Settled Minister of Plymouth, 1629–1636* (Boston: s.n., 1921), 14.

30. Ralph Smith to Hugh Goodyear, c. Spring 1629, from London, in D. Plooij, *The Pilgrim Fathers from a Dutch Point of View* (New York: New York

University Press, 1932), 92. This letter was written from London, before Smith departed for New England. In it he mentioned having known Goodyear for twenty-three years.

31. Ralph Smith to Hugh Goodyear, 1638, in Plooij, *Pilgrim Fathers*, 114. I have not been able to find any definitive details about his removals or his time spent in Europe. The online Clergy of the Church of England Database does list a "Radolph Smith" as curate and then preacher at Uffington in 1616–1617, and this could be the same man.

32. Hubbard, *History*, 97.

33. Gorton to Nathaniel Morton in Smith, *Ralph Smith*, 8–9.

34. Morton, *New-Englands Memorial*, 75.

35. Francis J. Bremer, *John Winthrop: America's Forgotten Founding Father* (New York: Oxford University Press, 2003), 166–167.

36. Morton, *New-Englands Memorial*, 77.

37. Fuller was comparing Endecott to Henry Barrow, a separatist who had been arrested along with John Greenwood in 1593, condemned, and executed. He had been a contemporary of Brewster's at Cambridge, and Brewster had carried with him to New England Barrow's book, *A Brief Discovery of the False Church* (1590).

38. Samuel Fuller to William Bradford, June 28, 1630, in *Governor William Bradford's Letterbook*, 56–57. Prior to the departure of the Winthrop fleet from Southampton, the emigrants gathered in March 1630 in the Church of the Holy Rood in Southampton. John Cotton, who had accompanied Coddington and other members of his St. Botolph's parish to the port, preached a sermon to the assembled group that was later published as *God's Promise to his Plantations* (1630). Following Cotton in the pulpit, John Winthrop preached the lay sermon on "Christian Charity," in which he called on those journeying to America to place the good of the community over their individual good. The printed version of Cotton's sermon does not contain the advice Coddington claims he offered that the colonists follow the lead of Plymouth, but that may have been omitted to avoid alerting the authorities to any such intent. It is likely that Cotton, who had become the minister at St. Botolph's, Boston, Lincolnshire, in 1612 might well have learned of the Scrooby-Leiden-Plymouth congregation from those who knew them prior to their departure, including during their imprisonment in Boston.

39. This phrase was not included in the copy of the letter from Fuller and Winslow to Bradford that the Plymouth governor published in *Of Plimoth Plantation*, but was in the complete letter as in *Governor William Bradford's Letterbook*, 57.

40. Samuel Fuller and Edward Winslow to William Bradford, William Brewster, and Ralph Smith, July 26, 1630, in *Governor William Bradford's Letterbook*, 57–58.

41. Samuel Fuller to William Bradford, June 28, 1630, in *Governor William Bradford's Letterbook*, 565–567.

42. Samuel Fuller to William Bradford, August 2, 1630, in *Governor William Bradford's Letterbook*, 58–59.

43. This is a point that Stephen Foster made in *The Long Argument: English Puritanism and the Shaping of New England Culture, 1630–1650* (Chapel Hill: University of North Carolina Press, 1991), pointing out that "the cast of mind" among English puritans at the time "virtually dictated that the churches of New England . . . would conform to a pattern that would be called Congregational," 154. But Perry Miller, in his *Orthodoxy in Massachusetts* (New York: Harper & Row, 1970 edition), 128, argued that the church in Salem would have been no different if Plymouth had never existed. Theodore Dwight Bozeman was even more explicit in arguing (*To Live Ancient Lives* [Chapel Hill: University of North Carolina Press, 1988], 115) that Plymouth was "pathetically unimportant."

44. Edward Winslow, *Hypocrisie Unmasked* (1646), 98–99. Two essays that argue for the importance of the Plymouth model are Slayden Yarborough, "The Influence of Plymouth Colony Separatism on Salem: An Interpretation of John Cotton's Letter of 1630 to Samuel Skelton," *Church History*, 51 (1982), 290–303; and Lewis M. Robinson, "The Formative Influence of Plymouth Church on American Congregationalism," *Bibliotheca Sacra*, 127 (1970), 232–240.

45. *Winthrop's Journal*, 39. See the discussion of this in Winship, *Godly Republicanism*, 152–153.

46. *Winthrop's Journal*, 48–49.

47. Hubbard, *History*, 180.

48. William Coddington, *A Demonstration of True Love unto You the Rulers of the Colony of the Massachusetts in New England* (London, 1674), 10.

49. John Cotton to Samuel Skelton, October 2, 1630, in Sargent Bush Jr., ed., *The Correspondence of John Cotton* (Chapel Hill: University of North Carolina Press, 2001), 141–149. The debate over the significance of that letter was begun with Miller, *Orthodoxy in Massachusetts, 1630–1650* (1933), and continued in Larzer Ziff, "The Salem Puritans in the 'Free Aire of a New World,'" *Huntington Library Quarterly*, 20 (1957), 373–384; and David D. Hall's introduction to his "John Cotton's Letter to Samuel Skelton," *William and Mary Quarterly*, 3rd series, 22 (1965), 478–480. See also Bush's discussion in *Cotton Correspondence*. Interestingly,

after John Robinson's death, Cotton would write to his friend Hugh Goodyear, wondering why the remnants of Robinson's congregation had not at the time merged with Goodyear's English Reformed Church of Leiden, suggesting that he saw the differences between them as insignificant. John Cotton to Hugh Goodyear, April 12, 1630, in Bush, *Cotton Correspondence*, 139–141.

50. The details, omitted by Winthrop in his *Journal* and Bradford in his history "Of Plimoth Plantation," is provided by Cotton Mather in *Magnalia Christi Americana; or, The Ecclesiastical History of New-England* (1853 edition), 1:128. See the discussion in David S. Lovejoy, *Religious Enthusiasm in the New World: Heresy to Revolution* (Cambridge, MA: Harvard University Press, 1985), 54–55.

51. *Winthrop's Journal*, 71.

52. Hubbard, *History*, 186.

53. Roger Williams to John Winthrop, before December 1632, in Glenn W. LaFantasie, ed., *The Correspondence of Roger Williams,* Volume I: *1629–1653* (Providence, RI: Brown University Press, 1988), 9.

54. In 1646 Bradford added to his account of the colony an observation in which he acknowledged that when he began to write his account "little did I think that the downfall of the Bishops, with their courts, canons and ceremonies, etc. had been so near" (OPP, 3r). For an excellent brief treatment of "The Puritan Revolution," in England that discusses the impact of the New England (and Dutch) congregational influence on events, see John Morrill's essay of that name in John Coffey and Paul C. H. Lim, eds., *The Cambridge Companion to Puritanism* (Cambridge, UK: Cambridge University Press, 2008), 67–88. I have dealt specifically and at length with the New England perspectives on and contributions to the debates in England in various works, but particularly in *Congregationalist Communion: Clerical Friendship in the Anglo-American Puritan Community, 1610–1690* (Boston: Northeastern University Press, 1994). For a recent work focusing on puritanism in this broader context, see Michael P. Winship, *Hot Protestants: A History of Puritanism in England and America* (New Haven: Yale University Press, 2019).

55. OPP, 181.

56. OPP, 16.

57. For Bradford's use of Pliny the Elder, see David A. Lupher, *Greeks, Romans, and Pilgrims: Classical Receptions in Early America* (Leiden: Brill, 2017), 232–233. Lupher effectively argues that Bradford was still optimistic when he completed writing his history of Plymouth, challenging darker interpretations of the Plymouth governor's mood.

Chapter 10

1. Richard Dunn, James Savage, and Laetitia Yeandle, eds., *The Journal of John Winthrop, 1630–1649* (Cambridge, MA: Harvard University Press, 1996), 44, hereafter *Winthrop's Journal*. Williams related the invitation and claimed it was unanimous in Roger Williams to John Cotton Jr., March 25, 1671, in Glenn W. LaFantasie, ed., *The Correspondence of Roger Williams* (Providence, RI: Brown University Press, 1988), 2:630.

2. Williams to Cotton, in LaFantasie, *Correspondence*, 2:630.

3. *Winthrop's Journal*, 50.

4. Williams to Cotton, in LaFantasie, *Correspondence*, 2:630.

5. *Winthrop's Journal*, 50. The influence of the Conant faction is noted in LaFantasie, *Correspondence*, 1:13.

6. Williams to Cotton, in LaFantasie, *Correspondence*, 2:630.

7. OPP, 193.

8. *Winthrop's Journal*, 81–83.

9. OPP, 195–196.

10. OPP, 193.

11. Nathaniel Morton, *New-Englands Memorial* (1669), 78. "Sebaptist" refers to someone who baptizes himself. Johnson did so because he rejected the efficacy of baptism as he had received it as an infant and as it was offered in the other churches of his day. Roger Williams appeared to be moving in this same direction when he rejected the authority of established churches.

12. OPP, 196.

13. See discussion by LaFantasie in *Correspondence*, 1:13. John Winthrop set forth Williams's controversial opinions in a letter to John Endecott, January 3, 1634, *Winthrop Papers, III* (Boston: Massachusetts Historical Society, 1943), 146–149.

14. Morton, *New-Englands Memorial*, 82.

15. For the disputes that led to Williams expulsion from the Bay, see Francis J. Bremer, *John Winthrop: America's Forgotten Founding Father* (New York: Oxford University Press, 2003), 249–252.

16. John M. Barry, *Roger Williams and the Creation of the American State* (London: Penguin Books, 2012), 215–216.

17. That underground is best approached in Peter Lake, *The Boxmaker's Revenge: "Orthodoxy," "Heterodoxy" and the Politics of the Parish in Early Stuart London* (Stanford, CA: Stanford University Press, 2001). See also David R. Como, *Blown by the Spirit: Puritanism and the Emergence of an Antinomian Underground in Pre-Civil-War England* (Stanford, CA: Stanford University Press, 2004).

18. The best study of that controversy is Michael P. Winship's *Making Heretics: Militant Protestantism and Free Grace in Massachusetts, 1636–1641* (Princeton: Princeton University Press, 2002). Puritans believed that the spirit could inspire readers of scripture to better understand the meaning of the text, though they cautioned against expressing too much certainty regarding such readings. Hutchinson went beyond what was permissible when she claimed that the Spirit spoke to her directly.

19. Winship finds some evidence that one of Gorton's supporters expressed radical views in challenging John Wheelwright, himself a supporter of Hutchinson; *Making Heretics*, 188–189.

20. Gorton's views and career are best set forth in Philip F. Gura, *A Glimpse of Sion's Glory: Puritan Radicalism in New England, 1620–1660* (Middletown, CT: Wesleyan University Press, 1984), ch. 10.

21. Smith's presence in Boston and his involvement in the synod were confirmed in a letter he sent to Hugh Goodyear back in Leiden; see Ralph Smith to Hugh Goodyear, 1638, in D. Plooij, *The Pilgrim Fathers from a Dutch Point of View* (New York: New York University Press, 1932), 114.

22. Writing in the eighteenth century, the Boston clergyman Charles Chauncy had access to a manuscript account of the synod in which he found that the Plymouth representative (Smith) had voted against the findings. Charles Chauncy, *Seasonable Thoughts on the State of Religion in New England* (1743), vii. Smith's support of some of the views of Roger Williams in Plymouth in 1632, coupled with his rejection of the synod's list of errors to be condemned, suggest that differences of opinion with Brewster and others in Plymouth may have contributed to his departure.

23. Morton, *New-Englands Memorial*, 108.

24. Samuel Gorton to Nathaniel Morton, Peter Force, ed. *American Archives* 9 vol (1837–1853), Volume Four, item 7.

25. Nathaniel B. Shurtleff and David Pulsifer, eds., *Records of the Colony of New Plymouth, in New England*, 12 vols. (New York: AMS Press, 1968) I, 101, 105. Gorton reported that during his first appearance, when he complained that one of the magistrates had spoken "hyperbolically," that individual had asked Elder Brewster, who was here to observe, what this meant, to which Brewster replied that Gorton had said he lied. Gorton to Morton, Force, *American Archives*, Volume Four, item 7.

26. Morton, *New-Englands Memorial*, 91–92.

27. William Bradford, "Of Plimoth Plantation," OPP, 13.

28. Examples of individuals who were received back into the church at Barnstable following excommunication are recorded in John Lothrop's

notebook ("Scituate and Barnstable Church Records," *New England Historical and Genealogical Register*, 10 (1856), 41.

29. Gorton to Morton, Force, *American Archives*, Volume Four, item 7.

30. Roger Williams to John Winthrop, March 8, 1641, in LaFantasie, *Williams Correspondence*, 1:215.

31. The financial aspects of the early history of Plymouth are the focus of Ruth A. McIntyre, *Debts Hopeful and Desperate* (Plymouth, MA: Plimoth Plantation, 1963). See also Nick Bunker, *Making Haste from Babylon: The Mayflower Pilgrims and Their World* (New York: Knopf, 2010), which focuses on the beaver trade in the economic history of the colony.

32. OPP, 109.

33. Lisa Brooks, *Our Beloved Kin: A New History of King Philip's War* (New Haven: Yale University Press, 2018), 55–56.

34. For more on this, see Brooks, *Our Beloved Kin*, and Christine DeLucia, *Memory Lands: King Philip's War and the Place of Violence in the Northeast* (New Haven: Yale University Press, 2018).

35. OPP, 210, 229.

36. OPP, 192.

37. Erin McGough, *Digging Duxbury: The Brewster Homestead's Archaeological Past* (Duxbury: Duxbury Rural & Historical Society, 2013), 9.

38. OPP, 192.

39. Jeremy Dupertuis Bangs, ed., *The Town Records of Duxbury, Bridgewater, and Dartmouth during the Time of Plymouth Colony, 1620–1692* (Leiden: Leiden American Pilgrim Museum, 2017), 9.

40. Jeremy Dupertuis Bangs, ed., *The Town Records of Marshfield during the Time of Plymouth Colony, 1620–1692* (Leiden: Leiden American Pilgrim Museum, 2015), 11.

41. Quoted in Chaplin Burrage, *The Early English Dissenters in the Light of Recent Research (1550–1641)*, 2 vols. (Cambridge, UK: Cambridge University Press, 1912), 2:301–302.

42. Francis J. Bremer, *Building a New Jerusalem: John Davenport, a Puritan in Three Worlds* (New Haven: Yale University Press, 2012), 100–101.

43. William B. Sprague, *Annals of the American Pulpit, Volume I* (1857), 49–50.

44. Richard Greaves, "John Lothrop," *Oxford Dictionary of National Biography*.

45. It is certainly likely that he had corresponded about his move with Brewster, but the absence of any surviving correspondence makes this conjecture.

46. This is interesting since one of John Cotton's complaints about the Salem church was that they received one of the members of Lothrop's London congregation to receive the sacraments while not giving the same privilege to William Coddington and others known to Cotton.

47. Jeremy Dupertuis Bangs, "Introduction," in Bangs, *The Seventeenth-Century Town Records of Scituate, Massachusetts* (Boston: New England Historic and Genealogical Society, 1997), 1:20.

48. "Scituate and Barnstable Church Records," *New England Historical and Genealogical Register*, 9 (1855), 279. These are records kept by Lothrop. Hereafter cited as Scituate Church Records (1855).

49. James Cudworth to John Stoughton, December 1634, in Bangs, *Scituate*, 3:43.

50. "Scituate and Barnstable Church Records," *New England Historical and Genealogical Register*, 10 (1856), 37. These are records kept by Lothrop. Hereafter cited as Scituate Church Records.

51. Morton, *New-Englands Memorial*, 71–72.

52. Scituate Church Records, 37–41.

53. Scituate Church Records, 39.

54. Scituate Church Records, 39.

55. John Lothrop to Thomas Prince (then governor of Plymouth), September 28, 1638, in Bangs, *Scituate*, 3:345.

56. Samuel Deane, *History of Scituate, Massachusetts from Its Settlement to 1831* (1831), 59–60. In his entry on Lothrop in the *Oxford Dictionary of National Biography*, Richard Greaves states that the problems in Scituate included "suspicions (which proved unfounded) of plotting between local residents and people in England." While Greaves states these were unfounded, it is worth noting that one of those who did not follow Lothrop to Barnstable was William Vassall.

57. OPP, 192.

58. H. Kirk-Smith, *William Brewster, "The Father of New England": His Life and Times, 1567–1644* (Boston, Lincolnshire: Richard Kay, 1992), 246, 248–249; Ashbel Steele, *Chief of the Pilgrims: The Life and Time of William Brewster* (1857), 367.

59. D. Plooij, *The Pilgrim Fathers from a Dutch Point of View* (New York: New York University Press, 1932), 100–120; Ralph Smith to Hugh Goodyear, 138, in Plooij, *Pilgrim Fathers*, 114. I thank Robert Charles Anderson for discussion of what "charge" he was referring to.

60. Morton, *New-Englands Memorial*, 73.

61. Jeremy Dupertuis Bangs, *Pilgrim Edward Winslow: New England's First International Diplomat; A Documentary History* (Boston: New England

Historic and Genealogical Society, 2004), 148–152. Winslow quoted on 149.

62. OPP, 214. There are two John Glovers in the Clergy of the Church of England database who may have been the Mr. Glover recruited by Winslow. One graduated from Oxford in 1616 and was ordained in that same year. The other John Glover also graduated from Oxford and was ordained in 1618.

63. OPP, 214. Bradford attributed Norton's decision to the fact that in Ipswich there "were many rich and able men and sundry of his acquaintance" (214).

64. OPP, 220. Reyner ministered to the church until 1654, when he spent the winter of 1654–1655 in Boston. There were some unspecified difficulties between him and the church, and when, following his return to Plymouth in the spring, the congregation refused to meet his terms, he left and settled in Dover, New Hampshire.

65. *Winthrop's Journal*, 199.

66. John Venn, *Alumni Cantabrigienses: A Biographical List of All Known Students, Graduates and Holders of Office at the University of Cambridge, from the Earliest Times to 1900*, Part I, volume 3 (1924), "Partridge, Ralph."

67. Cotton Mather, *Magnalia Christi Americana; or, The Ecclesiastical History of New England* (1858 edition), 1:404–405.

68. Morton, *New-Englands Memorial*, 72.

69. Jeremy Dupertuis Bangs, *Plymouth Colony's Private Libraries, as Recorded in Wills and Inventories, 1633–1692* (Leiden: Leiden American Pilgrim Museum, 2016), 233ff.

70. Williston Walker, *The Creeds and Platforms of Congregationalism* (Boston: Pilgrim Press, 1960 edition), 175, 184.

71. Morton, *New-Englands Memorial*, 74.

72. OPP, 219–220.

73. OPP, 242.

74. *Winthrop's Journal*, 398–399.

75. Bangs, *Scituate*, 31–37.

76. Some of the clergymen who served Plymouth colony churches are discussed in H. Roger King, *Cape Cod and Plymouth Colony in the Seventeenth Century* (Lanham, MD: University Press of America, 1994).

77. John Reyner and William Brewster to John Cotton and John Wilson, August 5, 1639, in Sargent Bush Jr., ed., *The Correspondence of John Cotton* (Chapel Hill: University of North Carolina Press, 2001), 291–293. Cotton's view in the *Pouring Out of the Seven Vials* is quoted by Bush, 291.

78. John Reyner to John Cotton, October 15, 1639, in Bush, *Cotton Correspondence*, 293–297; John Cotton to John Reyner, October 18, 1639, in Bush, *Cotton Correspondence*, 298–299.

79. OPP, 243.

80. *Winthrop's Journal*, 37–74.

81. Douglas Anderson, *William Bradford's Books: Of Plimmoth Plantation and the Printed Word* (Baltimore, MD: Johns Hopkins University Press, 2003), 200, and see Anderson's discussion of the three responses, 197–201.

82. OPP, 244–248.

83. OPP, 244–248. The unanimous opposition to ex officio oaths is not surprising, since puritans had fought the legality of such oaths imposed by English authorities against religious nonconformists.

84. OPP, 244–248. And see Anderson, *Bradford's Books*, 201–202 In keeping with scriptural injunctions, the animals that could be identified were killed in front of Granger prior to his execution and the animals then cast into a large burial pit. Similar cases occurred in the New Haven colony in 1641 and 1646; see Francis J. Bremer, *Building a New Jerusalem: John Davenport, a Puritan in Three Worlds* (New Haven: Yale University Press, 2012), 217–218.

85. OPP, 243.

Conclusion

1. One of the mysteries surrounding William Bradford's narrative "Of Plimmoth Plantation" is that he misdates the death of his friend and mentor, putting it in 1643 instead of 1644. Douglas Anderson notes this and suggests reasons in *William Bradford's Books: Of Plimmoth Plantation and the Printed Word* (Baltimore, MD: Johns Hopkins University Press, 2003), 203–204.

2. OPP, 253–254.

3. Nathaniel Morton, *New-Englands Memorial* (1669), 80.

4. Sargent Bush Jr., ed., *The Correspondence of John Cotton* (Chapel Hill: University of North Carolina Press, 2001), 291.

5. William Vassall, one of the disputants, wrote to John Cotton on April 6, 1644, mentioning a planned meeting at Partridge's house which had failed to occur. William Vassall to John Cotton, April 6, 1644, printed in Samuel Deane, *History of Scituate, Massachusetts from Its Settlement to 1831* (1831), 72–73.

6. OPP, 254.

7. "Modell of Church and Civil Power," printed in Robert Francis Scholz, "The Reverend Elders: Faction, Fellowship and Politics in the Ministerial Community of Massachusetts Bay, 1630–1720" (PhD, University of Minnesota, 1966), 61. For a discussion, see Francis J. Bremer, *Congregational Communion: Clerical Friendship in the Anglo-American Puritan Community, 1610–1692* (Boston: Northeastern University Press, 1994), 112. The focus of *Congregational Communion* is on the informal and formal means by which puritan clergy maintained and advanced unity.

8. *The Journal of John Winthrop 1630–1649*, edited by Richard S. Dunn, James Savage, and Laetitia Yeandle (Cambridge, MA: Harvard University Press, 1996), 102–103.

9. Smith's 1638 letter to Goodyear indicated he had been "much" in Boston, where, "besides our Synod," much of his business had been. There is no evidence to indicate if he still held the position of pastor in Plymouth at this time nor if he had been invited to the synod as a member of the Plymouth church. Ralph Smith to Hugh Goodyear, 1638, in D. Plooij, *The Pilgrim Fathers from a Dutch Point of View* (New York: New York University Press, 1932), 114. Edward Johnson, a contemporary, in his *The Wonder Working Providence of Sion's Saviour in New England* (1654), ed. J. Franklin Jameson (1910 reprint), 170–171, indicates that there were twenty-five lay and clerical representatives from throughout New England. While we know that Smith was there it is also possible that William Brewster may have been there as well.

10. The best discussion of this entire episode is Michael P. Winship, *Making Heretics: Militant Protestantism and Free Grace in Massachusetts, 1636–1641* (Princeton: Princeton University Press, 2002).

11. The errors were not identified as positions specifically held by members of the Hutchinson circle. For an excellent discussion see Winship, *Making Heretics*, 151–155. The list of errors and their confutation can be found in John Winthrop, *A Short Story of the Rise, reign, and ruine of the Antinomians, Familists, & Libertines* in David D. Hall, *The Antinomian Controversy, 1636–1638: A Documentary History* (Middletown, CT: Wesleyan University Press, 1968), 219–243.

12. Error 54 and the confutation are in Hall, *Antinomian Controversy*, 233–234.

13. *Winthrop's Journal*, 234.

14. Charles Chauncy, *Seasonable Thoughts on the State of Religion in New England* (1743), vii. The manuscript that Chauncy referred to is not known to still exist.

15. Good and up-to-date overviews of the struggle are Michael Braddick, *God's Fury, England's Fire: A New History of the English Civil Wars* (London: Allen Lane, 2008), and Blair Worden, *The English Civil Wars, 1640–1660* (London: Weidenfield and Nicholson, 2009).

16. See John Morrill, ed., *Oliver Cromwell and the English Revolution* (London: Longman, 1990), and *The Nature of the English Revolution* (London: Longman, 1993); Crawford Gribben, *John Owen and English Puritanism* (Oxford: Oxford University Press, 2017); Hunter Powell, *The Crisis of British Protestantism: Church Power in the Puritan Revolution* (Manchester: Manchester University Press, 2015); and Chad Van Dixhoorn, *God's Ambassadors: The Westminster Assembly and the Reformation of the English Pulpit* (Grand Rapids: Reformation Heritage Books, 2018).

17. OPP, 3r.

18. William Hooke, *New Englands Sence of Old Englands and Irelands Sorrowes* (1645), reprinted in Samuel H. Emery, *History of Taunton* (1893), 116–117. This was preached in Taunton, in the Plymouth Colony.

19. For days of humiliation and thanksgiving in regard to the English Civil Wars, see Bremer, *Congregational Communion*, 144–145. For such days in general, see Willam DeLoss Love, *The Fast and Thanksgiving Days of New England* (1895); and Richard P. Gildrie, "The Ceremonial Puritan: Days of Humiliation and Thanksgiving," *New England Historical and Genealogical Register*, 136 (1982), 3–16.

20. "Scituate and Barnstable Church Records," *New England Historical and Genealogical Register*, 10 (1856), 37–40.

21. Cotton quoted in Bremer, *Congregational Communion*, 147.

22. Winslow eventually died in 1655 while serving as one of Cromwell's commissioners engaged in the Protector's "Western Design," the attempted conquest of Spanish colonies in the West Indies. For a fuller discussion of the Western Design, see Carla G. Pestana, *The English Conquest of Jamaica: Oliver Cromwell's Bid for Empire* (Cambridge, MA: Harvard University Press, 2017).

23. All scholars of this period owe a debt of gratitude to Chad Van Dixhoorn for *The Minutes and Papers of the Westminster Assembly, 1643–1653*, 5 vols. (Oxford: Oxford University Press, 2012). I have discussed these issues more fully in *Congregational Communion*, especially chapters 6 and 7.

24. For radicalism in the English Civil War period, see Christopher Hill, *The World Turned Upside Down: Radical Ideas during the English Revolution* (London: Temple Smith, 1972); and Ann Hughes, *Gangraena and*

the Struggle for the English Revolution (New York: Oxford University Press, 2004).

25. I have discussed this further in Francis J. Bremer, *Lay Empowerment and the Development of Puritanism* (London: Palgrave Macmillan, 2015), esp. 112–116. And see Michael Braddick, *The Common Freedom of the People: John Lilburne and the English Revolution* (Oxford: Oxford University Press, 2018).

26. Bradford quoted Baillie in his "First Discourse," commenting that while there was no formal agreement for Massachusetts churches to follow that model, "if they of Plymouth have helped any of the first Comers in their theory by hearing and discerning their practices, therein the Scriptures [were] fulfilled that the kingdom of heaven is like unto leaven", OPP, 65.

27. Milton quoted in David S. Lovejoy, *Religious Enthusiasm in the New World: Heresy to Revolution* (Cambridge, MA: Harvard University Press, 1985), 51.

28. Edwards quoted in Hughes, *Gangraena*, 133. This work is the definitive study of Edwards and his book.

29. Edwards quoted in Hughes, *Gangraena*, 136.

30. For the career of Sarah Dudley Keayne, see Francis J. Bremer, *First Founders: American Puritans and Puritanism in an Atlantic World* (Hanover, NH: University Press of New England, 2012), 106–118.

31. William Rathband, *A Brief Narration of Some Church Courses . . . in New England* (1644), 46–47.

32. William Bradford, *First Dialogue (A Dialogue or the sum of a Conference between some young men born in New England and sundry Ancient men that came out of Holland and Old England Anno dom. 1648)*, in *Publications of the Colonial Society of Massachusetts*, vol. 22 (Boston, 1920), 124.

33. "First Dialogue," 134. In taking this line, Bradford was following the lead that had been provided by John Robinson, who, according to Edward Winslow, had told the emigrating colonists to "use all means to avoid and shake off the name of Brownist, being a mere nick-name and brand to make religion odious." Edward Winslow, *Hypocrisie Unmasked* (1646), 97–99.

34. Mark Sargent has pointed out how some of Bradford's criticism of Cotton was changed by his nephew Nathaniel Morton when Morton copied the dialogue into the Plymouth church records, presumably because John Cotton Jr. was about to assume a post as Plymouth's pastor. See Mark L. Sargent, "William Bradford's 'Dialogue' with History," *New England Quarterly*, 65 (1992), 389–421. I thank the Massachusetts Historical

Society for making a copy of Bradford's original manuscript available so that I could examine these passages in more detail.

35. "First Dialogue," 123, 120.

36. William Bradford, "A Dialogue or 3rd Conference between some Young Men born in New England, and some Ancient Men which came out of Holland and Old England, concerning the Church and the Government Thereof," ed. with a preface and notes by Charles Deane, reprinted from the *Proceedings of the Massachusetts Historical Society* (Boston, 1870), 51.

37. "First Dialogue," 118. John Davenport was perhaps the most emphatic of all New England's clergy in insisting that no assembly, conference, or synod of clergy could have authority over an individual congregation.

38. "Third Dialogue," 41.

39. "Third Dialogue," 39, 44.

40. "Third Dialogue," 48ff.

41. Thomas Lechford, *Plain Dealing, or News from New England* (1642), edited with an introduction by J. Hammond Trumbull (Boston, 1867), 94.

42. John Clarke, *Ill Newes from New England* (1652), reprinted in *Massachusetts Historical Society Collections*, 4th series, 2 (1854), 15, 96.

43. Williams quoted in Lovejoy, *Enthusiasm*, 59–60.

44. Lovejoy, *Enthusiasm*, 58.

45. William Coddington, *A Demonstration of True Love unto You the Rulers of the Colony of Massachusetts in New England* (London, 1674), 10.

46. "First Dialogue" 118–119.

47. Letter of the General Court (text is that approved by the Court of Assistants, which varied slightly from that of the Deputies), May 15, 1646, printed in Willison Walker, *The Creeds and Platforms of Congregationalism* (Boston: Pilgrim Press, 1960 edition with an introduction by Douglas Horton), 169.

48. Walker, *Creeds and Platforms*, 171.

49. *Winthrop's Journal*, 634–635.

50. *Winthrop's Journal*, 636–638. There is no comparable description of what brought the Salem church to acquiesce.

51. *Winthrop's Journal*, 688.

52. Walker, *Creeds and Platforms*, 175.

53. Walker, *Creeds and Platforms*, 184–188.

54. Bradford, of course, was still alive, but made no specific reference to the deliberations or conclusions of the assembly. His narrative "Of Plimmoth Plantation" ended with the events of 1645, the eve of the gathering, and went back and interjected his satisfaction with the course of the English

Civil Wars in 1646. Neither of his dialogues, composed in 1648 and 1652, deals with the event.

55. Partridge's account has never been published. The manuscript is in the collections of the American Antiquarian Society (Mather Papers, miscellaneous writings, B11 f10, Ralph Partridge, Model of Church Discipline) and will be transcribed and published online by the Hidden Histories project of the Congregational Library and Archives in Boston. But Henry Martyn Dexter printed some portions of the text in *The Congregationalism of the Last Three Hundred Years, as Seen in Its Literature* (1880). This is p. 445.

56. Text of the Platform in Walker, *Creeds and Platforms*, 219.

57. Partridge in Dexter, *Congregationalism*, 445.

58. Text of the Platform in Walker, *Creeds and Platforms*, 234.

59. "Scituate and Barnstable Church Records," *New England Historical and Genealogical Register*, 10 (1856), 38.

60. Partridge in Dexter, *Congregationalism*, 446.

61. Text of the Platform in Walker, *Creeds and Platforms*, 235–237.

62. Partridge in Dexter, *Congregationalism*, 446.

63. See chapter 4, earlier.

64. Discussion of those who were more tolerant is found in Bremer, *First Founders*, in the chapter on John Leverett.

65. In 1956 James Fulton Maclear published "'The Heart of New England Rent': The Mystical Element in Early Puritan History," *The Mississippi Valley Historical Review*, 42 (1956), 621–652. Maclear argued for a continuity between mainline puritanism and Quakerism, pointing out the importance of divine inspiration to each group. Like many historians, for a long time I denied any close connection between puritans and Quakers, but my realization of the importance of lay preaching has made me reconsider. Another scholar who drew this connection was Lovejoy, *Enthusiasm*.

66. Nathaniel B. Shurtleff, ed., *Records of the Governor and Company of the Massachusetts Bay . . . ,* Volume IV, Part I (1854), 122.

67. This is discussed at greater length in Bremer, *Lay Empowerment*, 100–104.

68. Mark Peterson, "The Plymouth Church and the Evolution of Puritan Religious Culture," *New England Quarterly*, 66 (1993), 575–576.

69. For a discussion of this reverse migration, see Bremer, *Congregational Communion*, 179ff. The quote from Mather is on 179–180. See also Susan Hardman More, *Pilgrims: New World Settlers and the Call of Home* (New Haven: Yale University Press, 2008).

70. Morton, *New-Englands Memorial*, 109.

71. Mather, *Magnalia*, 1:405.

72. Morton, *New-Englands Memorial*, 76.

73. The appreciation of Southworth is from Morton, *New-Englands Memorial*, 57. Cotton was available since charges of an illicit sexual liaison while he was in New Haven had dogged him and led most churches to shun him.

74. Edward Winslow to John Winthrop, November 24, 1645, *Winthrop Papers, Volume V: 1645–1649* (Boston: Massachusetts Historical Society, 1947), 55–56. See the discussion in George D. Langdon, *Pilgrim Colony: A History of New Plymouth, 1620–1691* (New Haven: Yale University Press, 64–65). Vassall was a supporter of a similar petition presented to the Massachusetts General Court by Robert Child and others in 1646.

75. "Third Dialogue," 57.

Bibliographical Essay

Primary Sources

The starting point for understanding the history of the Plymouth congregation and its role in New England is William Bradford's *Of Plimoth Plantation*. Written by the colony's longtime governor, it was used in manuscript by various colonial historians, including Cotton Mather and Thomas Prince. The volume disappeared at the time of the American Revolution, presumably carried off from the library where it was kept by British soldiers who evacuated Boston in 1776. It made its way to the library of the Bishop of London, where it was discovered in the nineteenth century. The first publication of the work was in 1856. In 1897 the manuscript was returned to America and deposited in the Library of the Commonwealth of Massachusetts. Since then there have been five additional publications, the last edited by Samuel Eliot Morison and published in 1952. A new edition in two forms—online and print—will be published in 2020 under the aegis of the New England Beginnings partnership with the joint sponsorship of the Colonial Society of Massachusetts and the New England Historic and Genealogical Society. This features correction of past transcription errors, a presentation of the text as Bradford intended, up-to-date annotation, and an essay providing the Native perspective on the subject.

Bradford devoted relatively little attention to the religious dimensions of the story, but was far more expansive in discussing that topic in three "dialogues" or "conferences" he composed in the form of "some ancient men which came out of Holland and Old England" answering questions about religion and church government posed by "some young men in New England." The first of these was published in *Publications of the Colonial Society of Massachusetts*, volume 22: *Plymouth Church Records, 1620–1859, Part I* (Boston: Colonial Society of Massachusetts, 1920). The second manuscript has been lost. The third dialogue was printed in *Proceedings of the Massachusetts Historical Society*, volume 11. Bradford also shared views in poems that he wrote, which have been collected and published in Michael G. Runyan, ed., *The Collected Verse of William Bradford* (St. Paul, MN: John Colet Press, 1974). Bradford collected numerous letters dealing with the colony's origins and history, some of which he incorporated into his history, but he omitted some parts in that manuscript. Only a small portion of this collection has survived, published as

"Governor Bradford's Letter Book," *Collections of the Massachusetts Historical Society*, III (1794).

A variety of other contemporary publications deal with this history. *A relation or journal of the beginning and proceedings of the English plantation settled at Plimoth in New England* (1622), commonly known as *Mourt's Relation*, is available as *A Journal of the Pilgrims at Plymouth: Mourt's Relation*, edited by Dwight B. Heath (New York: Corinth Books, 1963). Edward Winslow wrote *Good Newes from New England* (1624), available in a modern edition as *"Good News from New England" by Edward Winslow: A Scholarly Edition*, edited by Kelly Wisecup (Amherst: University of Massachusetts Press, 2014). Winslow provided further insights in Edward Winslow, *Hypocrisie Unmasked* (1646). Nathaniel Morton, Bradford's nephew, used some of his uncle's papers in writing *New-England Memoriall, or, A brief relation of the most memorable and remarkable passages of the providence of God manifested to the planters of New-England in America* (1637). A critical contemporary view is found in Thomas Morton (no relation to Nathaniel), *New England Canaan* (1637).

Primary sources for understanding the religious beliefs and practices of the Plymouth congregation include the works of John Robinson. A collection is *The Works of John Robinson, pastor of the Pilgrim Fathers*, edited by Robert Ashton (London: J. Snow, 1851). Robert Cushman's *The Cry of a Stone: A Treatise Showing What Is Right Matter, Form and Government of the Visible Church of Christ* reprinted from edition of 1642, edited by Michael R. Paulick, transcription and annotation by James Baker (Plymouth, MA: General Society of Mayflower Descendants, 2016), sets forth the principles on which the congregation was formed. Of value in understanding the social gospel of the congregation is Robert Cushman, *A Sermon Preached at Plimoth in New-England December 9, 1621*.

Secondary Sources

A useful overview of puritanism and puritan beliefs is Francis J. Bremer, *Puritanism: A Very Short Introduction* (New York: Oxford University Press, 2009). A good narrative overview is Michael P. Winship, *Hot Protestants: A History of Puritanism in England and America* (New Haven: Yale University Press, 2019). The best study of the congregation in England and the Netherlands is Jeremy D. Bangs, *Strangers and Pilgrims, Travelers and Sojourners: Leiden and the Foundations of Plymouth Plantation* (Plymouth, MA: Society of Mayflower Descendants, 2009). Timothy George, *John Robinson and the English Separatist Tradition* (Macon, GA: Mercer University Press, 1982), is the best study of the congregation's pastor.

There are a large number of books that deal with various aspects of the colony without paying much if any attention to religion. An exception is

Robert Charles Anderson's *The Mayflower Migration: Immigrants to Plymouth Colony, 1620* (Boston: New England Historic and Genealogical Society, 2020). Anderson's *The Pilgrim Migration, Immigrants to Plymouth Colony, 1620–1633* (Boston: New England Historic and Genealogical Society, 2004) is an invaluable biographical dictionary of all who arrived in the colony in those years. John Demos, *A Little Commonwealth: Family Life in Plymouth Colony* (New York: Oxford University Press, 1970); Darrett Rutman, *Husbandmen of Plymouth: Farms and Villages in the Old Colony, 1620–1692* (Plymouth, MA: Plimoth Plantation, 1968); and James Deetz and Patricia Scott-Deetz, *The Times of Their Lives: Life, Love, and Death in Plymouth Colony* (New York: W. H. Freeman, 2000), deal with various aspects of the social history of the colony.

George Langdon's *Pilgrim Colony: A History of New Plymouth, 1620–1692* (New Haven: Yale University Press, 1966) is the most comprehensive overview of the colony's history. Nathaniel Philbrick, *Mayflower, A Story of Courage, Community, and War* (New York: Viking, 2006), is a well-written narrative that focuses largely on relations with the Natives. Nick Bunker's *Make Haste from Babylon: The Mayflower Pilgrims and Their World, a New History* (New York: Alfred A. Knopf, 2010) is insightful on the economic dimensions of the story and, in particular, the fur trade. Rebecca Fraser's *The Mayflower: The Voyage, the Families, and the Founding of America* (New York: St. Martin's, 2019) focuses on one of the more important colonists, Edward Winslow. This can be complemented with Jeremy D. Bangs, *Pilgrim Edward Winslow, New England's First International Diplomat* (Boston: New England Historic and Genealogical Society, 2004). A new evaluation of the colony's nemesis Thomas Morton is Peter C. Mancall, *The Trials of Thomas Morton: An Anglican Lawyer, His Puritan Foes, and the Battle for New England* (New Haven: Yale University Press, 2019). The impact of the colony on America is explored in John Turner, *They Knew They Were Pilgrims: Plymouth Colony and the Contest for American Liberty* (New Haven: Yale University Press, 2020).

A number of recent works shed important new light on the Native population of New England (New Haven: Yale University Press, 2018), which is far broader in scope than the title suggests; Lisa Blee and Jean M. O'Brien, *Monumental Mobility: The Memory Work of Massasoit* (Chapel Hill: University of North Carolina Press, 2019); and David J. Silverman, *This Land Is Their Land: The Wampanoag Indians, Plymouth Colony, and the Troubled History of Thanksgiving* (New York: Bloomsbury, 2019). A forthcoming work of interest is Andrew Lipman, *Squanto's Odyssey* (New Haven: Yale University Press, forthcoming).

Index

For the benefit of digital users, indexed terms that span two pages (e.g., 52–53) may, on occasion, appear on only one of those pages.

Note: Tables and figures are indicated by *t* and *f* following the page number (edited)